FOOLPROOF PERSPECTIVE DRAWING

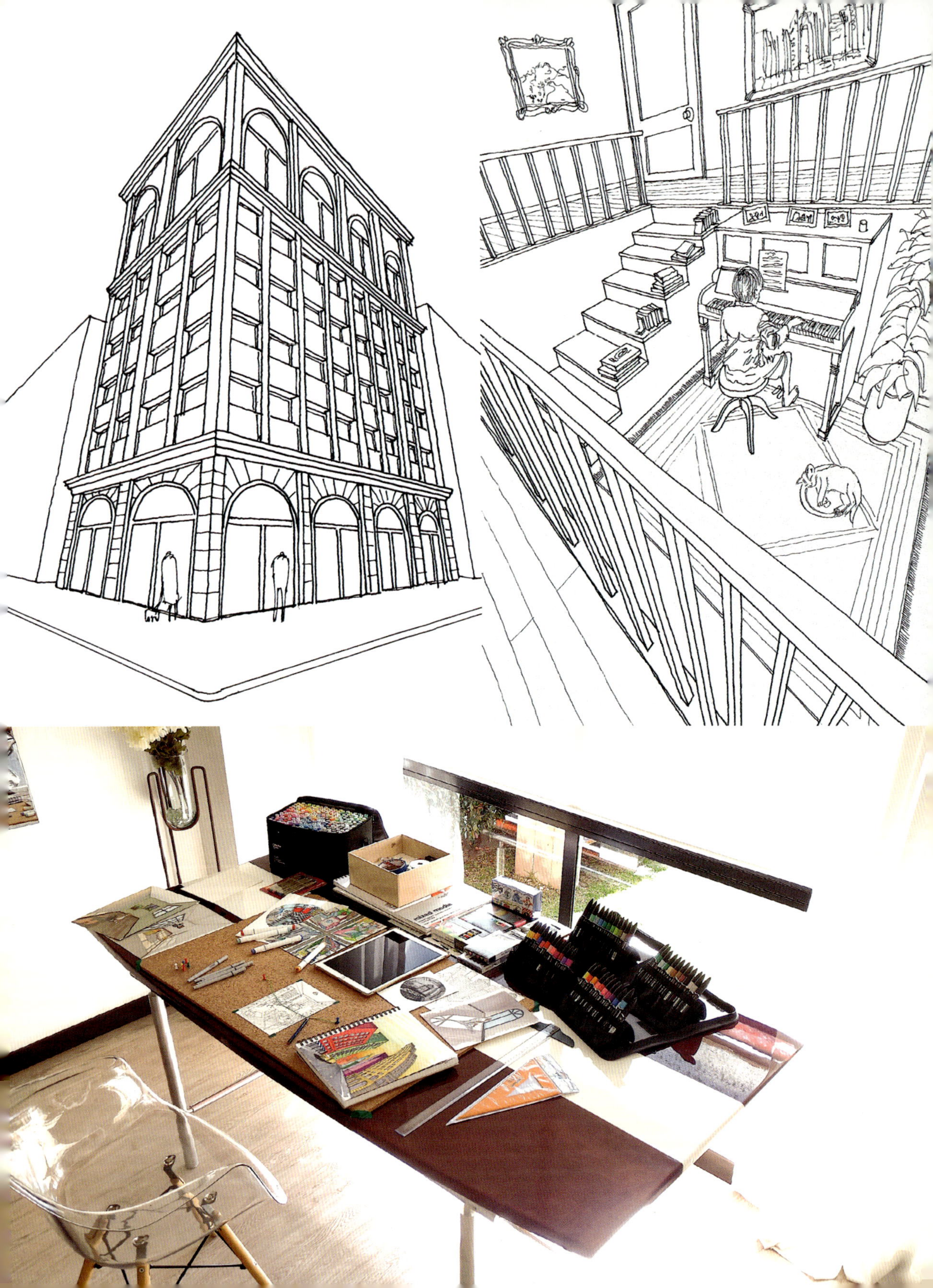
mixed media

FOOLPROOF PERSPECTIVE

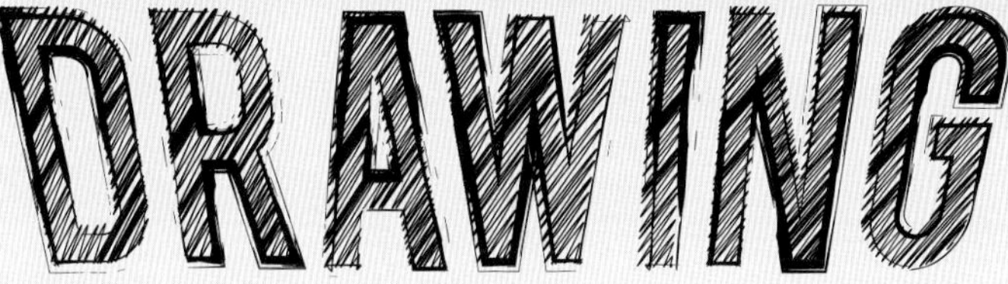

Your ULTIMATE GUIDE to Creating Lifelike Buildings, Cities and Scenes

ROBERTO BERNAL

Creator of @bkartchitect01

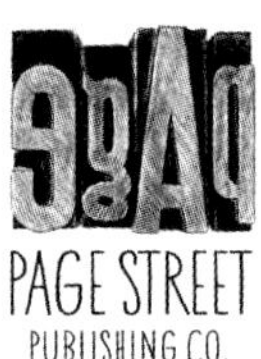

PAGE STREET
PUBLISHING CO.

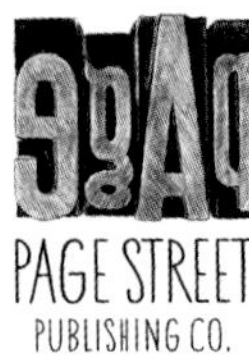

First published in 2024 by
Page Street Publishing Co.
27 Congress Street, Suite 1511
Salem, MA 01970
www.pagestreetpublishing.com

Distributed by Macmillan, sales in Canada by The Canadian Manda Group.

28 27 26 25 24 1 2 3 4 5

ISBN-13: 978-1-64567-859-5
ISBN-10: 1-64567-859-8

Library of Congress Control Number: 2023942732

Edited by Sadie Hofmeester
Cover and book design by Laura Benton for Page Street Publishing Co.
Photography by Roberto Bernal

Printed and bound in the United States of America

Page Street Publishing protects our planet by donating to nonprofits like The Trustees, which focuses on local land conservation.

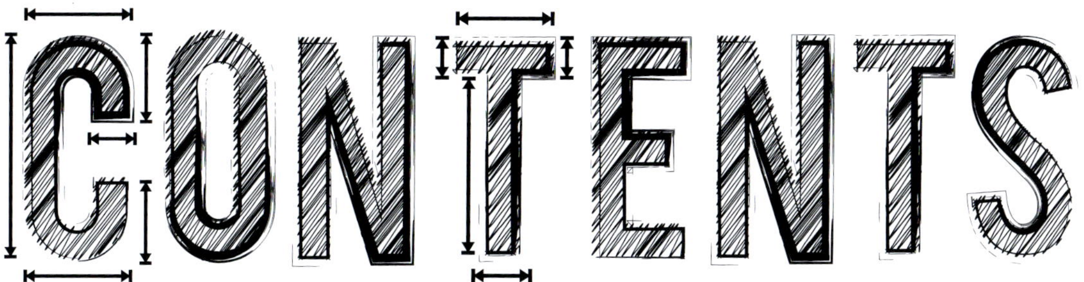
CONTENTS

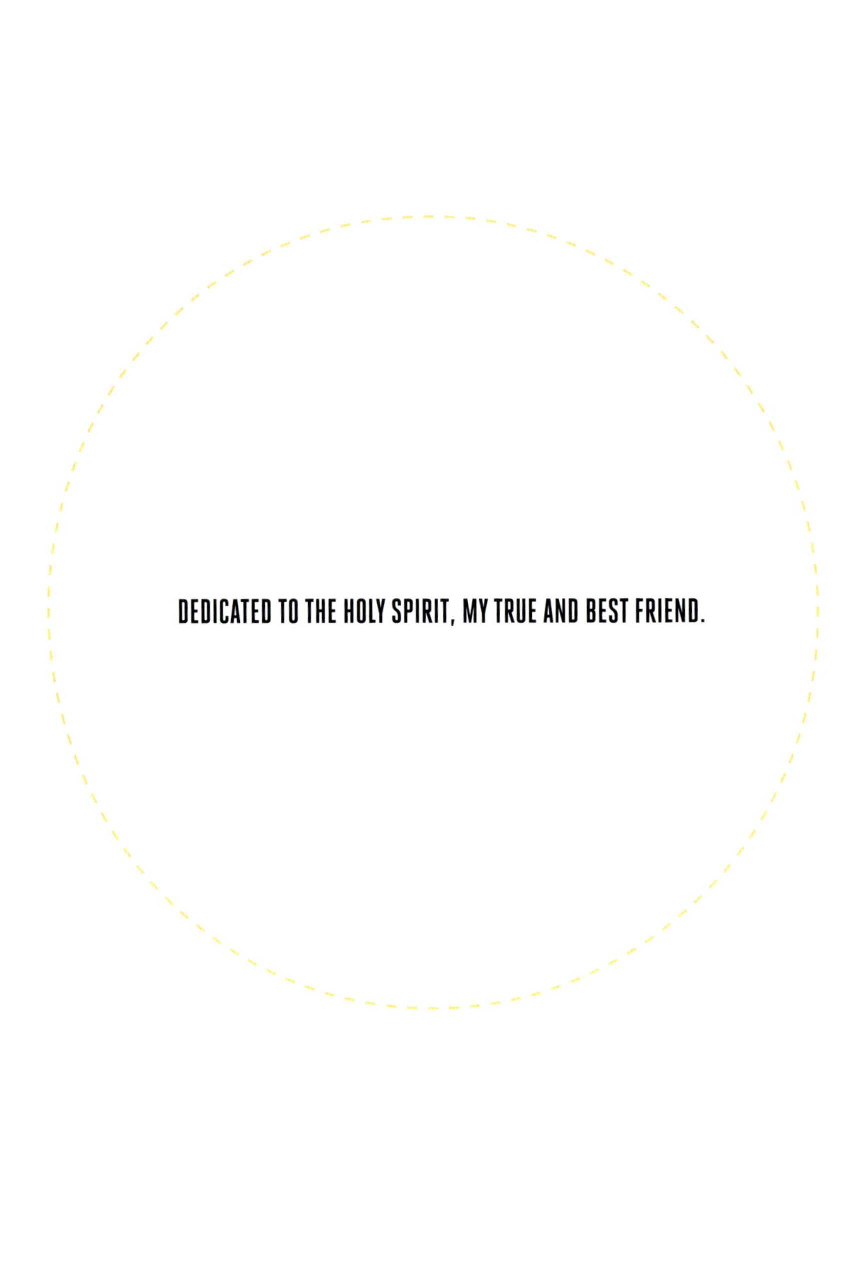

DEDICATED TO THE HOLY SPIRIT, MY TRUE AND BEST FRIEND.

INTRODUCTION

This book is, in many ways, the kind of book I would have wanted to find when I was starting to learn perspective drawing. It is a summary of my more than twenty years of experience as an architect and artist.

I went to architecture school in my home country, Colombia. After graduation, I worked as an architect for a couple of years, but soon realized that the job was much more about budgets, permits, management and business than what I really enjoy, which are the artistic and creative aspects. So, I started shifting my career in that direction by working at a furniture shop. This allowed me to design and create while also being able to sell my artwork, because who would say no to that, right? I really enjoyed the job, and slowly, my work as an artist gained more strength, and I was perfectly okay with that.

Of course, with my background as an architect, my art always gravitated in that direction, and my fascination for perspective was present from the start. One day, I found a video of a guy working in two-point perspective using an elastic string. I was blown away. It was so intuitive, visual and easy to learn. I started thinking: *Would it be possible to do this with one, three, five and other types of perspectives?* So, I experimented with strings, pins, elastics and every other thing I could find, and I posted my journey on social media. The response to those videos was overwhelming. People were very interested in how this worked and wanted to learn more. I was getting messages saying things like, "Where were you when I was in art class?", "Why didn't they teach me like this?", "I never understood perspective until I saw this video . . ." and so on. So now, I dedicate a lot of time to teaching people how to use these techniques. My approach is to put the fun back in art and to work smarter, not harder.

I want this book to be as practical as possible—stripped of every method and rule that I have ultimately discovered to be useless, or at least non-essential. My main goal is that you feel at ease when you are in front of blank paper and want to translate your ideas into lines. This is a 100% hands-on type of book, so I want to encourage you to follow these projects step by step. You will be amazed by how fast you will be drawing things you did not think possible before. It does not matter if you have some previous knowledge about perspective or if you know nothing at all; my advice is to work through the book without any preconception and with an open mind.

Some people have a basic idea of how perspective works, but they still struggle with how to make it do what they want and not the other way around. Being able to tame the rules of perspective so that you know exactly what you need to do to create the exact kind of view that you want is essential for any artist, architect, designer, illustrator or animator.

I have found so many people along the way who dropped out of art school, quit painting and drawing or even changed careers entirely because of perspective. I not only want to prove to you that it is not hard to learn or master, but that it is extremely fun and fulfilling.

I will lead you step by step from very simple shapes all the way to complex scenes, staircases and even city street landscapes. So, if you are ready, grab a pencil and some paper and dive right in!

DIPPING YOUR TOES INTO PERSPECTIVE DRAWING

I hope you are as excited to start learning as I am to start teaching! You will only need the very basic materials listed below to work through this book. But first, I will mention some important pointers.

I normally draw the horizon line with pencil, so I can erase it easily afterward, but in the first chapters of this book, I will use a pen so it can be visualized clearly. In the same way, I usually just draw a little pencil dot to mark the vanishing point(s), but for educational purposes, in the first lesson, I will use a red X.

I finish all the sketches in the book with fine-point pens. I find them optimal for detailing and teaching. However, the idea is that you appropriate these techniques and adapt them to your own style, so feel free to finish your sketches with pencils, colored pencils, markers, watercolors or any other media that you prefer.

Every project in this book requires paper, a pencil, masking tape, a fine-point pen, an eraser and a corkboard. Some projects will require the use of thumbtacks, string, elastic strings and/or paper clips. Those projects will have a corresponding icon to let you know you need to gather these additional supplies:

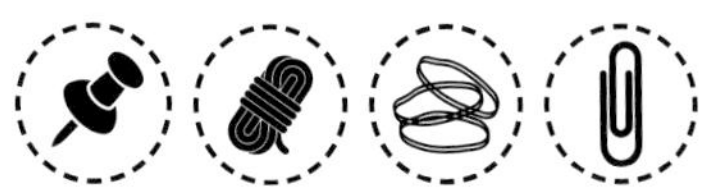

The paper format I use for all but one of the sketches in this book is half A4. That is roughly 5.8 x 8.3 inches (15 x 21 cm). Unless otherwise stated, the paper should be in a horizontal/landscape orientation. For the final project (page 150), I used a larger square format because I wanted to add a lot more detail. That paper was 10 x 10 inches (25 x 25 cm).

MATERIALS

Paper: Any sketch paper will do the trick. Drawing is an incredibly personal experience and choosing the right paper for you is part of the process. Experiment with different mediums and brands until you find that perfect combination that works for you. Not all pencils are created equal and not all papers receive the pencil in the same way. There are subtle differences that you will see as you practice and that is also a part of learning, so have fun experimenting. I personally use regular printer or notebook paper for fast sketches or when I am brainstorming. If I am creating content, working on a commission or drawing for a print, I prefer Bristol, Durex or watercolor paper. I like these because they are super white and that works very well with black-and-white ink drawings—my preferred sketching technique. Regardless of brand, I recommend a paper quality higher than 180 grams and one that is not overly textured; these papers hold up well over time and are also ideal for inking.

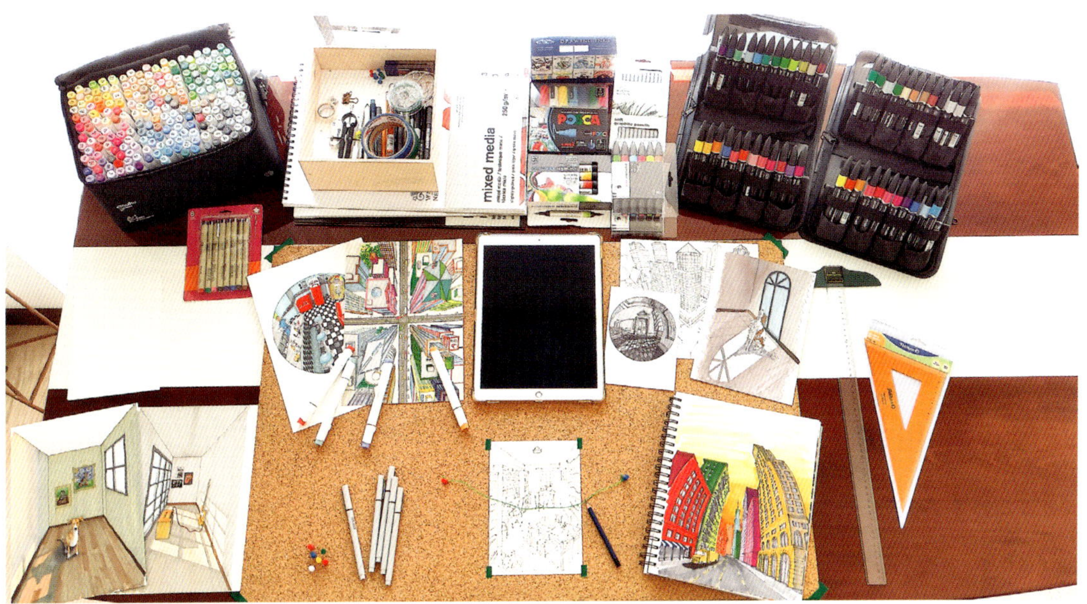

Pencils: I normally prefer to use harder pencils (2H to HB) to do my sketches, because I can erase them easily without leaving smudges. I will almost always erase all pencil lines and leave only the ink. If you are going to use pencil as your main medium, you should use at least 5H and up to 8B.

It is important to work on the amount of pressure you put on the paper when drawing. Looser, softer markings lead to a cleaner paper and more controlled and smoother lines. A good exercise for this is filling a paper with parallel lines drawn very softly in all directions as if you were hatching its whole surface. The pencils I normally use are Berol or a Pilot Shaker mechanical pencil. I just love the balance of the Pilot and the fact that you do not need to push the button but just shake it to move the lead forward is a huge plus for me.

PRO TIP: I normally sharpen my pencil with a knife and not a sharpener. It is easier to get a longer, thinner tip that works very well for details and for shadowing with the tip tilted down. Keeping the knife pointed away from yourself for safety, make gentle cuts around the pencil, trying to keep them as even as possible all the around, so you get a nice centered tip. Do not make the tip too pointy, because it will break with your first line and you will start your drawing with a smudge. Always draw the first line on a separate piece of paper to make sure the pencil is ready.

Masking Tape: There are many types of masking tape and I recommend getting the types that are specifically manufactured for arts. Scotch®, 3M® and Mr. Pen® are all good options. They will prevent damage and tears to your paper and if you are working with watercolors or any other wet medium, they will also avoid leaks better and keep the color line nice and crisp. Because I primarily work in black and white, I normally just use small pieces of tape on the corners of the paper to keep it in place.

Fine-Point Pens: Pens are a whole universe. There are countless brands of fineliner pens on the market and again, my recommendation is that you try a couple and see which one works best for you and your drawing style. My personal favorites are Microns®, but if I cannot get my hands on them for any reason, I will go for Staedtlers®, Pilot® or Winsor & Newton™. These all have long-lasting, hard tips that do not get damaged easily and are practically smudge free.

Erasers: Any white pencil eraser will work perfectly. However, I encourage you to use the eraser as little as possible. When you are a heavy eraser user, somehow your drawing becomes more careless. I force myself to draw in ink as much as possible, because it makes me extra careful with every single line to make sure it is correct. It is a marvelous exercise.

Corkboard: I normally use a corkboard under my paper. I find that its texture and hardness are perfect for sketching, and it allows me to pin my elastics without any trouble. Not only that, but I can make small adjustments to the position of the vanishing points easily. My preferred size is 14 x 20 inches (35 x 50 cm). Of course, it ultimately depends on the size of your work. I use a thickness of at least ¼ inch (6 mm) so that the thumbtacks have a good grip.

Thumbtacks: In this book, I will be using regular thumbtacks, but I recommend trying to get ones with the thinnest possible tip to minimize the damage to the paper. You will see me using thumbtacks with large heads for instructional purposes, but a small head will make it easier to maneuver around them.

String: I prefer sturdier string built for long duration. Any type of kite string will do. If you cannot find kite string you can also look for a thick sewing thread, or very thin non-hairy wool.

Elastic Strings: I have tried many different types of rubber bands in my journey with elastics. The ones that I find work best are elastic strings. They are coated, and often used for kids' crafts. They come in rolls, so you can cut them to any size you need. I use colored elastic string in this book, but it also comes in white.

Paper Clips: I use paper clips when working with elastic strings so I can move them around to the correct position. Any regular paper clip will do the trick, but I personally use jumbo-sized ones, because they feel better in my fingers. After your elastic string is in position, insert a paper clip through it starting from its outermost tip and following its shape until reaching its center.

Optional—Markers: If you want to add more excitement to your perspective drawings, you can add color with markers (or any other preferred medium, like colored pencils or watercolors). I personally use alcohol markers from Ohuhu®, Winsor & Newton and Copic®.

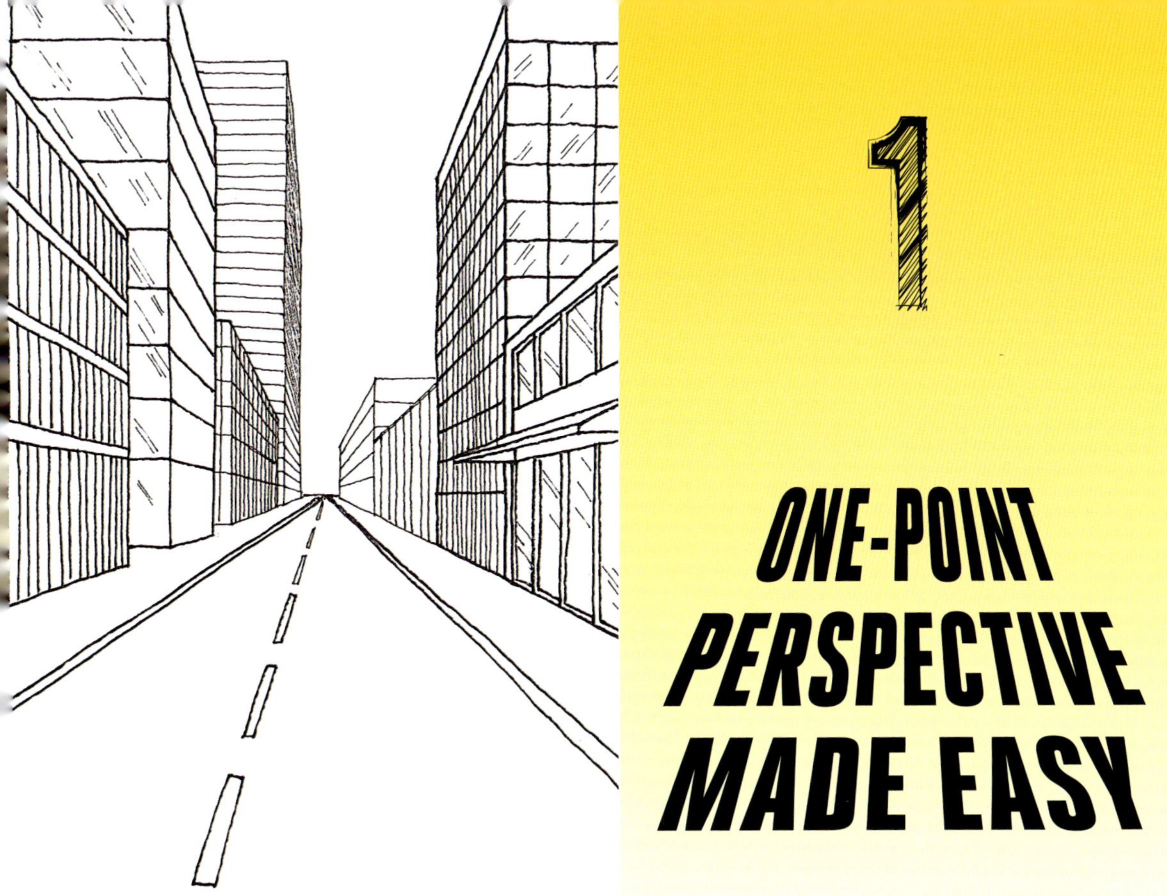

1 ONE-POINT PERSPECTIVE MADE EASY

In this chapter, you will learn everything you need to know about one-point perspective and how to use it effectively to create drawings with correct proportions and a great sense of depth. One-point is by far the most versatile type of perspective and it can be applied to any urban or natural landscape imaginable. I use this technique extensively in my own work because I find it extremely fun and it is a perfect way to generate a sense of connection between the artist and the observer.

As an architect, I gravitate toward urban scenes with mainly straight horizontal and vertical lines, but in this chapter, you will also be learning how to apply one-point perspective to nature and organically curved objects (Sketching a Natural Landscape, page 34). I will show you how to draw basic and complex objects and how to place them in space (Coffee Break, page 24).

One of the most dreaded things to draw for architects, artists and illustrators are staircases. In Drawing a Simple Staircase (page 44), I will let you in on a couple of secrets and hacks that have helped me tame this wild beast over the years. And finally, you will be drafting your first urban sketch (Beginner's City Landscape, page 55), and this will let you see firsthand the endless possibilities that one-point perspective offers. The best part about this sketch is that it will be done using the string technique, and that will open up a whole new facet of perspective drawing. At the end of this chapter, you will have a very clear idea of how one-point perspective works and will be able to draw pretty much anything you can think of by applying the simple tips and rules I will show you.

LESSON: ONE-POINT PERSPECTIVE 101

Though many can find perspective drawing intimidating, one-point perspective is actually very simple and straightforward. It is used to create the sensation of depth and realism in your drawings so that they don't look flat and dull. It is made up of three main elements that I will cover in this lesson, and then you will be ready to start drafting your first perspective drawing! As I mentioned in the introduction to this chapter, this is arguably the most versatile of all perspective techniques, and it is definitely my first choice when doing a fast sketch or drafting a quick design idea. Although you can draw pretty much anything using this technique, it is perfect for things like urban sketching, interior design concept views, product portfolios, floor plans and layouts, urban planning designs and so on.

The three central elements that make up one-point perspective are: the horizon line, the vanishing point and lines.

HORIZON LINE: This line represents the height of the observer's eyes and is fundamental in helping determine the kind of view you want to achieve. This is very important when learning to draw. You must be able to determine exactly how you want the final drawing to look before even making the first line. The horizon line allows you to do just that. It is basically just a horizontal line that you can place anywhere on the paper, but its position will dramatically change the outcome.

In our first example (Picture 1), I have placed it exactly in the middle of the paper. That is where it will be most of the time, because it allows for a vertically centered view, which is very pleasing to the eye. If you draw something directly on the horizon line, it will appear as if you were looking at it at the exact same height of your eyes. On the other hand, if you draw above it, it will look as if that object was higher than your head and you were looking up at it. The opposite will happen if you draw below it. You will see this in more detail later.

When you put the horizon line near the top of the paper (Picture 2), the whole drawing will look as if you were above the objects you are portraying, looking down at them. And if you move it to the lower part of the page (Picture 3), it will feel as if you were below the whole scene looking up. I will show you some examples of how this works on the following page.

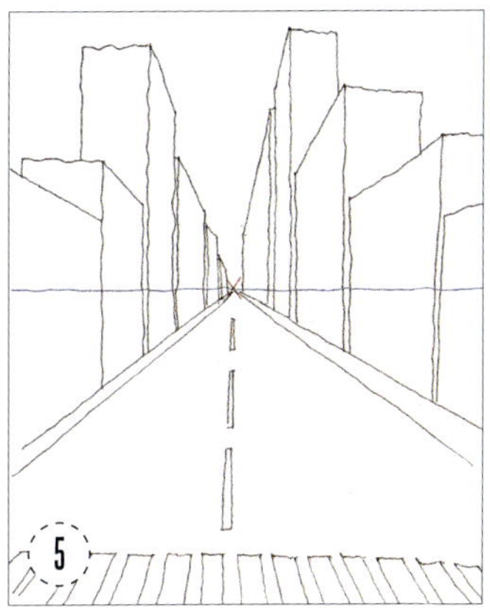

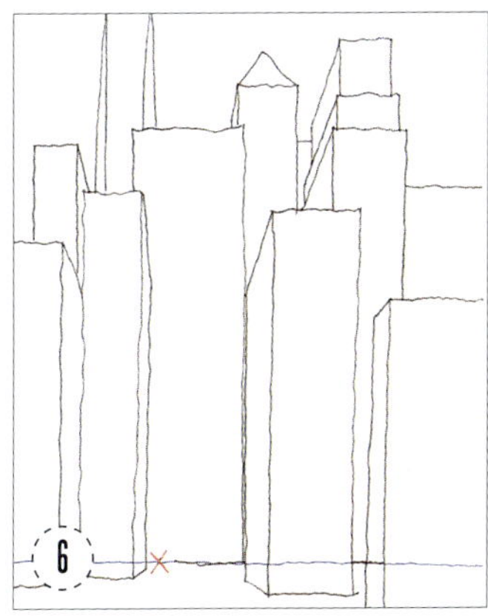

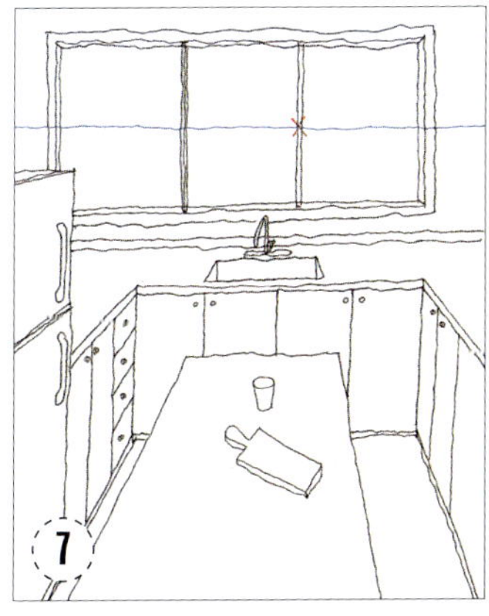

VANISHING POINT: The vanishing point is where all the lines that go in the same direction as the observer's eyesight come together in a single point. (This will be easier to understand after I explain the third element.) You can place the vanishing point anywhere on the horizon line (even outside the paper if the view you need calls for it). In Picture 4, you can see I placed the vanishing point right in the middle. This position will allow for an easily balanced and centered composition. But again, you don't want to always default to the center; think about the overall view you want before deciding where to place the vanishing point.

Let me show you a couple of examples of how the position of both the horizon line and the vanishing point may change the way you perceive a drawing. In Picture 5, you can see that both elements are very close to the center and the drawing feels exactly like that: balanced and centered. The observer is standing in the middle of the street and he can see half of the landscape above his eyesight and half below.

Picture 6 has a very low horizon line and an off-center vanishing point. You can immediately feel the difference. Now, the observer is standing at a slightly lower position than the buildings he is looking up at. He is also standing a little bit to the left and that causes the landscape to appear slightly to his right.

Finally, Picture 7 shows what happens when the horizon line goes to the top of the paper and the vanishing point moves to the right. Now, you have more of a closed-circuit television (CCTV) kind of view. The observer is in an elevated position looking down at the kitchen. Notice how you can see more of the floor on the right of the island because the observer is closer to that side.

All of this means that the height of the horizon line determines how high or low you want the observer to be, and the position of the vanishing point determines how far left or right you want them standing.

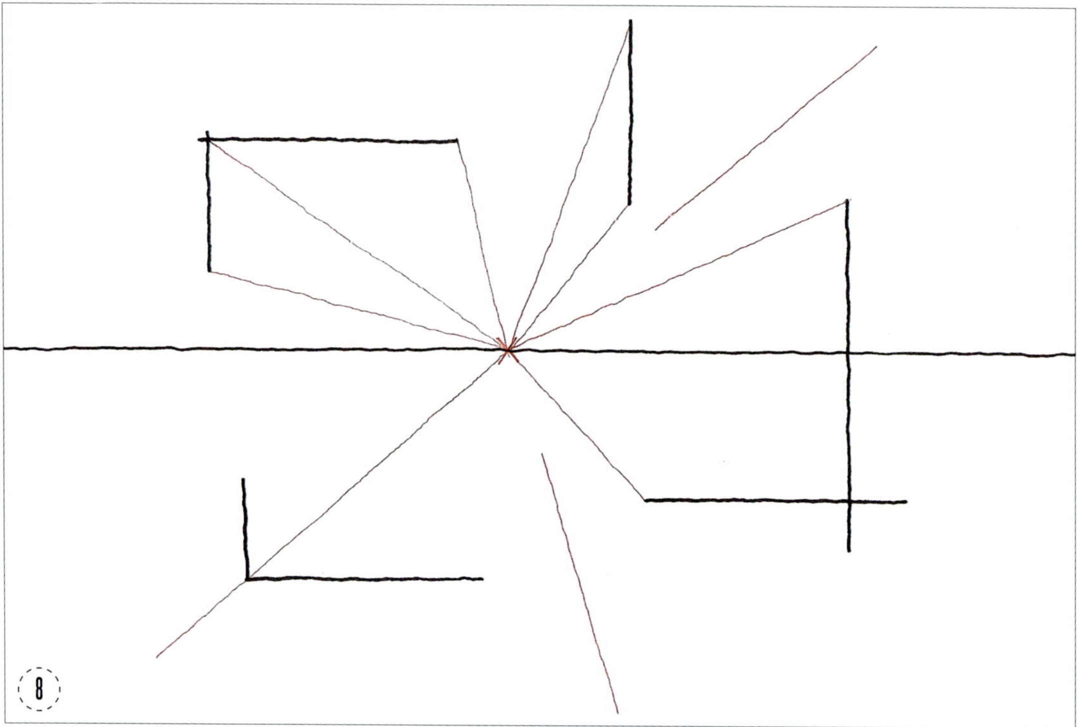

LINES: The third and final element are horizontal, vertical and vanishing lines. Lines compose the actual drawing you are creating. The horizon line and the vanishing point will most likely not be visible in the final drawing, but lines will, and they can be classified in three different types (Picture 8):

1. **Horizontals:** Lines that go straight from left to right
2. **Verticals:** Lines that go straight from down to up
3. **Vanishing lines (or lines going to the vanishing point):** Lines that have the same direction as the observer's eyesight when looking straight at the vanishing point (red). These lines will have different angles depending on their position in space but if continued, they will always join at the vanishing point.

You can appreciate that there are numerous interactions that can occur between these different lines: They can cross, they can be placed one under the other, they can exist on one side of the horizon line or on both, but the most important interaction of all is when they are joined at their ends. When they join, shapes start to form and that is the goal. You can already see that this set of almost random lines are starting to give a sense of depth and dimension that draws your eyes to that center point. That ability to turn a flat piece of paper into a seemingly three-dimensional drawing is what perspective is all about.

In the first project, you will explore how to draw the most basic shapes and understand how they are placed in space according to their relation to the horizon line and the vanishing point. These basic shapes are the foundational bricks that you will use to build more complex objects afterward. By the end of this project, you will have a very clear idea of the way one-point perspective works.

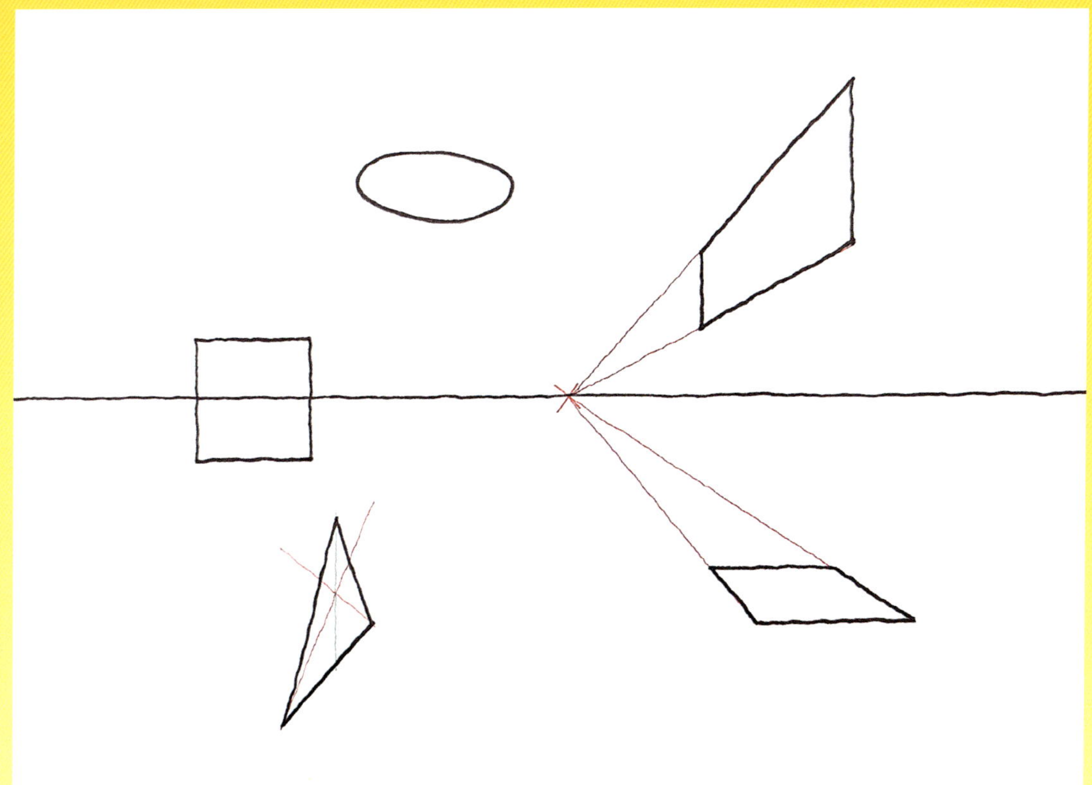

PROJECT: DRAFTING BASIC SHAPES

Now, it is time to do your first sketches and I am really excited about it! The ability to create something out of thin air and putting it on paper is empowering and life changing—even more so if you are sharing it with other people. In this project, you will be learning how to draw the simplest shapes you can make in perspective. They will later become the foundation for all the other work in this book. But don't worry, because I will be guiding you through every step of the process. If this is your first time trying perspective, I urge you to have fun and don't try to make the drawing perfect. In my world, imperfect is fine as long as you are learning and enjoying.

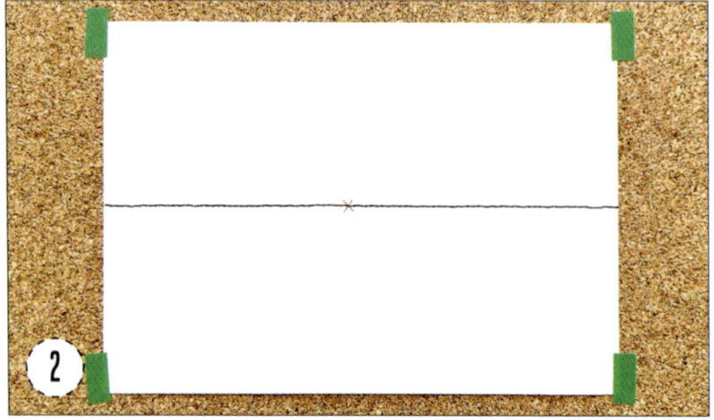

STEP 1: Fix the paper to the corkboard with the masking tape, or directly to the table if you do not have a corkboard.

PRO TIP: When using masking tape, make sure to press it on your clothing first, to take a little bit of the excess glue off before using it on the paper. This will prevent tearing or damage to the corners of your paper when you take it off.

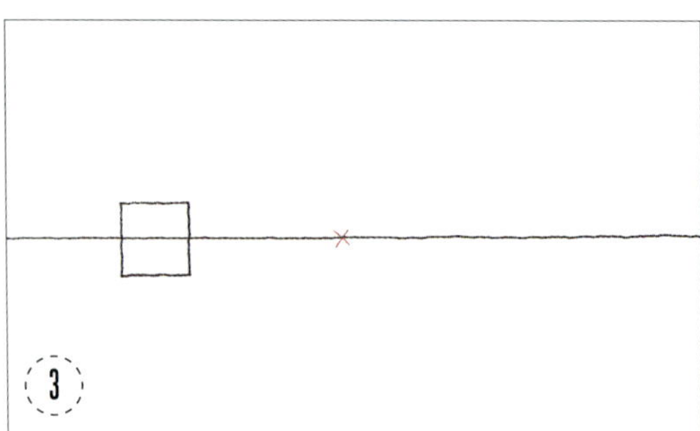

STEP 2: Now, get your pencil ready. Use it to draw a horizon line and vanishing point (red X) in the middle of the paper. I am drawing free hand, but if you want to use a ruler in these first exercises that is okay.

STEP 3: Next, draw a square to the left of the vanishing point, directly over the horizon line. It can be as big as you want. Rectangles and squares are the easiest and most useful of shapes to draw. This one represents a squared plane or surface.

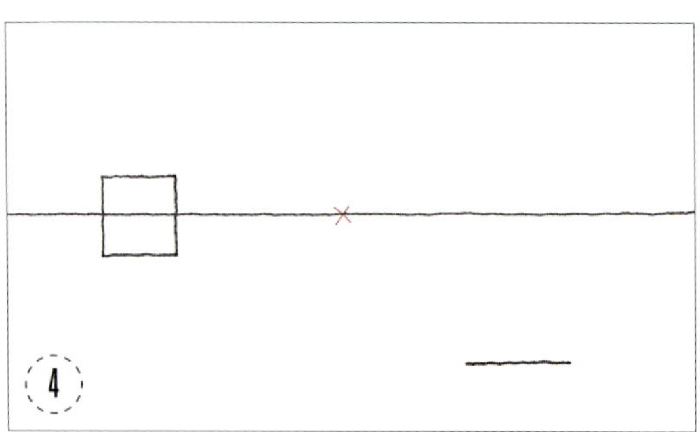

STEP 4: Draw a horizontal line below the horizon line and to the right of the vanishing point. This will be the start of another squared plane, but in this case, oriented in the same direction as the floor you are standing or sitting on.

STEP 5: Now add a couple of lines from the ends of the line you drew in Step 4 going to the vanishing point. Because these red lines go in the same direction as the observer's eyesight, they need to go to the vanishing point.

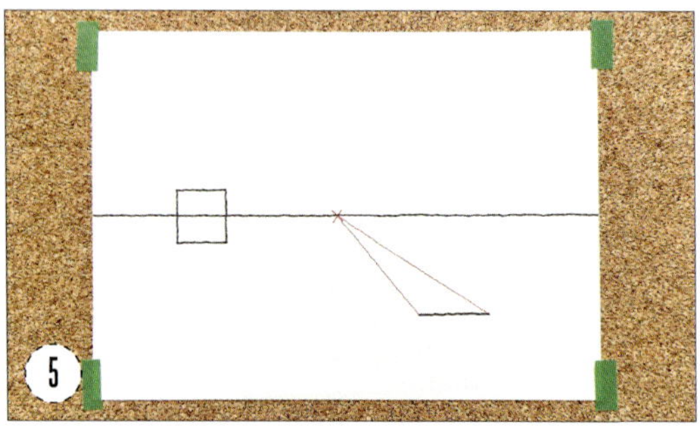

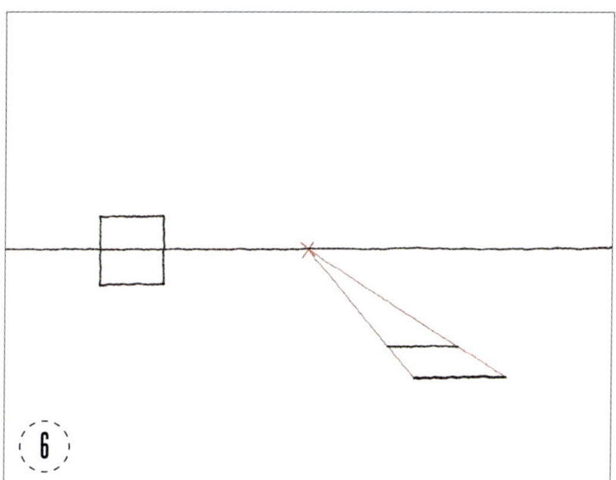

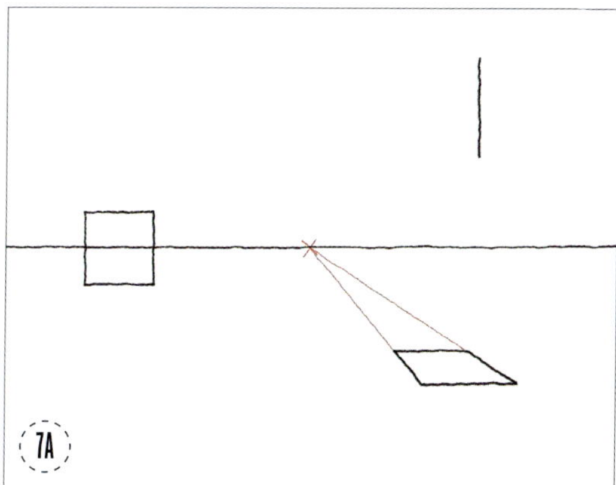

STEP 6: To finish up the square, simply draw another horizontal line between the two vanishing lines you drew in Step 5. This squared plane could very well be a tile on the floor or a carpet, or any other surface with the same orientation as the floor. And you can see in this picture, the square looks and feels like it is bigger in the front and smaller as it goes back in space. However, these two black lines would have the exact same measure in real life. The back one just looks smaller because it is farther away from you.

But what if you want to draw a plane that is not "on the floor" but "standing up" and above you? Okay, here is how to do just that.

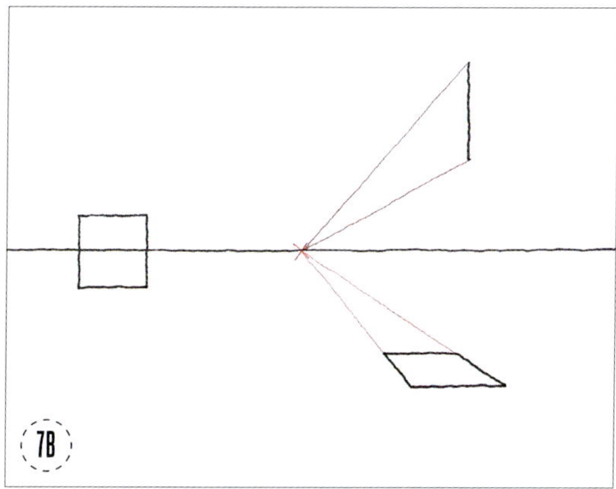

STEP 7: To draw a vertical plane, start with a vertical line instead of a horizontal (Picture 7a), and then repeat the exact same process as in Steps 4 through 6, drawing two vanishing lines from the ends (Picture 7b) and closing with another vertical (Picture 7c). In my example, I made a longer plane that looks more rectangular than square just by spacing the two verticals a bit more. This shape could be a wall or a glass window. By placing it above the horizon line it looks as if it were above your head.

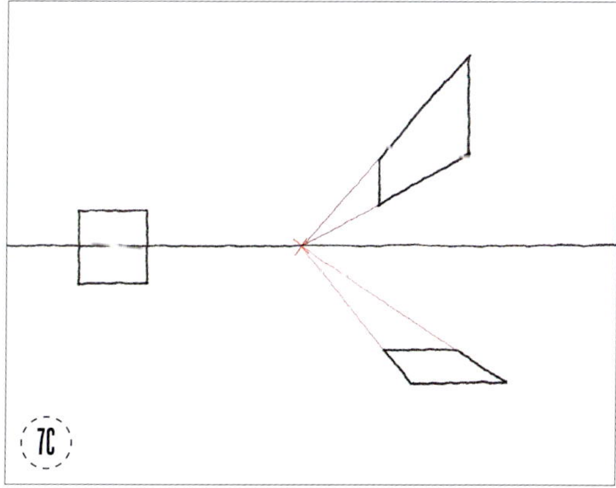

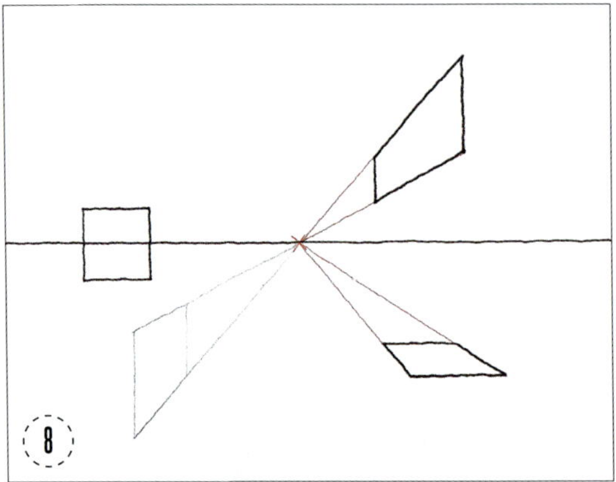

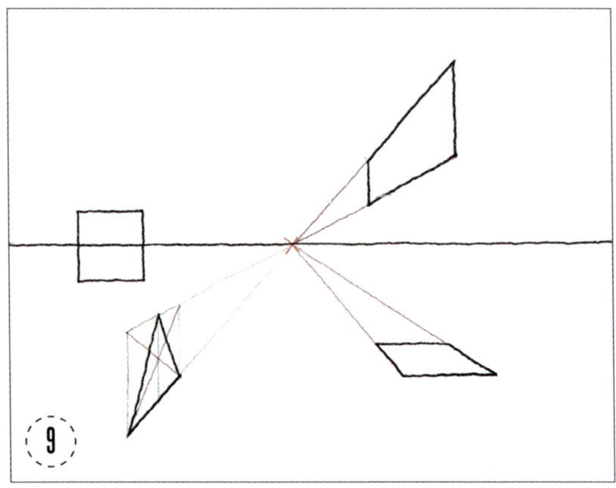

STEP 8: Now let me show you how to draw a triangle that has a centered tip. For objects that have lines in directions other than straight horizontal or straight vertical, or that are curved, you will use a technique that I call "the container plane." Start by drawing a vertical plane in the same way that you did in Step 7. Place this new container plane below the horizon line and to the left of the vanishing point.

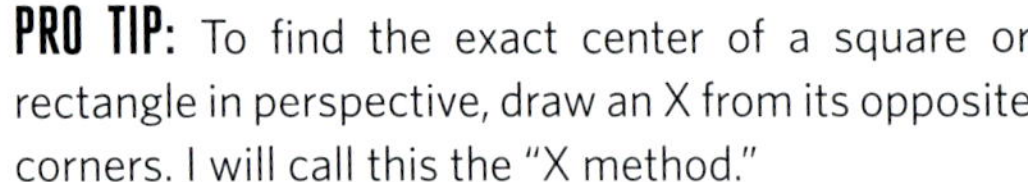

PRO TIP: To find the exact center of a square or rectangle in perspective, draw an X from its opposite corners. I will call this the "X method."

STEP 9: After defining the container plane, use the X method below to find its center and sketch a vertical line through the center point. This new line lets you know where the centered tip of the triangle should be. To finish the triangle, just draw a couple of lines from both bottom corners of the container plane to the center point of the top line. To polish it up, erase all your construction lines.

STEP 10: Finally, create a circular plane above the horizon line. Start by drawing a squared container plane above the horizon line like you did in Steps 4 through 6 (Picture 10a). Lightly sketch a circle within the container plane (see the Pro Tip below). Keep in mind that because of the perspective the circular plane is going to look more like an ellipse than a circle (Pictures 10b and 10c).

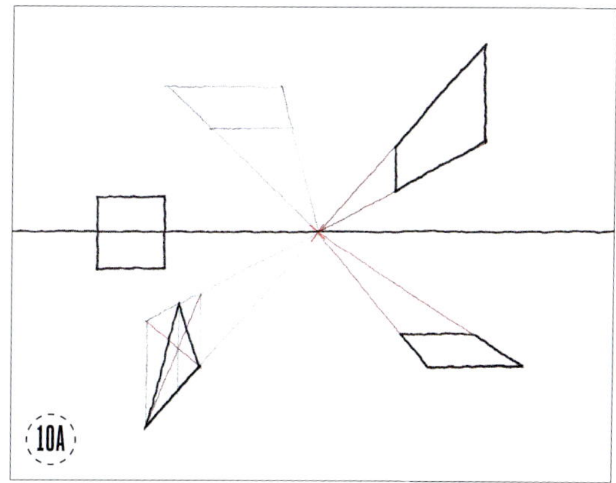
10A

PRO TIP: When drawing a circle or ellipse shape inside a plane, hover your pencil lightly with its tip gently touching the paper in circular motions, until you see and feel that it is right and that the edges of the circle/ellipse are touching the sides of the box (Picture 10b). Then you can trace over the best lines in pen (Picture 10c).

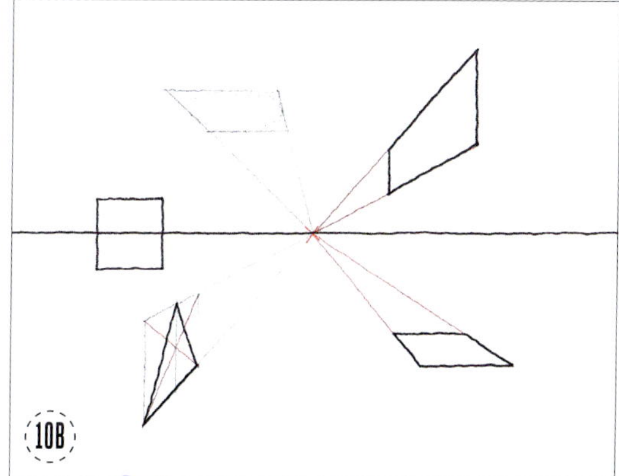
10B

And now you've done it! Before you move on, notice how all objects seem to be "traveling" toward the vanishing point and that creates a strong sense of depth in the drawing. Although they are on a two-dimensional surface like paper, they feel like they belong in a three-dimensional space. That is exactly what perspective is supposed to do. Squares, triangles and circles might not be the most exciting things to draw, but they are the foundational shapes you will later use to draw buildings, towers and trees.

Congratulations on finishing your first project! I hope you enjoyed it as much as I did and that you now have a good understanding of the basic rules of one-point perspective. In the next lesson, you will build on this knowledge to draw some more complex and interesting objects.

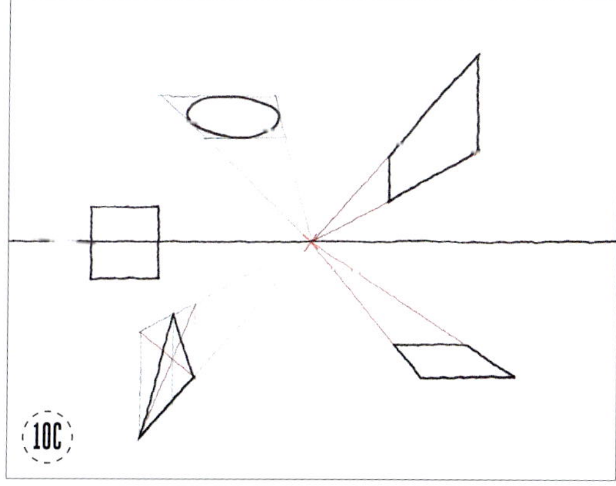
10C

LESSON: HEIGHT, DEPTH AND SPATIAL AWARENESS

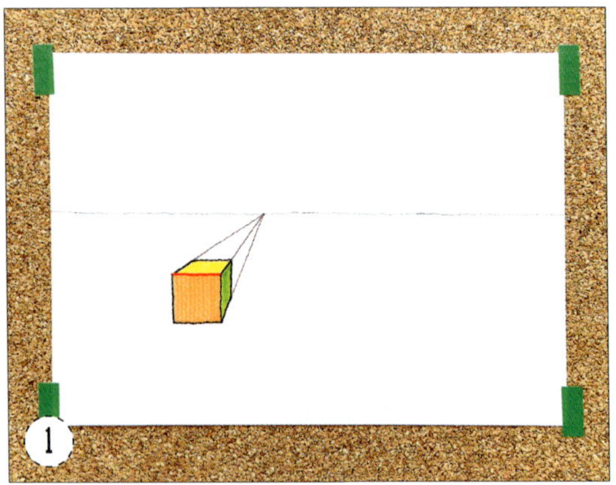

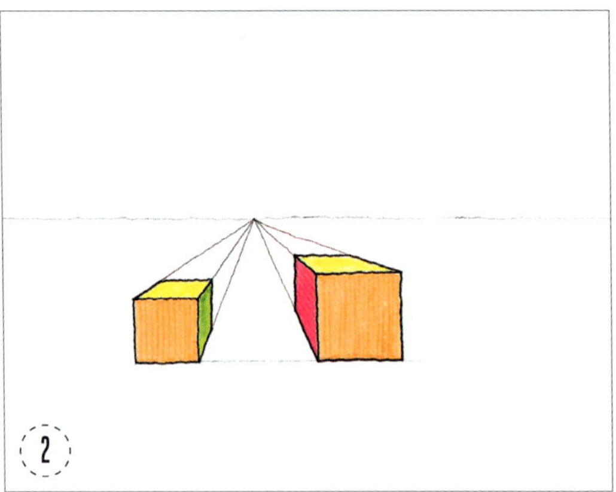

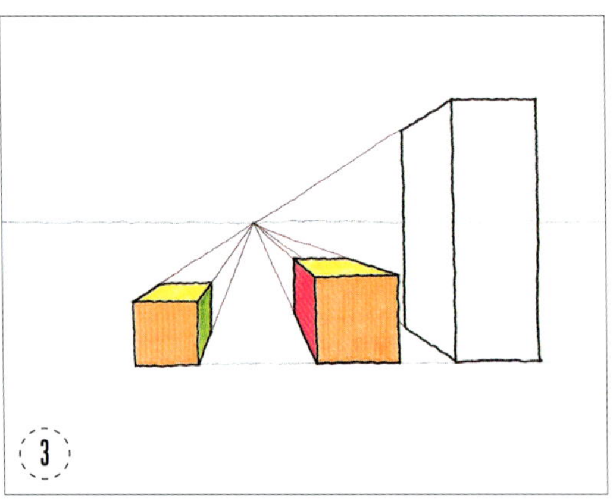

Now that you know the basics of one-point perspective, in this lesson, I want to show you how space works within a blank sheet of paper when using one-point perspective. You will learn how to position objects exactly where you want them and use them to create a three-dimensional space on a flat surface. This knowledge will be extremely valuable in your drawing journey because it will allow you to be in control of every line you draw. You will learn how to draw tall and short objects, make them bigger or smaller, place them in a high or low position and decide if you want them to appear close or far from the observer. And that is exactly what you need to be able to transfer your ideas to the paper without any technical struggle.

Picture 1 shows the simplest and most useful three-dimensional figure you can learn to draw in perspective: a cube. In this example, you can see that I drew it by joining three squared planes. I started with the one facing the observer directly (orange). Then I drew the horizontal one that forms the top (yellow), joined to the first one by its upper vertex (red line). And finally, I added a vertical plane that forms the right side (green) and is attached to the first two by one of their vertices.

If you want to make it bigger, all you have to do is increase the size of the front-facing side (Picture 2). This cube is on the right side of the vanishing point, so you can see its left side (fuchsia) instead of the right one. Now, I will take that same cube and make it taller, so that it becomes a vertical rectangle. To change an object's height, you need to draw longer vertical lines (Picture 3). See that the figure now goes above the horizon line and that means that you will not be able to see its top any more—only its front and left sides.

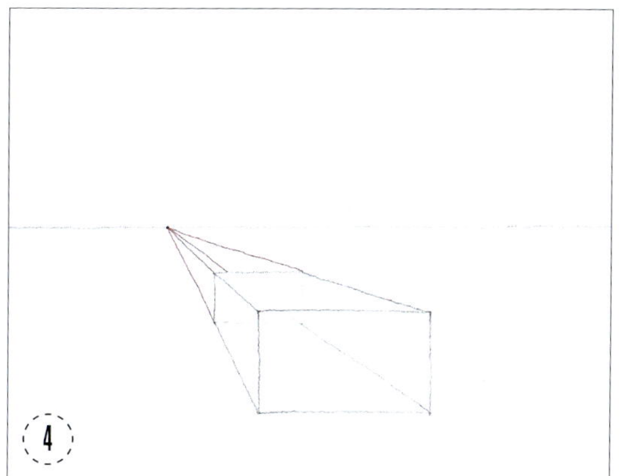

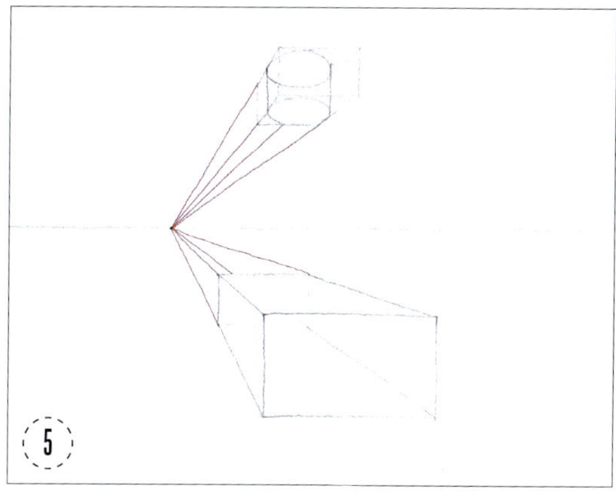

Once you can create three-dimensional objects, the next step is to learn how to move those objects around the space and place them wherever you want. The horizon line is the clue for vertical placement. Picture 4 shows a rectangular box below the horizon line; you can see that it appears to be under the observer's eyeline. The further down from the horizon line you place it, the lower it will appear. Exactly the opposite occurs when you draw above the horizon line.

In Picture 5, you can see a cylinder inside a container box that looks like something that would be hanging high above your head in the space. In the same way you used container planes in the previous project to insert planes that are not made up of 90-degree angles or straight lines, you will use container boxes to insert three-dimensional objects that have those same characteristics. I will show you how to build some of those objects step by step in our next project, don't worry.

PRO TIP: When drawing your construction lines and container planes/boxes, make sure to draw them lightly in pencil. This will make erasing them after you're done outlining your borders in a fine-point marker much easier.

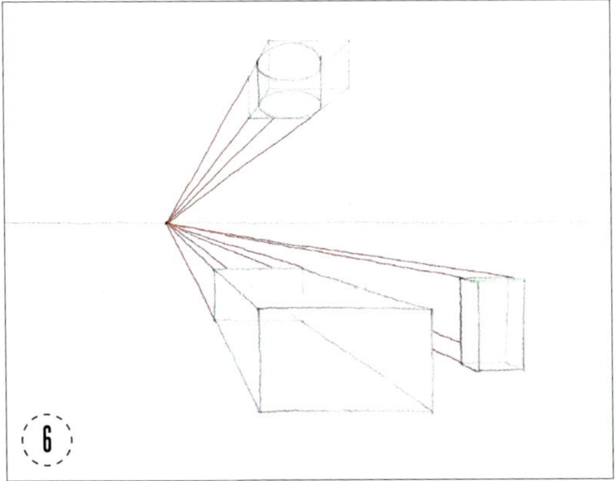

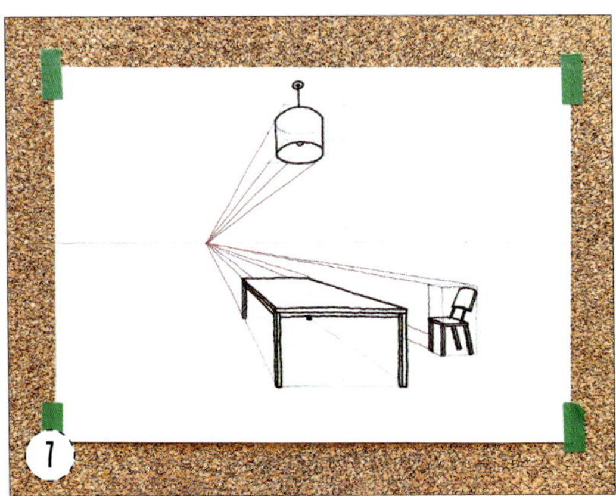

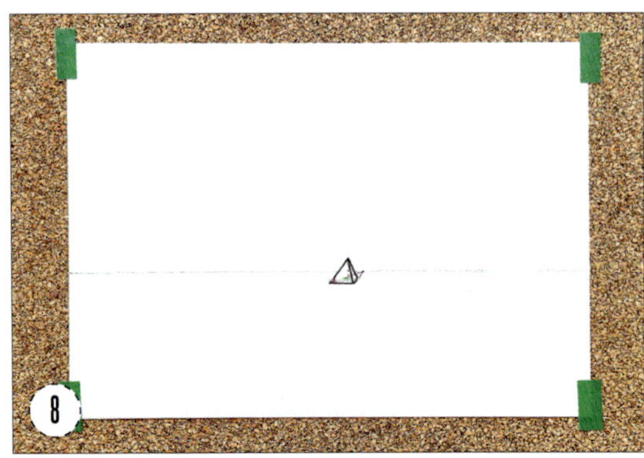

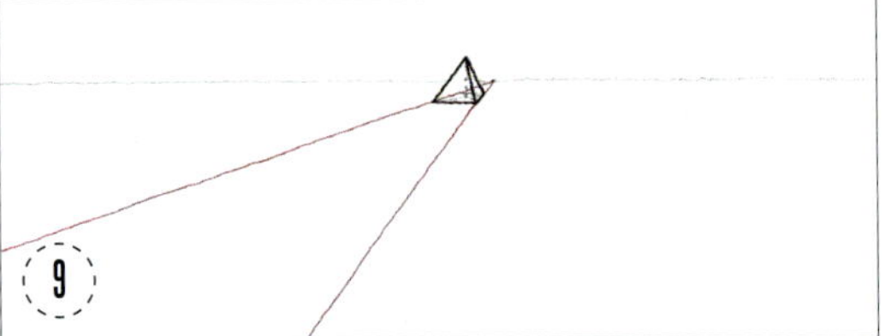

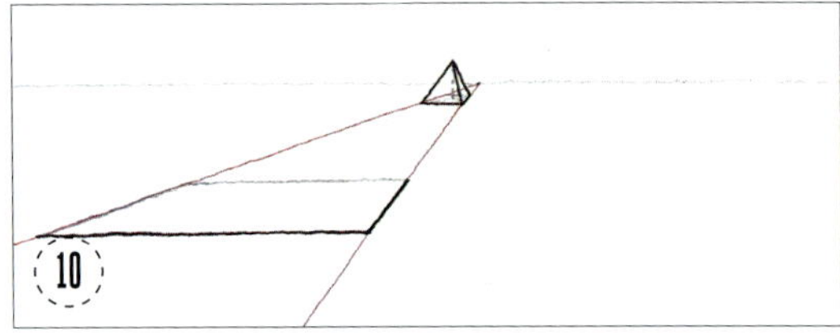

Horizontal placement is much easier because all you have to do is move your objects farther right or left. Picture 6 shows an example of this. Just by placing a new rectangular box farther right, it looks as if it is to the right of the first object. I then added details to transform all those boxes into a dining room with a chandelier (Picture 7). With a few additional steps, you will be able to do the same very soon!

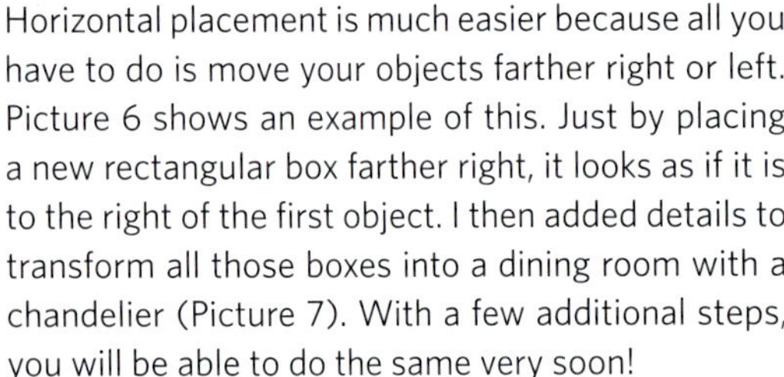

It is one thing to know how to move objects horizontally and vertically around the space. But when it comes to perspective, the real power comes from learning how to move objects closer and farther away. This ability to create depth using variations in distance from the observer is at the very heart of artistic creation.

Picture 8 shows a small pyramid. There are two possible explanations for it being small. The first is that it is a tiny object sitting fairly close to the observer. The second is that it is actually rather big, but is very far away so it looks small. For the sake of this lesson, suppose that it is the second option.

I will show you how to bring that pyramid closer. I am not going to change its dimensions; I am just going to move it closer. The first thing that I will do is extend the lines that come from the vanishing point and form its base all the way until they go off the paper (Picture 9). I could draw the pyramid anywhere between those two lines and it would have the same width as the original. Picture 10 shows its new base. You can see I only outlined the front horizontal line and the right side of the new base because I know the other two will be invisible once I complete the figure.

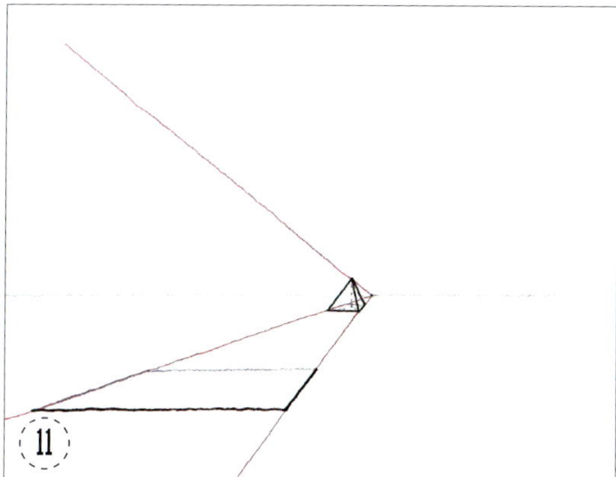

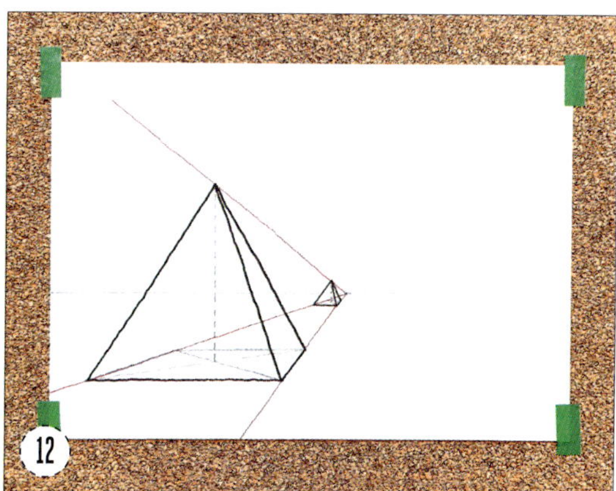

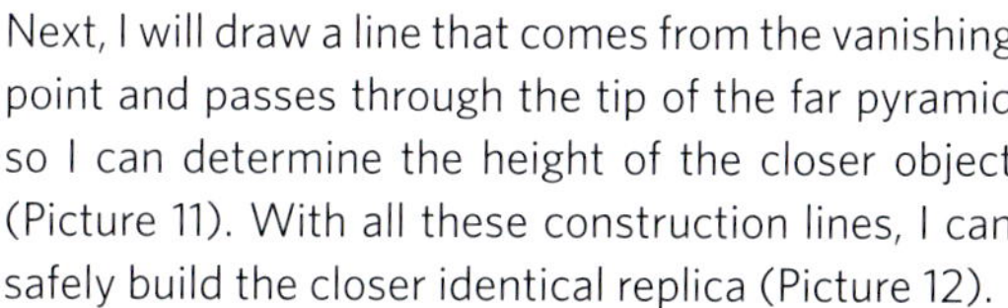

Next, I will draw a line that comes from the vanishing point and passes through the tip of the far pyramid so I can determine the height of the closer object (Picture 11). With all these construction lines, I can safely build the closer identical replica (Picture 12).

What if you want to do the opposite, and go from near to far away? I am going to begin with an object that is very close—so close that it even goes off the paper (Picture 13). It is a very slim and tall rectangle. To make it, I drew two pairs of lines (in red), one for the base and one for the top. Each pair of vanishing lines passes through both external borders of its top and bottom planes. So, I used them to draw the external borders of the top plane and then verticals coming down from the three visible vertices.

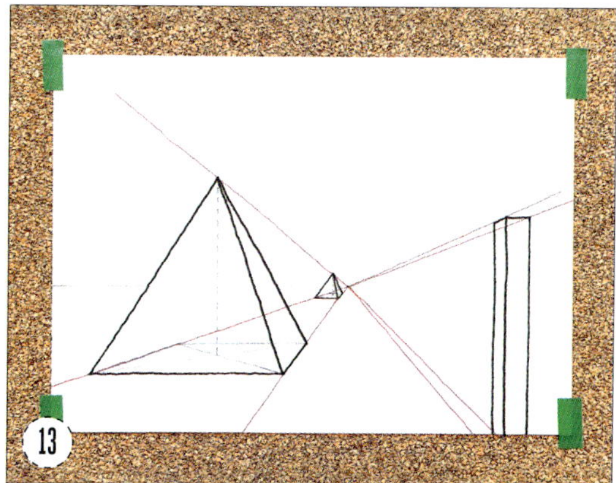

I will use these construction lines in the same way I did with the pyramid to draw exact replicas that stand progressively farther away from the observer (Picture 14). This is the process that you would use to draw a fence or a line of electric posts on the side of a highway.

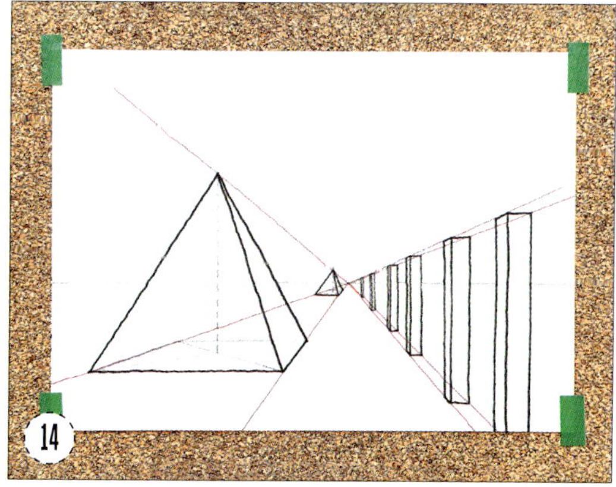

PRO TIP: This repetition of objects technique is incredibly useful. Later in the book, you will see me applying it to palm trees and light posts (pages 29 and 32 respectively), but you can use it to replicate any repetitive set of objects that are aligned in the direction of the vanishing point.

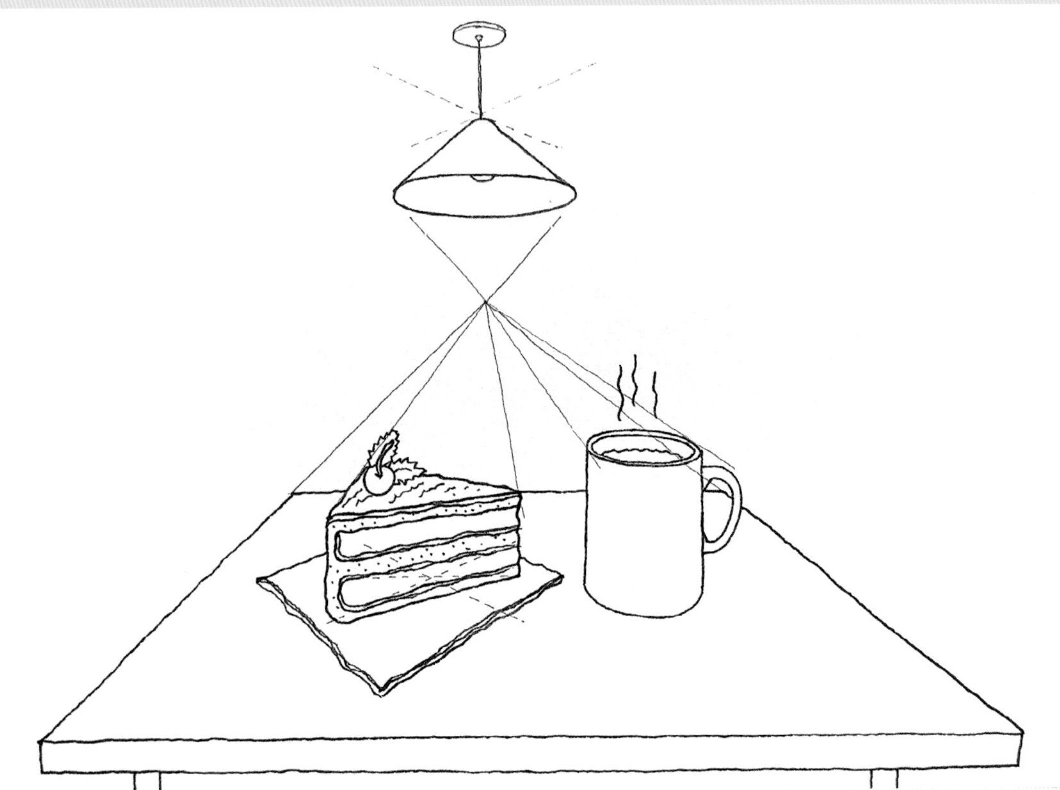

PROJECT: COFFEE BREAK

The secret of drawing is learning how to combine simple elements to build more complex ones. Every object you see, no matter how intricate, can be divided into smaller, simpler parts. In this project, you will use the basic shapes that you have learned so far and use them to create more complex objects (in this particular case, a slice of cake and a steaming cup of coffee). Then you will study how to place them in different parts of the space, for instance, placing a napkin on a table that stands on the floor or hanging a lamp from a ceiling rather than having it float in space.

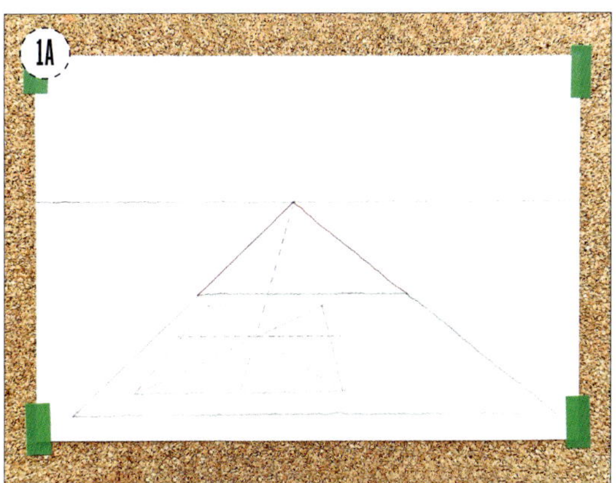

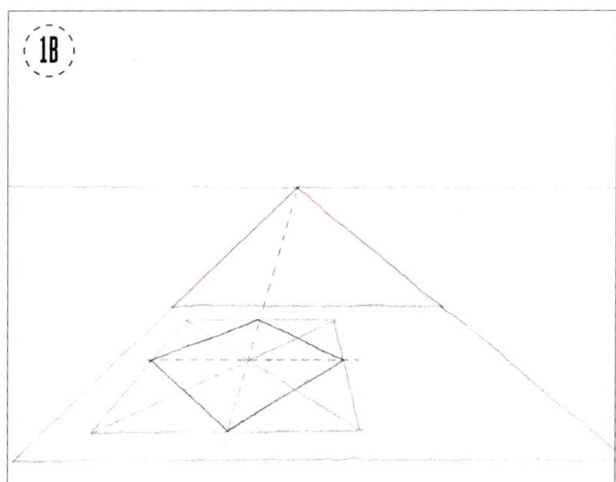

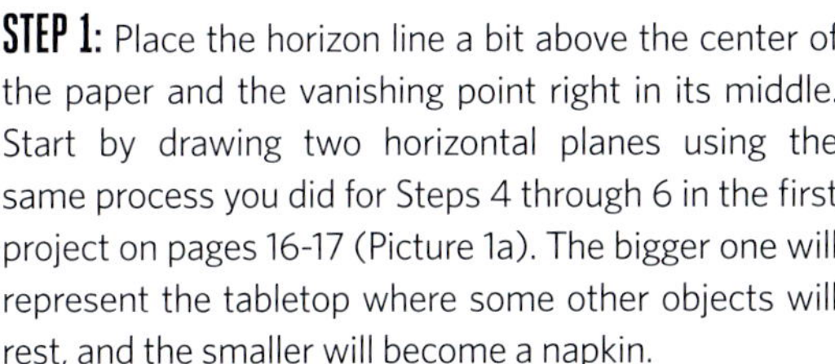

STEP 1: Place the horizon line a bit above the center of the paper and the vanishing point right in its middle. Start by drawing two horizontal planes using the same process you did for Steps 4 through 6 in the first project on pages 16-17 (Picture 1a). The bigger one will represent the tabletop where some other objects will rest, and the smaller will become a napkin.

I think the composition will look better if the napkin does not have the same orientation as the tabletop, so I am going to turn it 45 degrees so that it looks like a rhombus rather than a square (Picture 1b). You can see that I found the middle of the plane using the X method (page 18) and drew two dotted lines that pass through it: one horizontal and one that goes all the way to the vanishing point. Picture 1b shows how I joined those four middle points to form the rhombus. Keep in mind when doing this that the rhombus will be significantly smaller than the original square.

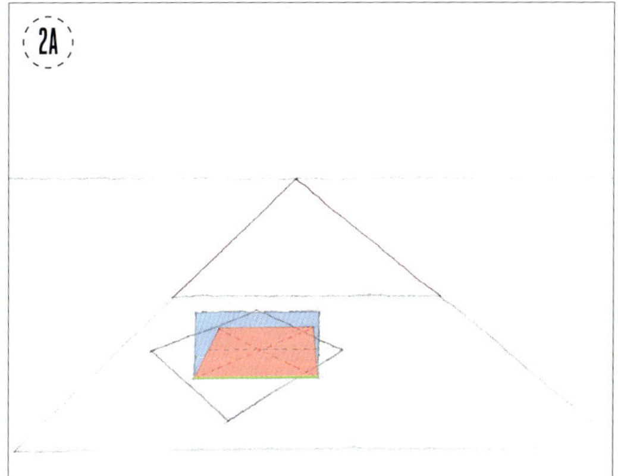

STEP 2: Now you will draw a container box that will turn into a cake slice. Draw another horizontal squared plane on top of the napkin (red in Picture 2a). Then draw a vertical front-facing plane (blue) that has the same width as the first one. They are joined together by one of their vertices (green).

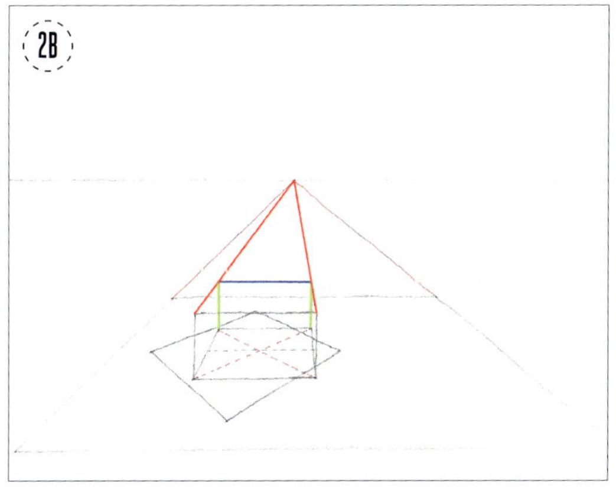

(Step 2 continues)

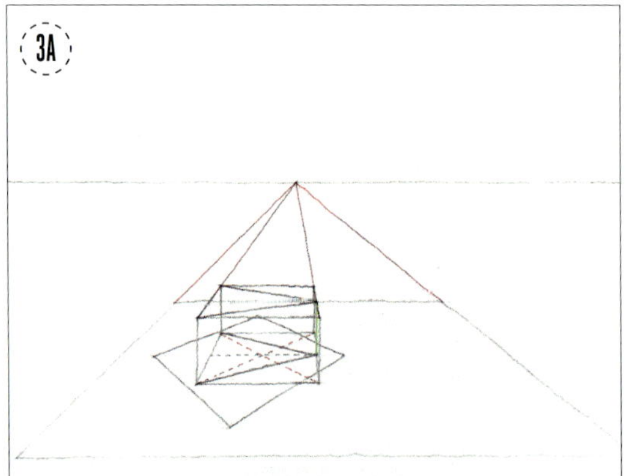

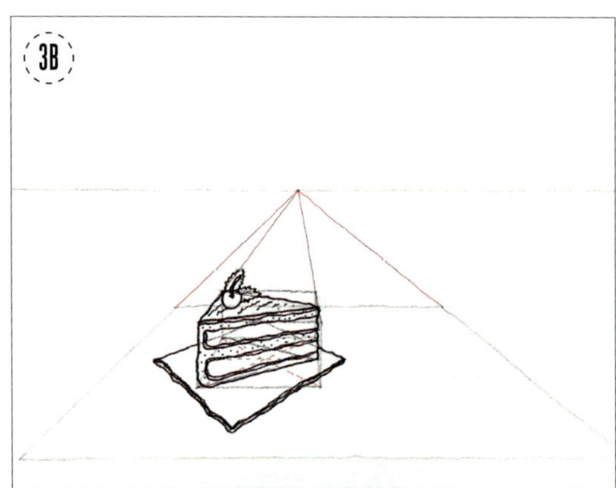

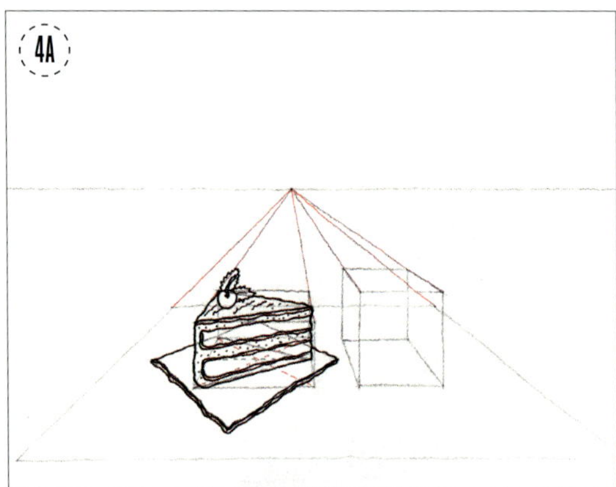

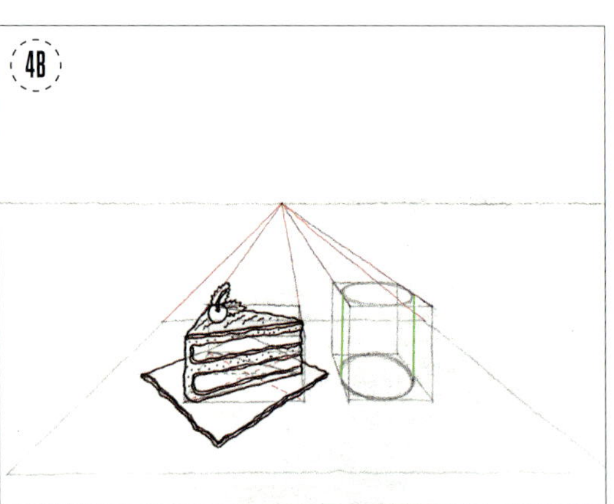

Next, draw a couple of lines from the top corners to the vanishing point (marked in red in Picture 2b). Draw two vertical lines (green) going from the back corners of the horizontal plane all the way up until they reach the red ones. Now all you need to do is join the top tips of those two last lines with a horizontal (marked in blue) and the box is ready.

STEP 3: Draw a centered-tip triangle on both the bottom and top planes of that box. (Check out Steps 8 and 9 of the Drafting Basic Shapes project on page 18 if you need a reminder on how to do this.) Join both tips of the triangles with a vertical line (green), and you have a cake slice-shaped figure (Picture 3a).

Now you can use the outline as a reference to draw all the delicious details (Picture 3b). Soften all the edges to make it more cake like and top it with a cherry and a couple of mint leaves. I also did very loose lines on the napkin to mimic its texture.

STEP 4: Draw another box on top of the table following the same instructions from Step 2 (Picture 4a). This time make it narrower and taller because this one will be a coffee cup. Then you can draw a couple of circles (ellipses) on the top and bottom planes (Picture 4b) and join them by their outermost edges with a couple of vertical lines (marked in green).

STEP 5: Add a few details to finish up this part of the drawing. Add a double line on the rim of the cup to give it thickness, and just below, a wavy line that mimics the liquid in it. For the handle, I chose an ear-shaped one, but you can change the design if you want. Because this handle faces straight to the right (meaning that it has been inserted in a front-facing plane), it doesn't have to follow the rules of perspective: it simply exists in the same plane as the side of the mug facing the observer. Because of this, you can draw the handle as big or small as you want and with any shape you prefer. Finally, draw a long rectangular front-facing plane as the edge of the table and add a couple of table legs.

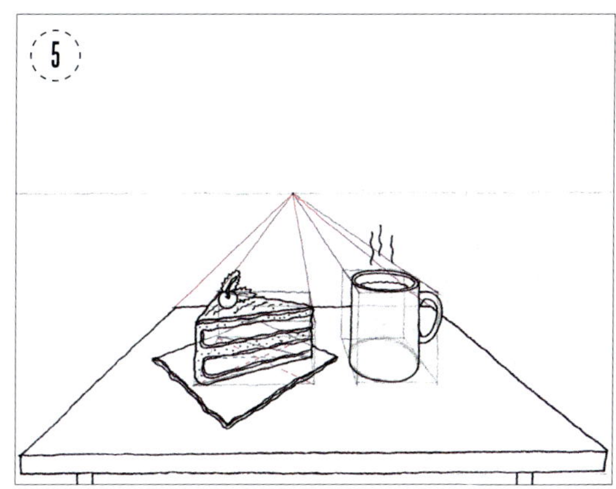

STEP 6: Now you need to balance the composition by drawing something on the upper part of the paper. I am thinking a conical ceiling lamp would be a perfect addition. Draw another container box in the middle of the paper above the horizon line. Find the center of the top plane and draw an ellipse on the bottom one.

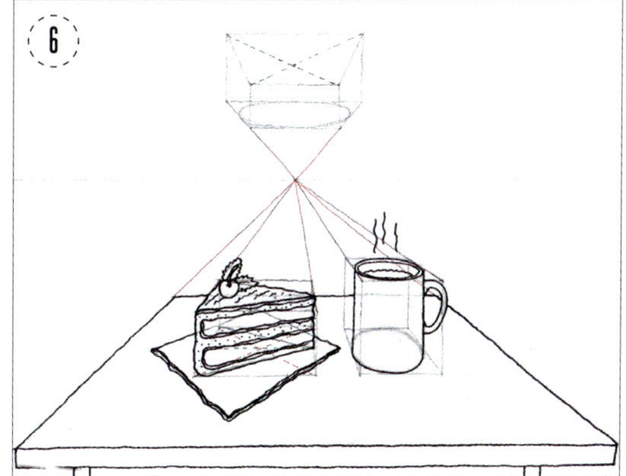

STEP 7: Sketch a couple of lines from the center point of the top plane to the outermost edges of the ellipse on the bottom. That is how you draw a cone in perspective. I finished it up by adding a straight vertical line that represents the cable and a circular plane as the fixture that holds it to the ceiling. To create that circular plane, I first drew a squared container plane and inserted an ellipse in it. I then drew a double line in the front to give it thickness.

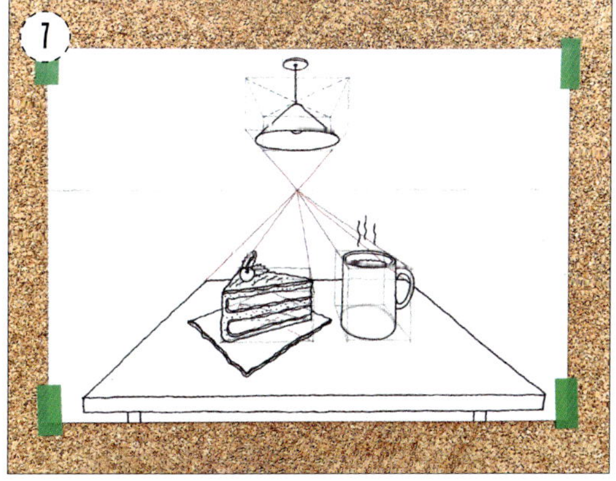

I hope you had fun drawing this little project. Without really noticing, you just learned how to draw a cube, a cylinder, a cone, a rectangular box and a triangular prism. With these figures, you can create pretty much anything you want. So, pat yourself on the back because you are on the right track to mastering perspective!

LESSON: PUTTING NATURE IN PERSPECTIVE

Perspective is made up of straight lines and sharp angles, so you may be wondering how to use it to draw organic, curved and textured objects like the ones seen in nature. Well, that is exactly what I will show you in this lesson, and the good news is that everything you have learned so far will absolutely allow you to draw natural landscapes. As free as it is, nature still has to obey the same rules of perspective.

To make it easier to explain, I will divide natural landscapes in two parts: background and foreground.

The Background: By definition, a portrait of nature is immense and goes as far as the eye can see. Some objects will be drawn beyond the horizon line, and perspective will not affect them directly. They will make up the background.

The Foreground: In the foreground are the objects that exist between the observer and the horizon line. They will be drawn according to the laws of perspective that you already know.

Now, I will show you a couple of examples of how this works. First, I will create an ocean landscape beginning with the horizon line, vanishing point and the background (Picture 1). I did not use perspective at all to draw the mountains in Picture 1. I just drew them as big and high as I wanted to, because mountains do not need to have a size ratio with any other object nor do they need to have a specific shape. This applies to all objects that do not have an implicit scale (like mountains, rocks, waterfalls, rivers and lakes) in both the background and foreground. These natural things have no implicit scale without something to compare them with, meaning that you can draw a mountain, but it is not until you add an object with an implicit scale, like person or a car, besides it, that you know if you've drawn a hill or Everest.

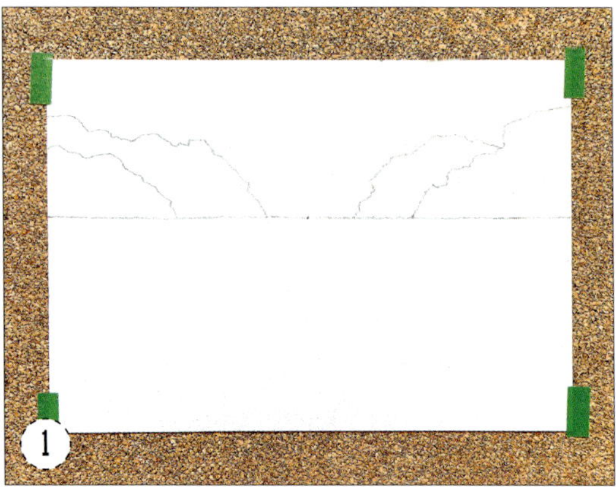

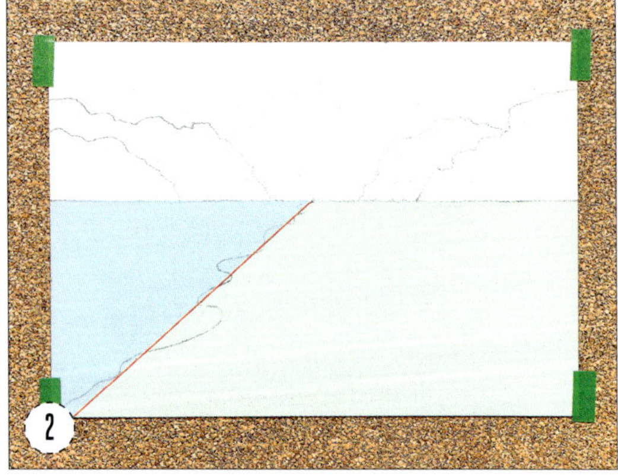

Next, I am going to start the foreground making two big decisions that will be crucial for the rest of the drawing. First, I will determine the seashore line. To do so, I am going to draw a line from somewhere around the bottom left corner of the paper going to the vanishing point (red line in Picture 2) and then draw a curvy line following its direction that mimics the waves. This first line has a huge impact on the overall composition of the sketch because it divides the foreground in two big blocks (water and land, shown in blue and green respectively) and draws the eye of the observer straight to the vanishing point.

Second, I will draw a palm tree. Because it is the first object, I have absolute freedom to decide its size. But, from now on, every other object will have to be drawn in proportion to it. To create my palm tree, I drew two slightly bent vertical lines that form the trunk (Picture 3). At their top, I drew a series of palm leaves with arched top lines and wiggly bottom ones. Some circles or ovals beneath them will mimic coconuts. Now, I want to fill the beach with some more palms and I am going to show you how to repeat an object and determine its size according to its position within the landscape.

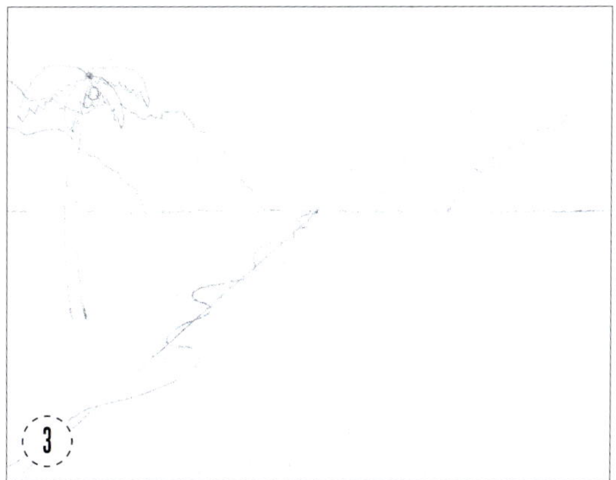

In Picture 4, you can see how I drew two lines from the palm tree going to the vanishing point (red)—one of them from the bottom and the other one from the top. The vertical distance between those two lines at any given point (blue lines) is the height of the palm tree in that position. You can use the very same height for any other one that you put in the same horizontal position, as the green lines show.

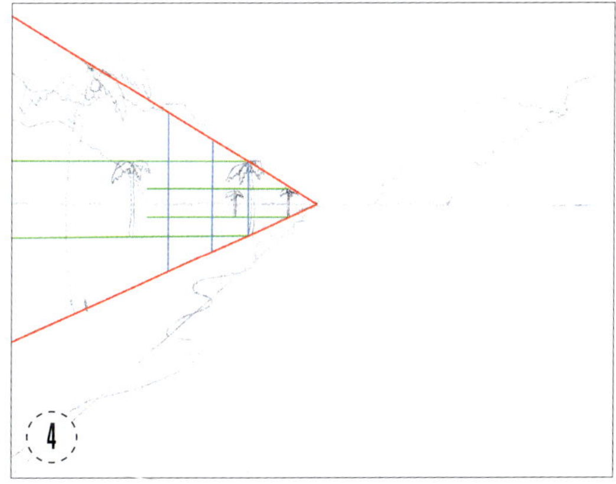

I also want to draw a dock and I will use a horizontal plane to do it (Picture 5). Docks have many sizes and shapes. This one will be a rather small one and I am eyeballing it in relation with its distance to the observer and the size of the palm trees. Its left end goes off the paper and the right one goes to the vanishing point. All the boards in the dock also go to the vanishing point because they are parallel.

I gave the dock some thickness by adding a very slim and long front-facing plane, where you can see all the fronts of the boards, and then another one at the right end going to the vanishing point. Finally, I added a cylindrical dock leg that you can see underneath submerged in the ocean. The bottom of the leg is a bit curved because it is round and a couple of wiggly elliptical lines around it make it look like it goes into the water.

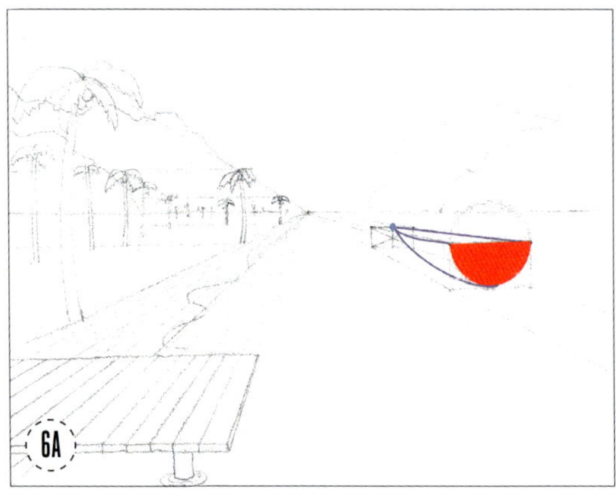

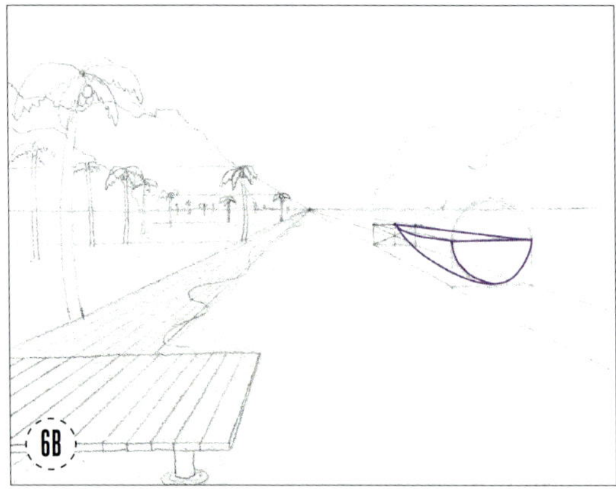

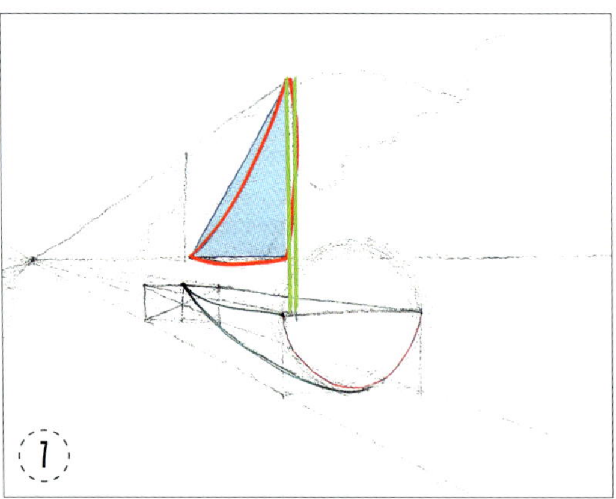

To balance the composition, I will draw a small sailboat on the right, using a container box to do so (see the Height, Depth and Spatial Awareness lesson on page 20 to remember how container boxes work). I want to make the boat big enough that it does not look like a toy, but small enough that it has a nice proportion with the rest of the objects. However, boats come in all different sizes so I am not worrying too much about it.

Picture 6a and 6b depict how I built the boat. Picture 6a shows how I turned its back plane (red) into a semicircular one and marked the top center point of the front one (blue dot). Next, to create the body of the boat, I drew curved lines (purple) going from the top corners of the back semicircular plane and from its lowest point all the way to that center point in the front (Picture 6b).

For the mast, I drew two vertical lines (green in Picture 7) and attached to the mast a triangular plane going to the vanishing point that will form the sail (blue). But sails are not straight, so I used it as a reference to draw curved lines that mimic the fabric being blown by the wind (red).

Finally, I inked the whole drawing and added some texture lines to help understand what material the objects and surfaces are made of (Picture 8). Particularly see how I covered the lower part of the boat with water by drawing a wavy line around its bottom. And you cannot forget some seagulls.

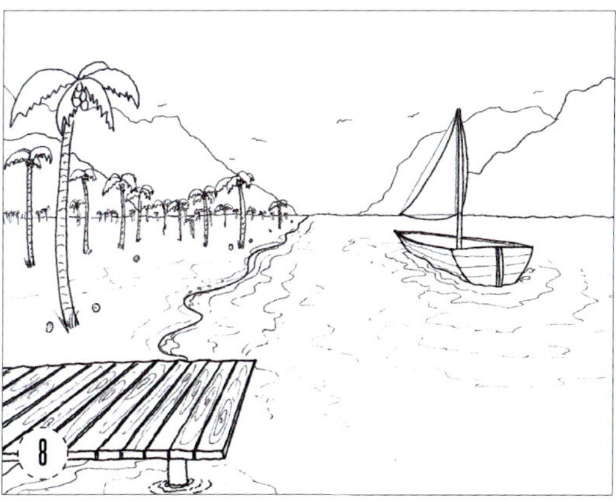

PRO TIP: Draw the objects that are closer to the observer with thicker lines and make them thinner as they go farther away. This helps create the feeling of depth.

The second example of putting nature into perspective is a landscape that includes a lake and a road. I decided to place the horizon line a bit above the center of the page to achieve a view as if the observer was in a slightly high position, which works very well for landscapes. The vanishing point is off center to the right to make space for the lake on the left. I will start setting the mood with a hilly background made up by random, slightly inclined, very loose lines that seem to be getting farther and farther away (Picture 9). To achieve the depth in the hills, draw them on top of each other, letting some spots overlap and dip behind one another. I also drew the first two lines of the foreground that will soon become a road.

When you want to draw a body of water like a pond, a lake or a pool, you need to build a horizontal plane that contains it. That way you make sure that it sits flat in space and the water is not going to spill over. You can see in Picture 10 that I drew a rectangular horizontal plane with the bottom left corner going off of the page (red). I then drew a wavy line using that plane as a reference, imitating the shore of a lake. The lake does not have to be strictly within the plane's boundaries; just use it to help you figure out the inclination that it should have. I then sketched some rocks and bushes on its shore. Both these objects have the same characteristics as mountains; they can have any size and shape imaginable, so just have fun with them.

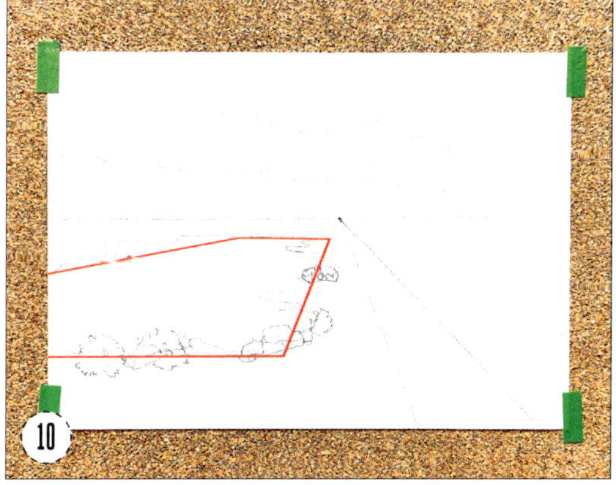

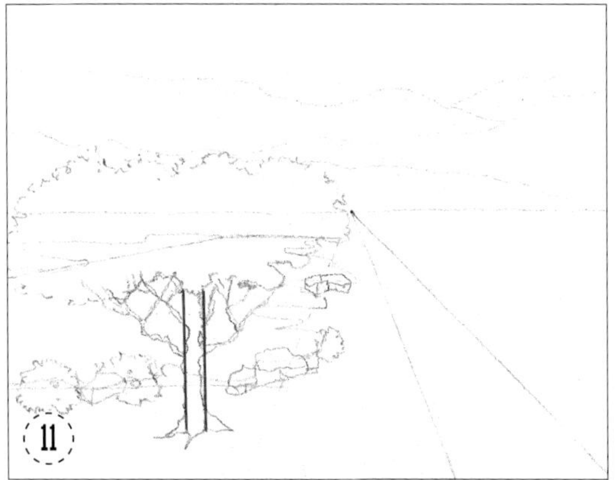

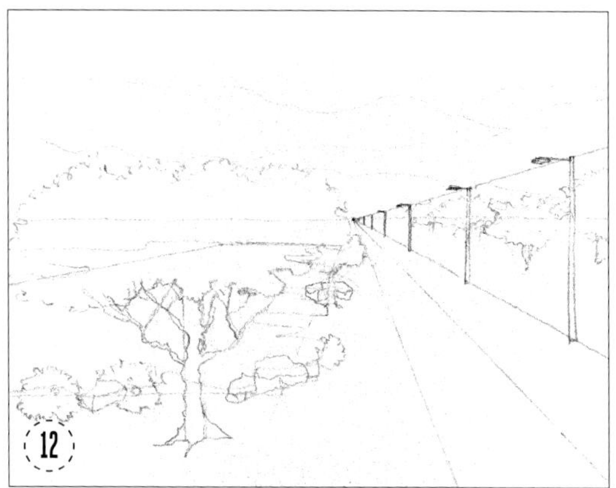

PRO TIP: The focal point is that object or person that you want to be the main character of the drawing or painting. Having a focal point helps a lot to figure out the general composition because the rest of the elements should be helping it shine. Always think about your composition before drawing the very first line.

Next, I will draw a tree between the lake and the observer. I want this tree to be the focal point of the drawing, so I will make it big. I always start trees by drawing their trunk with two vertical lines (red in Picture 11). I use them as a guide to draw more organic shapes, copying the texture of bark, and then I add smaller branches meandering toward the top. It is always a good idea to have reference pictures so you can see how things actually look. For the leaves, I made random wiggly lines that follow the outside shape of the whole body of the tree.

Trees have many different shapes and sizes, but usually trees in the same region have roughly the same characteristics, so I am going to draw some more trees using the first one as a reference, just as you did with the palm trees on page 29 (Picture 12). This picture also shows how I used a technique you studied in the Height, Depth and Spatial Awareness lesson (page 20) to draw a series of light posts at the right side of the road. Each one is made up of two vertical lines that form the post, a horizontal line at the top and a small squiggly object at its end that looks like the lamp. I like my sketches to look very loose and relaxed so I never detail objects much, but feel free to make yours as detailed as you want.

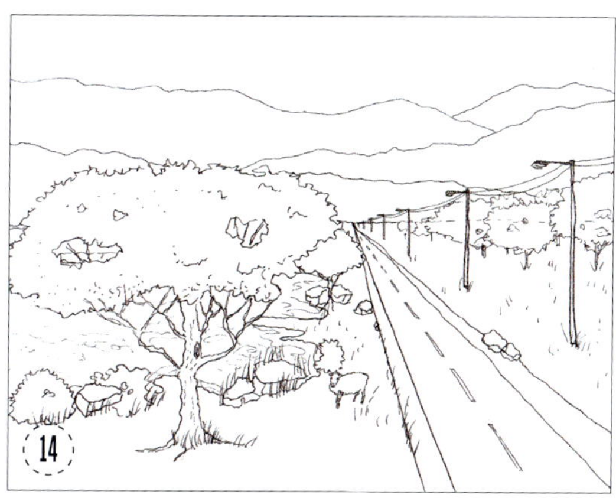

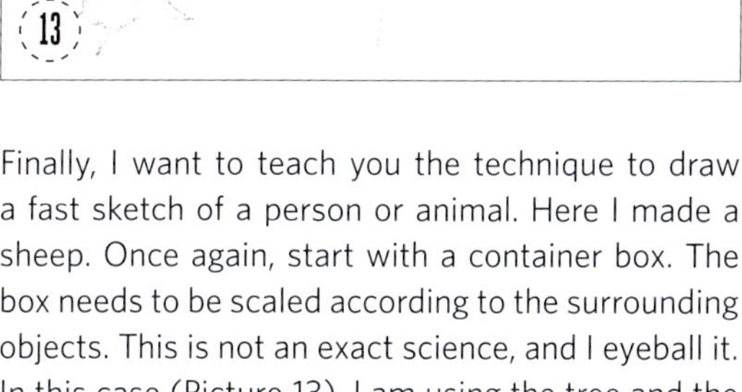

Finally, I want to teach you the technique to draw a fast sketch of a person or animal. Here I made a sheep. Once again, start with a container box. The box needs to be scaled according to the surrounding objects. This is not an exact science, and I eyeball it. In this case (Picture 13), I am using the tree and the road to figure out its size.

Inside the box, I will sketch the basic shapes that make up the body of the sheep as circles or ellipses (red). Now it is much easier to insert the different body parts of the sheep inside those ellipses. Use a reference picture to figure out the exact position of the eyes, ears and legs, and, of course, make the body a bit squiggly to mimic the texture of the wool.

When you are satisfied with how your drawing looks, finish it up with all the details you want. Notice how I have drawn everything in pencil so far, just to make sure that I am happy before inking the final version. Picture 14 shows the finished result. Notice how I created a lot of layers: (1) the tree and road in the first plane, (2) the lake and sheep right behind it, (3) light posts to the right, (4) trees behind the light posts, (5) the same road far in the distance, and (6) the mountains in the background. Many layers is exactly what you want to create the sense of depth in your landscapes.

Many people feel insecure when drawing organic and curved objects in perspective. But if you use container boxes or planes to do it, you will feel much safer drawing inside their boundaries.

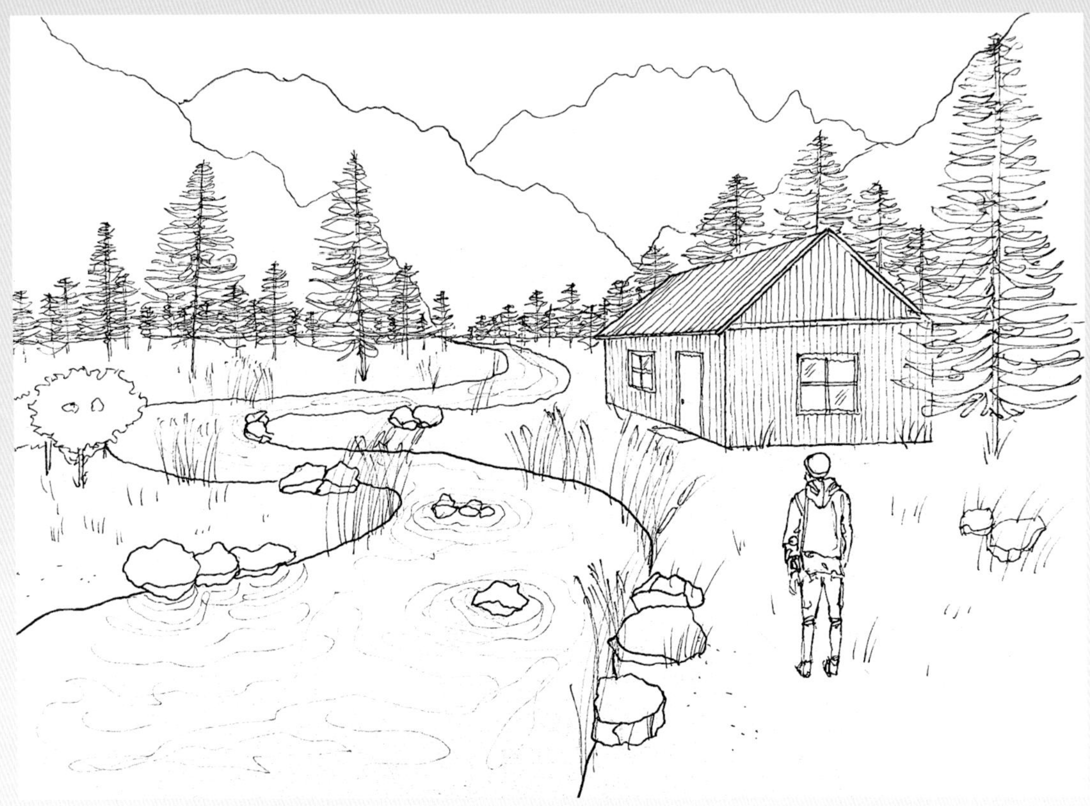

PROJECT: SKETCHING A NATURAL LANDSCAPE

Now, I will show you how to draw your very first woodland sketch. Remember that it does not have to be perfect. Perfection is only achieved by repetition and practice, so right now, just focus on understanding and having fun. This sketch will allow you to explore the power of trusting your container boxes and planes when experimenting with organic lines as you create a meandering stream, pine trees, a cozy cabin and a hiker observing the whole scene.

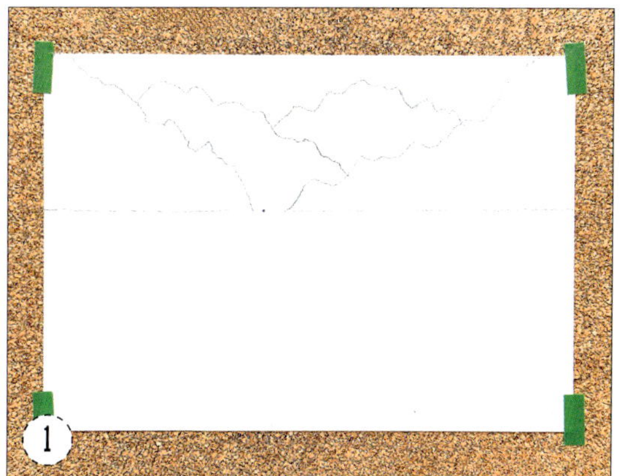

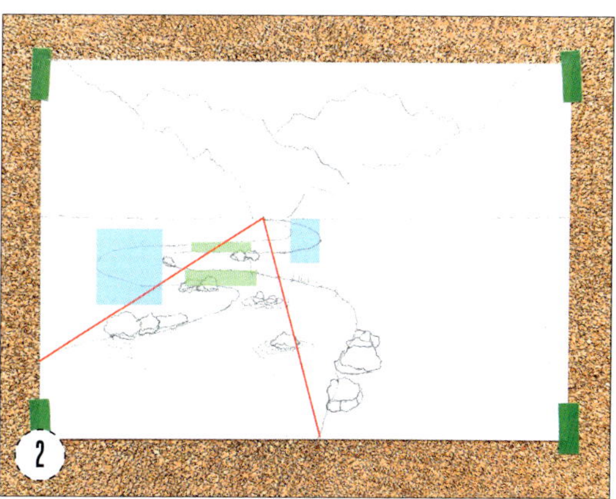

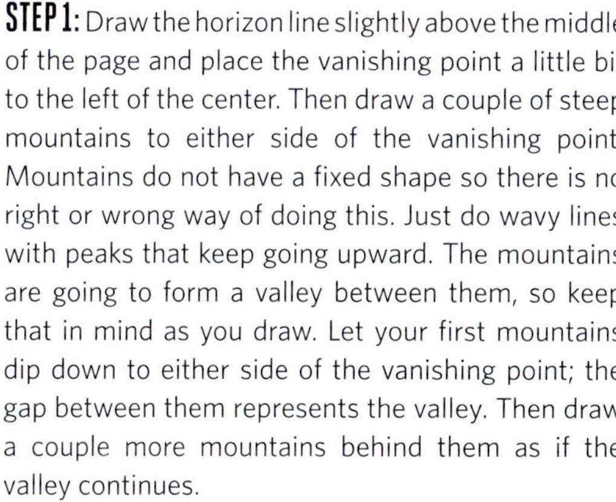

STEP 1: Draw the horizon line slightly above the middle of the page and place the vanishing point a little bit to the left of the center. Then draw a couple of steep mountains to either side of the vanishing point. Mountains do not have a fixed shape so there is no right or wrong way of doing this. Just do wavy lines with peaks that keep going upward. The mountains are going to form a valley between them, so keep that in mind as you draw. Let your first mountains dip down to either side of the vanishing point; the gap between them represents the valley. Then draw a couple more mountains behind them as if the valley continues.

STEP 2: Draw a couple of straight lines (red) coming from the vanishing point toward the left corner of the paper. Use them as a reference to draw a pair of winding lines representing a stream. As the stream gets closer to the observer, the distance between the banks should be progressively bigger and match that of the two straight lines. This is the same method you would use to draw a curvy road or a hiking path.

Note that when you draw something like this, you will always see the sections facing the observer directly (shaded in blue) wider than those that run across (shaded in green). This is an effect of perspective and the same reason you always see a horizontal square plane wider than deeper. Now add some stones at the stream's shore to create ambience.

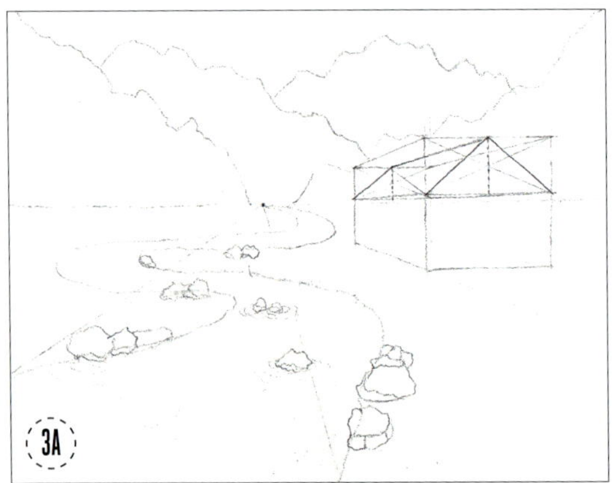

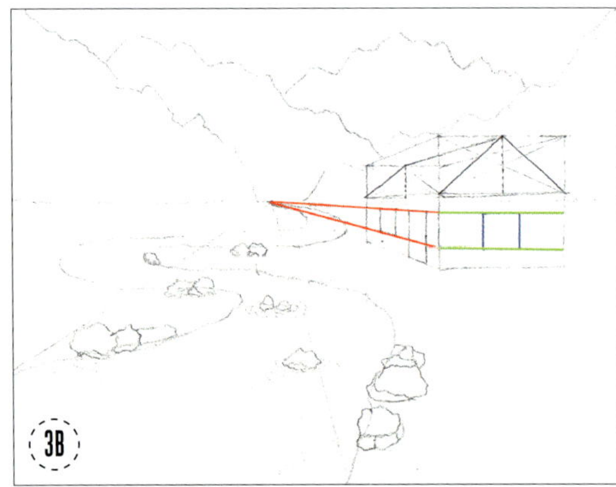

STEP 3: Now you will put a cabin in the empty space on the right. Draw a rectangular box and a triangular box exactly on top of it (Picture 3a). Next, put a door-shaped plane (vertical rectangle) on the left side of the bottom box (Picture 3b). The lower side of that plane should be aligned with the bottom line of the cabin. Now draw a squared plane at its left side aligned with the top of the door, which will become a window. Add another window on the side of the box facing the observer.

I want both windows to be the same size and height. To transfer the height from one side of the container box to the other, draw a couple of lines from the vanishing point that touch its top and bottom borders and go all the way to the corner of the cabin (red in Picture 3b). In the corner, wrap them around by continuing them horizontally on the front-facing plane (green). Add a couple of vertical lines (blue) to complete the square, and now you have two identical windows on both sides. The cabin is the first object with an identifiable size in the drawing, so it is going to determine the scale of every other object.

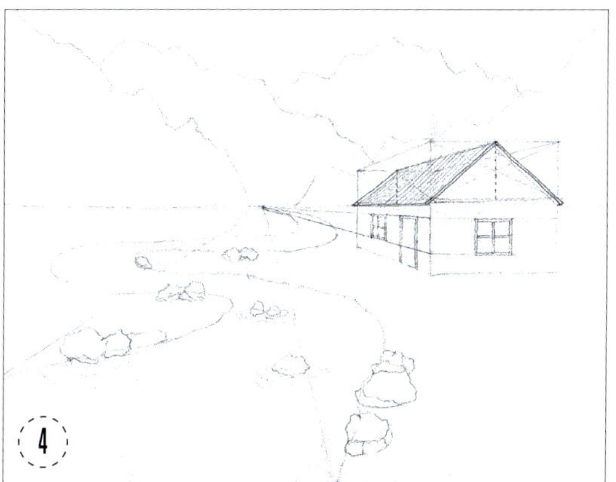

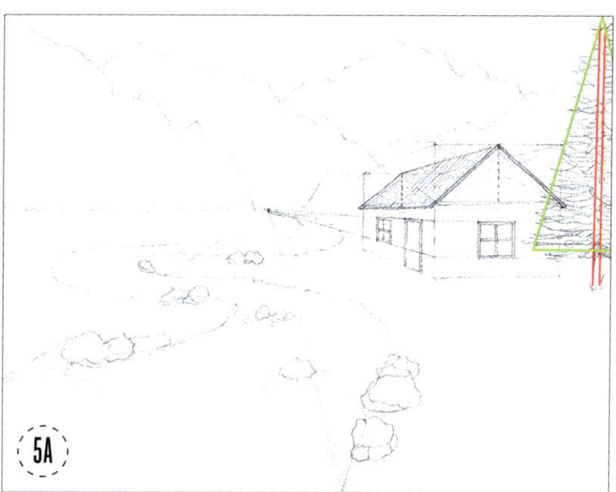

STEP 4: Now that the basic shape of the cabin is done, add some details. Add double lines in the planes you just drew to create frames for the door and windows. Also, draw a double-lined cross on each window to give them a rustic cabin vibe. In the roof, add double lines on the front to give it volume and extend it a little bit past the front and back walls so that it looks more real. Then, fill it with lines parallel to the inclination of the roof imitating boards or straw.

STEP 5: Next, decorate the scene with some pine trees. Draw the first one in front and to the right of the cabin. Use its size as reference and assume it is at least double the height of the top of the roof. Start with a couple of vertical lines (red) that represent the trunk (Picture 5a). Then draw wiggly, shaky lines coming in and out of it in a triangle-shaped manner (green) all the way to the top. Now, fill the landscape with many more trees using the repetition of objects technique (see the Height, Depth and Spatial Awareness lesson on page 20 and the Putting Nature in Perspective lesson on page 28) (Picture 5b).

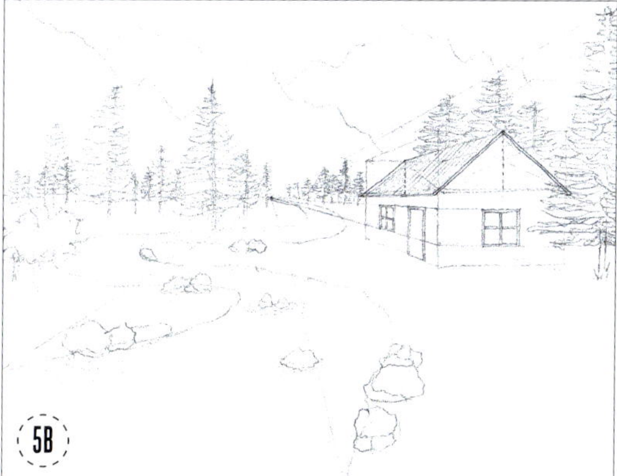

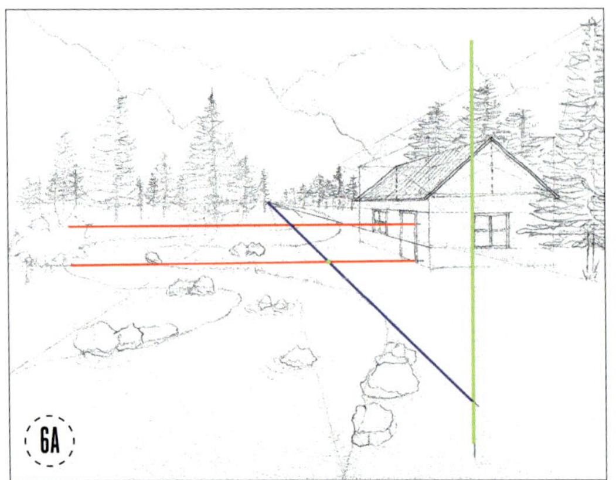

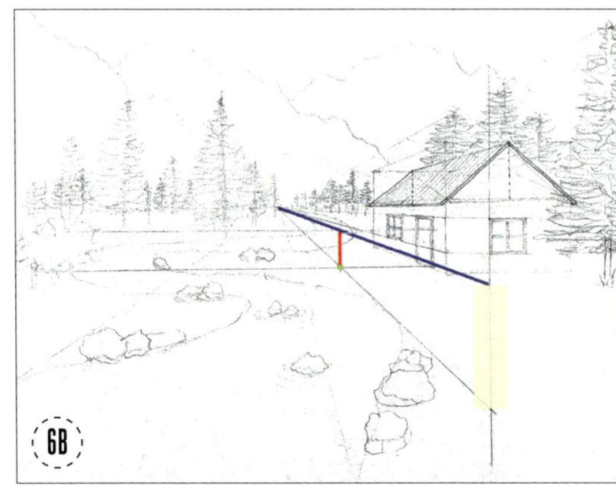

STEP 6: The finishing touch of the drawing is going to be a human figure. How do you decide the size of a person (or any other object with an identifiable size) in an almost finished sketch? Pay close attention because this technique I am about to show you will become one of your most treasured secrets. The first thing you need to do is find an object that you can easily compare with a human. In this case, I would recommend the door. Next, sketch a couple of horizontal lines with the assumed height in comparison to it (red in Picture 6a). The average person is roughly three quarters of a standard door.

Now, draw a vertical line in the place where you want the person to be (green in Picture 6a). Then draw another line that starts somewhere in that vertical where you want their feet to be touching the ground and goes all the way to the vanishing point (blue in Picture 6a). That line is going to intersect with the lower of the two horizontals that you made first. From that point (green in Pictures 6a and 6b), draw a vertical line (red) to the upper horizontal line (Picture 6b). From there, draw a line from the top of your new vertical (red) that goes to the vanishing point and extends all the way to the vertical line of the initial position you chose for the person (blue in Picture 6b). The distance between those two lines (yellow in Picture 6b) determines their height in that particular position.

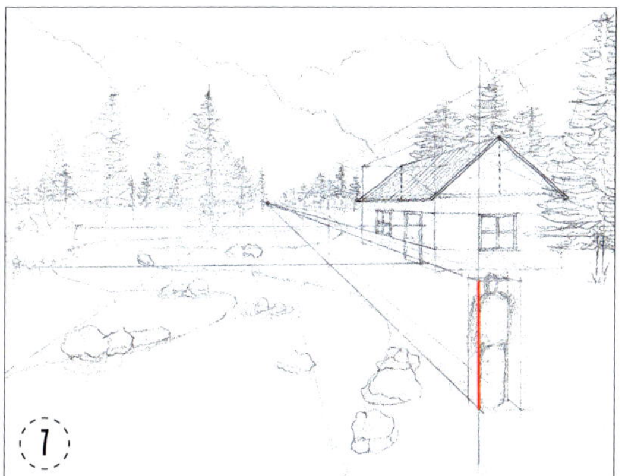

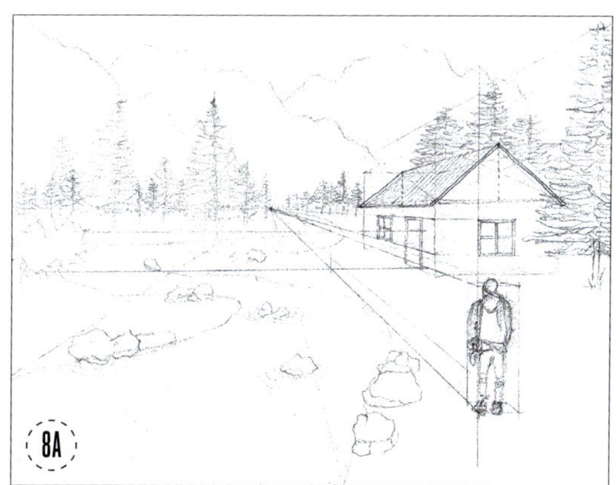

STEP 7: Using that vertical as the first corner, draw a box that contains the person. Inside of it, draw ellipses dividing the person into their most basic parts.

STEP 8: Now you can use those ellipses as a guide to draw the person's details (Picture 8a). For more details on sketching human figures in perspective, see the Vertical Vanishing Points lesson on page 101. Finally, ink the whole drawing when you are happy with everything (Picture 8b).

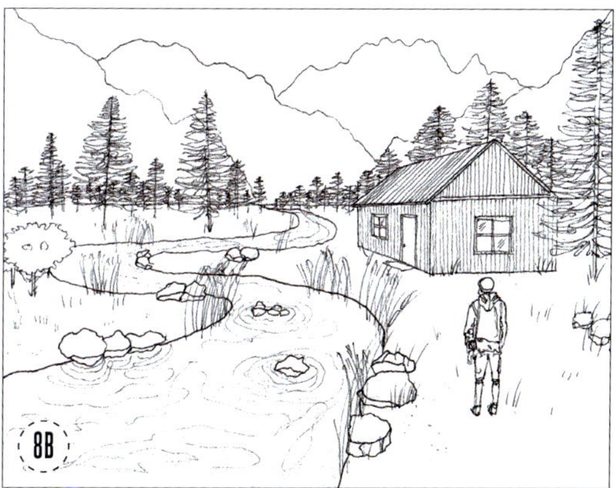

You are now ready to get out there, draw an awesome natural landscape and leave your friends' minds blown!

LESSON: CONQUERING DIAGONAL LINES

Diagonals are incredibly important in drawing. More than you may think. Particularly for architecture sketching, where you need to be able to draw things like ramps, staircases, roofs, half-opened doors, objects leaning on walls and so on. So far, you have seen glimpses of diagonal lines, for example to create a triangular box or a pyramid. But in this chapter, I want to teach you in detail how to draw diagonals and use them for very practical purposes.

Perspective is easiest with lines that are perpendicular to each other, because as you have seen, you only need to think about the three main directions: straight horizontal, straight vertical and going to the vanishing point. When the angles of lines start changing, people start struggling. I am going to show you a painless way of dealing with this. To do this, you will create your first interior perspective.

By definition, interior perspective implies creating a space within which to put the observer. I start with the simplest of spaces: a big blank box with straight walls. I place both the horizon line and the vanishing point in the very center of the paper (Picture 1). Then, I will make a couple of diagonal lines (red) from opposite corners of the paper creating an X. Those lines cross right at the vanishing point.

Now the paper is divided in four triangular planes: left (orange), top (blue), right (yellow) and bottom (green). Imagine for a moment that you are inside a rectangular-shaped tunnel and the vanishing point represents its end as far as your eye can see. The orange section would be its left wall, the blue one its ceiling, the yellow its right wall and the green one its floor.

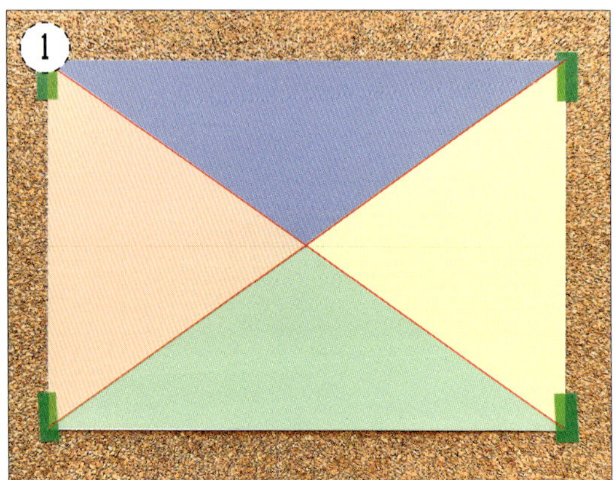

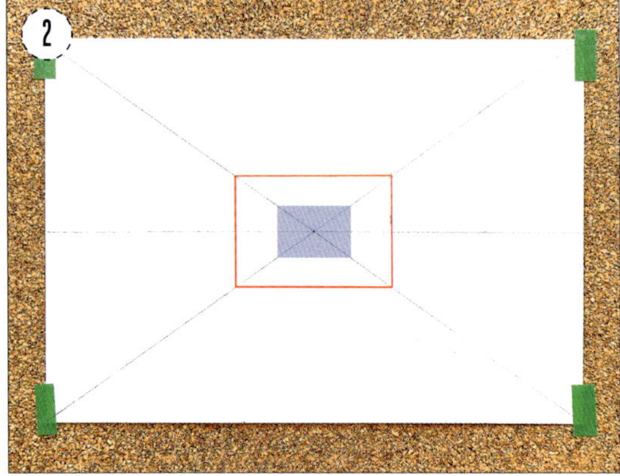

I do not know about you, but being inside a tunnel that long makes me a bit uneasy, so I want to draw a wall that limits its depth. A front-facing plane will do that job perfectly. I will build it by joining the diagonals with straight vertical and horizontal lines (red in Picture 2). That plane can be as big or small as you want. The smaller and closer to the vanishing point you draw it (for example, the blue plane in Picture 2), the deeper the room will be. Now that I have completed the room, I will start drawing the inside.

The first thing I want to show you is how to draw an object leaning on a wall. A standing mirror is a perfect example of this. I will start with a vertical rectangular container box that sits right where the left wall meets with the floor. To do that, place the bottom left corner of the box anywhere on the diagonal (green dot in Picture 3). Then I drew the two diagonals of the mirror that start on the floor and finish up on the wall (red in Picture 3). Next, I join those two with lines that go to the vanishing point (blue in Picture 3). Notice that if you want the mirror to look closer to the wall, you need to draw a shallower box.

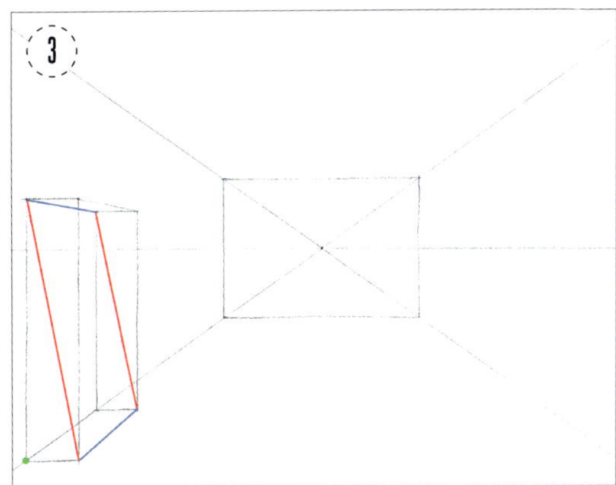

To finish the mirror, I want to give it a frame all around. So, I drew a very long and narrow plane on the front to give it thickness (green in Picture 4). Then, I drew an X on its front (blue) and used the X to draw a smaller plane inside of it by joining those diagonals. See how I started with a line parallel to its left side (red) and then went all around using the vanishing point?

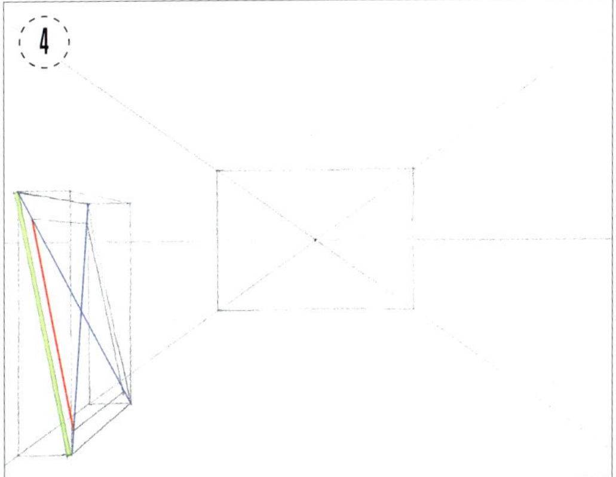

Picture 5 shows the result. I added some diagonal lines on the mirror to create the illusion of a reflective surface.

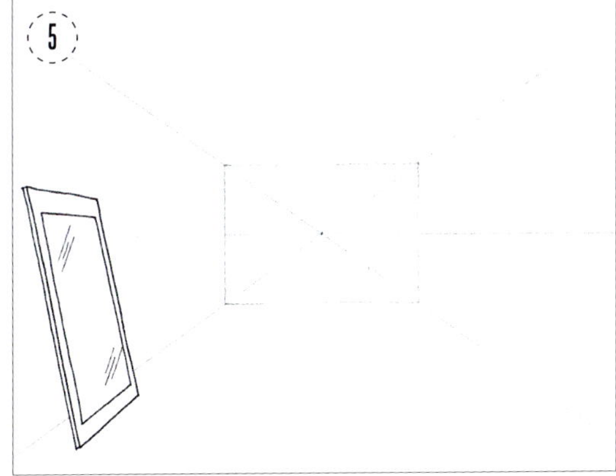

Another kind of diagonal you are going to be using a lot are the ones used to draw half-open doors. I get so many messages from people who struggle with the correct way of determining the angle and size of a door that is not shut. With this method, you will not have that problem.

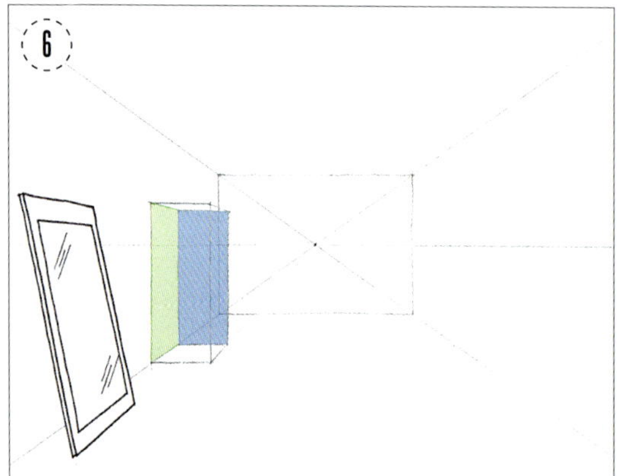

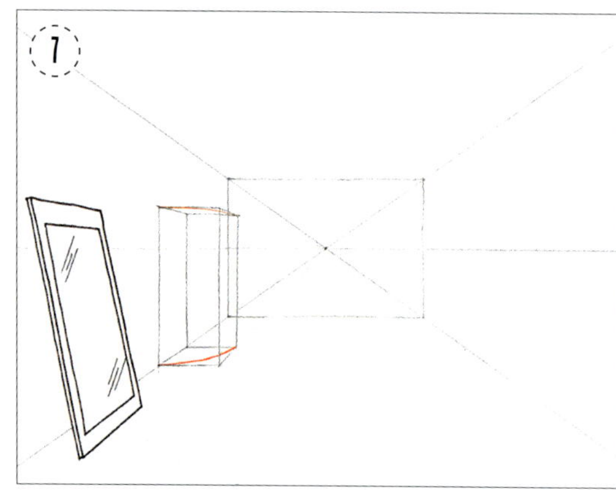

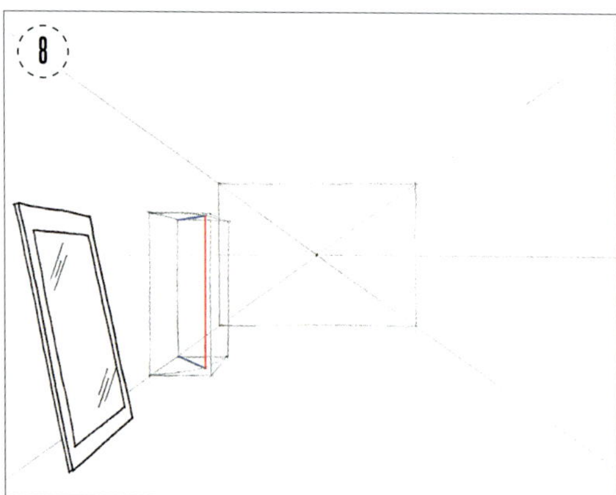

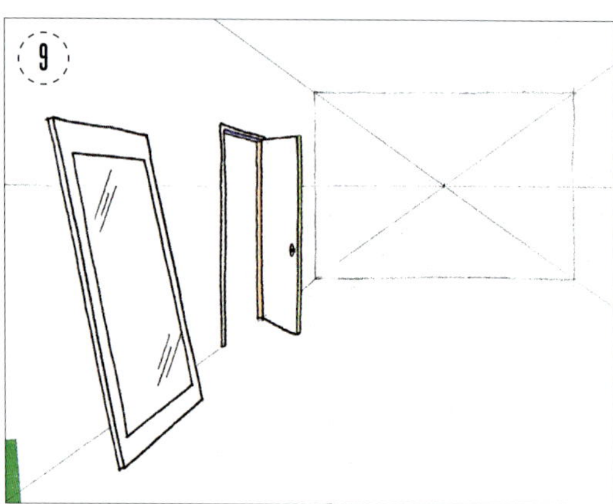

I begin by drawing a container box with a squared base (Picture 6). This box will be positioned in the same wall as the mirror, so I aligned its bottom-left corner with the same diagonal. This box will determine the height of the door; I am going to assume that the mirror next to the door is a full body mirror, so I'll draw my box just a little bit taller than it. Now I want you to imagine that the plane of the box touching the wall (shaded in green in Picture 6), is the door when it is shut. That means that when it is opened to 90 degrees, its position changes to the plane in the back (shaded in blue).

If I draw a couple of arcs (red in Picture 7) in the upper and lower planes of the container box, I will be able to find the path of the door as it goes from closed to open. Now, I just have to choose the opening angle that looks best and draw it. To do that, I draw a vertical line (red in Picture 8) in my selected position joining the two arcs. From its ends I draw a couple of lines (blue) to the hinging corners of the door's plane.

The final touches for the door include adding thickness by drawing a thin long plane to the edge of the door (shaded in green in Picture 9). I also drew double lines around the plane in the wall to mimic the frame. In this position, I would also be able to see the depth of the frame in the wall for the upper and right sides of the door opening (shaded in blue and orange). That is drawn with a couple of planes joined at the top corner. You will see this in detail later, so do not worry. I also drew a simple handle for the door.

The third example of diagonal planes I want to show you is the kind used to create ramps, roofs and staircases. For this part of the lesson, pretend that there is a hall leading to another room in the upper right corner of the back wall (Picture 10). To draw the hall, I erased from the corner a front-facing plane the size of the hall (shaded in green). Then I continued the ceiling diagonal until it hid behind the wall (red). I also drew a line from the bottom-right corner of the hall going to the vanishing point (blue). These two lines create the illusion of the hall continuing to somewhere else.

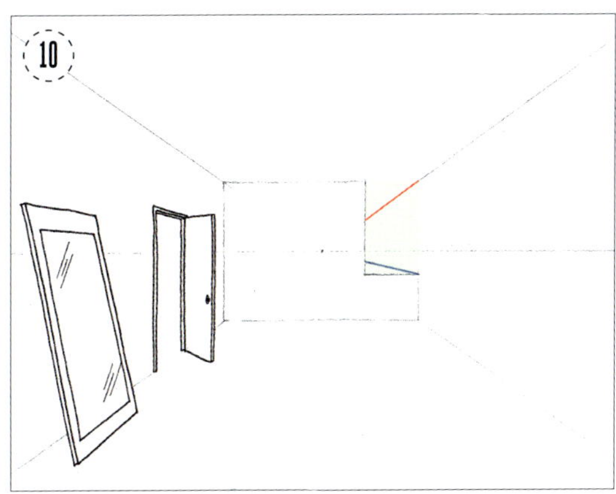

I think there should be a ramp to reach that hall. Again, the first step is to build a container box (Picture 11). It has the height of the wall below the hall and the width of the hall itself. I can make it as long or short as I would like. The longer the box, the less steep the ramp will be. Now I can draw the diagonals (red), and I almost immediately create the ramp.

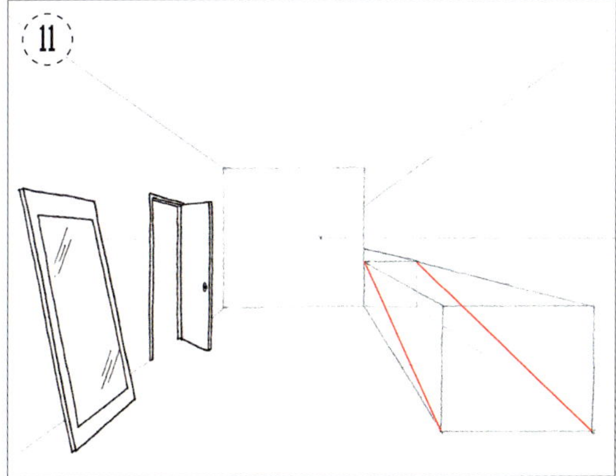

Picture 12 shows the drawing completed. I erased all container boxes and reference lines.

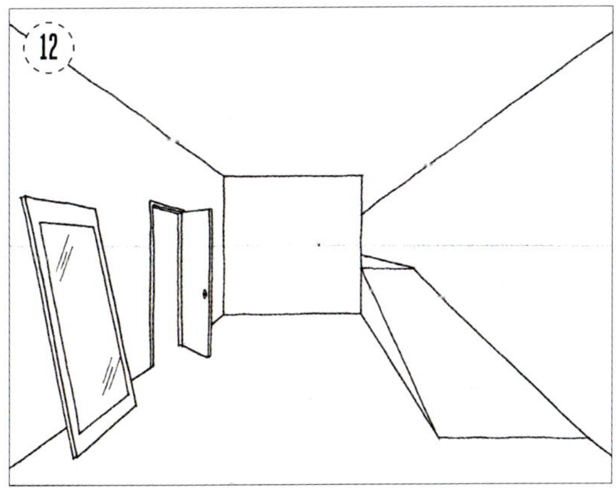

Get ready for a very exciting project ahead where you will use all these concepts to draw your first staircase.

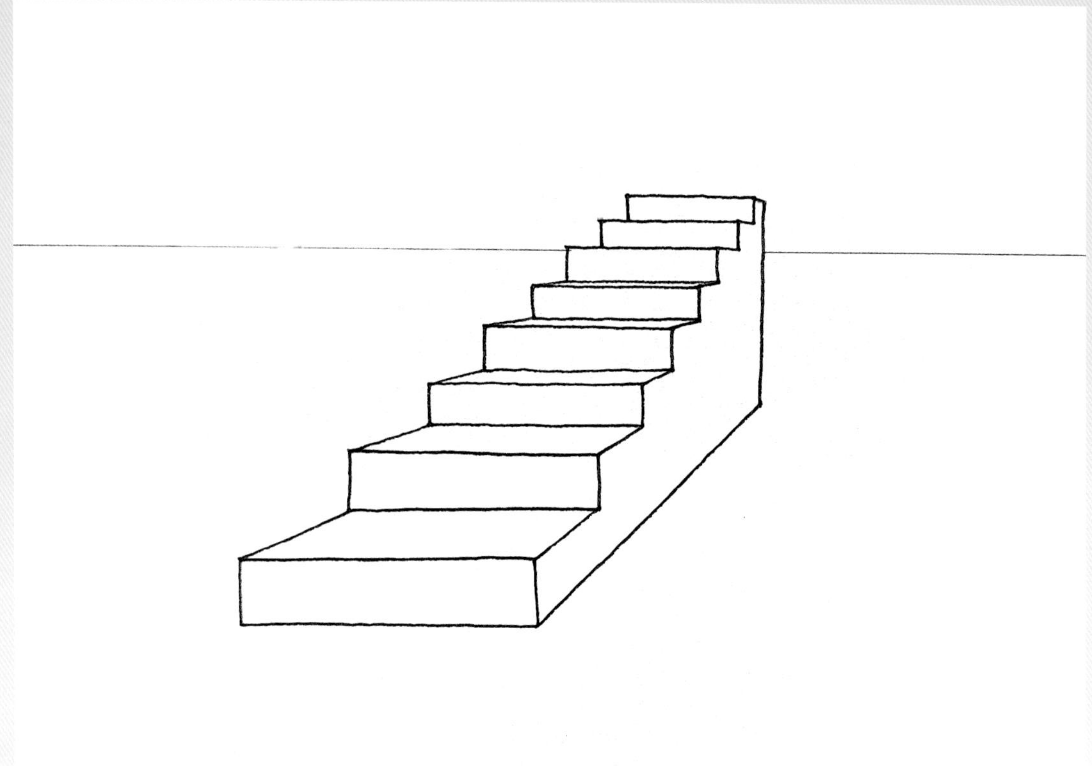

PROJECT: DRAWING A SIMPLE STAIRCASE

People around the world have a natural fascination with staircases. Historically, they have been focal points of castles, monuments, parks, paintings, photographs and every other means of human expression. I personally am obsessed with them, and I want to teach you how to draw them without losing your mind. Students are terrified of them, but there is absolutely no need to panic. I will lead you with baby steps and start with the easiest type: a straight staircase.

PRO TIP: Staircases can be more or less steep, but a 2:3 ratio is the most common worldwide. This means that for every two units of any measure that you have to climb (vertically), the staircase needs three units to develop (horizontally). For example, if the height of the staircase is 6 feet (1.83 m), it should be 9 feet (2.74 m) long.

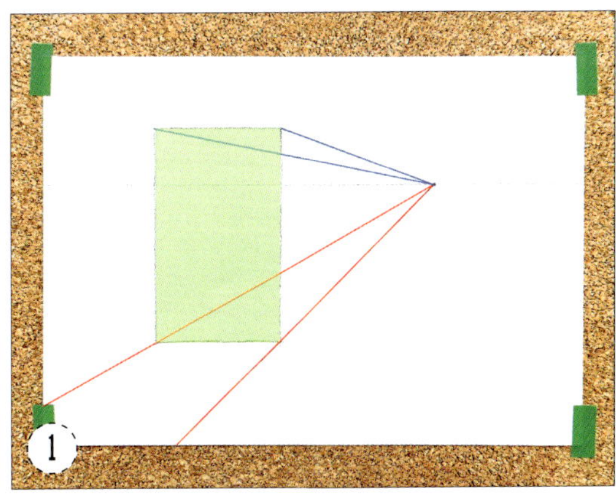

STEP 1: Draw the horizon line slightly above the center of the paper and the vanishing point to the right. Sketch a couple of lines (red) from the vanishing point toward the left corner of the paper. The distance between those two lines is the width of the staircase.

Next, draw a rectangular front-facing plane (shaded in green) that has the height of the staircase. Make sure that it goes above the horizon line so you can see how it looks when that happens. Now, add lines (blue) from the two top corners of the plane to the vanishing point.

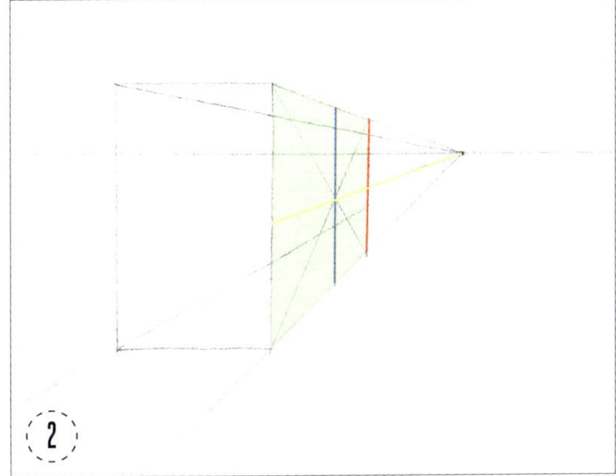

STEP 2: So far this is the normal process to build a container box, but now I will show you how to build it with the proportions needed according to the Pro Tip. Draw a line (red) on the right side of the box as if you were going to draw a squared plane (shaded in green). Find its center by tracing an X on it and draw a vertical line (blue) passing through the center. Add another line (yellow) that starts In the vanishing point and passes through the center.

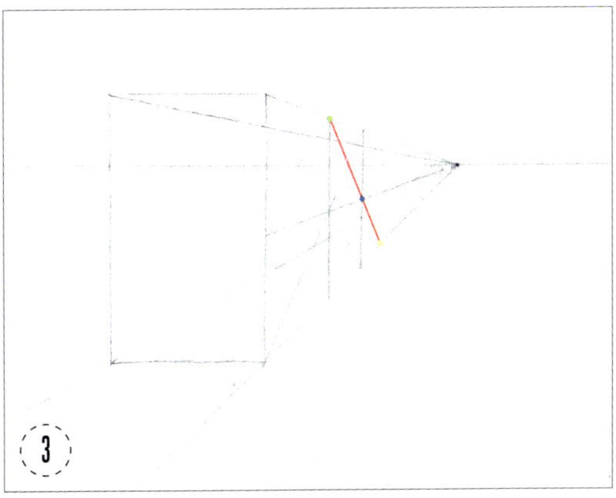

STEP 3: Now draw a line (red) from the upper end of that middle vertical line (green dot) passing through the intersection of the red and yellow lines from Step 2 (blue dot). The point where it touches the floor line that goes to the vanishing point (yellow dot) marks the exact 2:3 ratio needed.

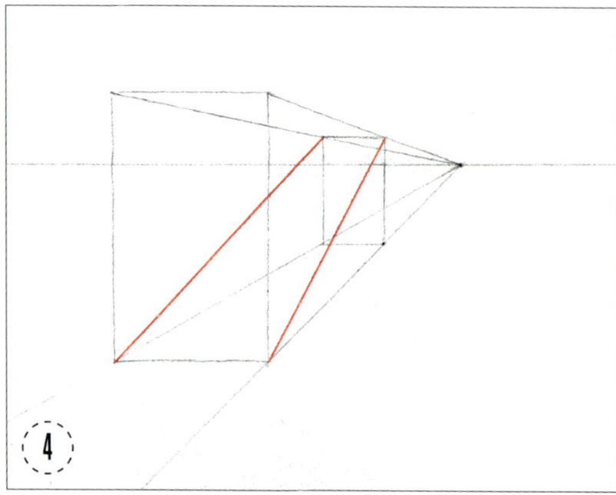

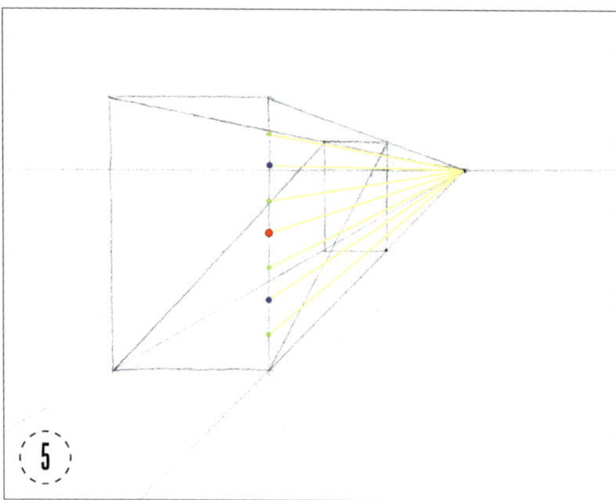

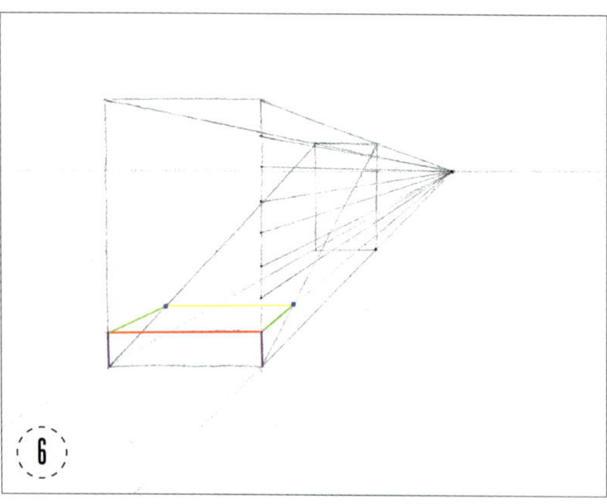

STEP 4: Now you can complete the container box using that point as a reference of its length, then erase all construction lines. Steps 1 through 3 will not be necessary once you develop the ability to eyeball the approximate proportions of the container box. But it is always nice to know the proper way of doing it. Next, draw two diagonals (red) on both long sides of the box.

STEP 5: Now you need to determine the height of the steps. Normally you would do this by dividing the total height you need to climb by 7 inches (18 cm), which is the normal height of a step. That would be the number of steps you need in your staircase. In this case, I have decided to do eight steps.

To find the height of each step, divide the closer vertical vertex of the box in eight equal parts. I usually find the middle of the line (red dot), then the middle of each half (blue dots), and finally, the middle of each quarter (green dots). From each one of those dots, draw a line (yellow) going to the vanishing point.

STEP 6: Here comes the fun part: Building the steps. Sketch a horizontal line (red) from the height of the first step going up all the way to the other side of the box. From both its ends, draw a couple of small verticals (purple) to the bottom corners of the box, and two lines (green) going to the vanishing point until they meet with the diagonals you added in Step 4. And then join those two meeting points (blue) with another horizontal (yellow). You just completed the first step!

STEP 7: For the second one, you need to add a couple of small verticals (blue) from the end corners of the first tread. The one on the right will find the height of the second step and stop there. The one on the left has the exact same height. Now repeat Step 6; that is, join them with a horizontal (red). Then, draw two small lines (green) to the vanishing point until they meet the diagonal and join them with another horizontal (yellow).

STEP 8: From this point on, all you have to do is repeat Steps 6 and 7 all the way to the last step before going above the horizon line. You will notice the treads seem narrower as they come closer to the horizon (shaded in green). Once they go above it, you will not be able to see them at all because they surpassed your eyesight height. Then it becomes even easier.

STEP 9: For the treads that go above the horizon line, draw two vertical lines (blue) just as you did in Step 7. Join them with a horizontal (red) and from its right end a small line (green) going to the vanishing point until it meets the diagonal.

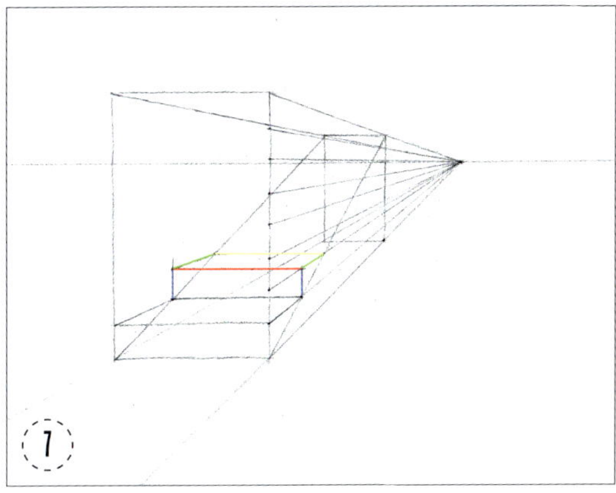

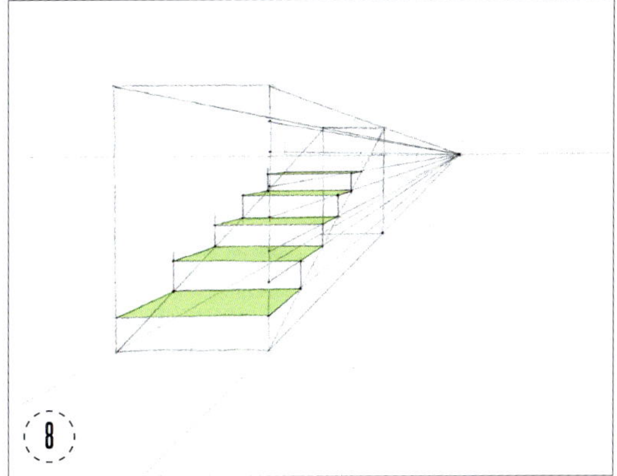

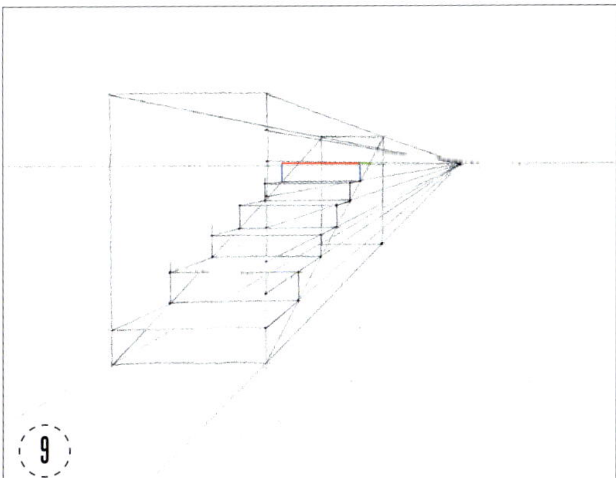

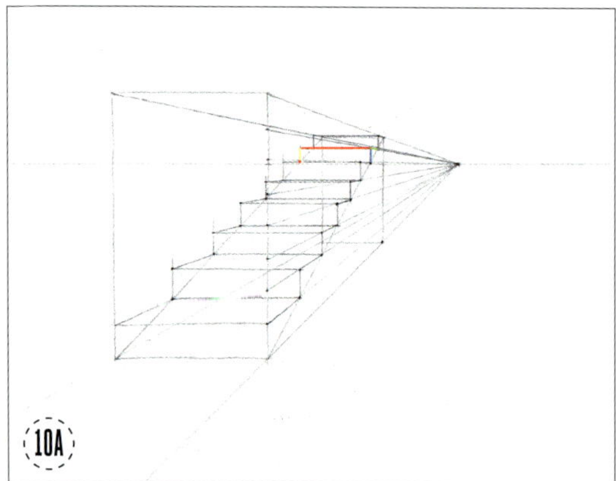

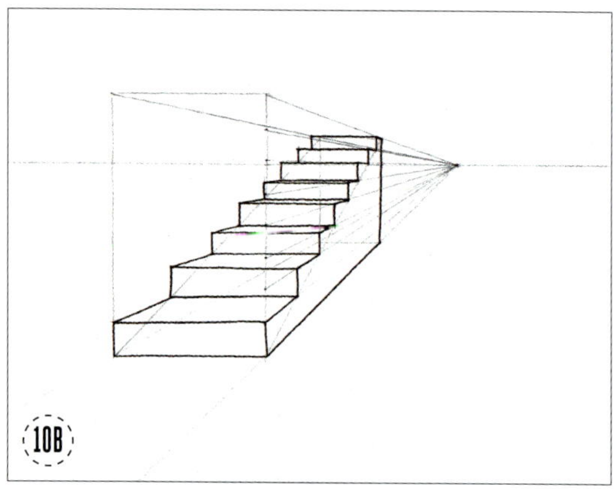

STEP 10: Use this process from there until the end of the staircase: Draw two vertical lines—one from the end of the last tread on the right until it meets the height of the following step (blue in Picture 10a), and another one (yellow) with the same height from the intersection of the last horizontal and the diagonal (red dot). Then, join them with a horizontal (red) and from its right end, a small line (green) going to the vanishing point until it meets the diagonal. Picture 10b shows the finished result.

Congratulations on finishing your very first staircase drawing! I really hope you enjoyed it. Now it is time to get your string ready because you will see how to do one-point perspective faster and easier.

LESSON: URBAN SKETCHING WITH STRING

This is what you have been waiting for: drawing with a string! Up to this point, I have covered the basics of one-point perspective and by now, you have a pretty good idea of how it works. Now, I want to show you how to use a string to work smarter and not harder.

If you are doing relatively simple drawings like the ones you have done so far, it is okay to use a ruler or reference lines. However, for more complex drawings, this poses several problems. First, having to align your ruler with the vanishing point to draw every single line is extremely time consuming and to be honest, quite annoying. If you are using reference lines to draw freehand, it is going to take you a lot of time as well. Then, there is the problem of cleanliness. Moving your ruler around and filling your drawing with reference lines will leave the paper smudged and needing a lot of cleaning up afterward. Finally, strings have an additional bonus that is priceless: fun! This technique gives you freedom and safety. Freedom to work without the need of rulers and safety to know that every single vanishing line you draw has the correct angle. Those two things combined make the overall experience much more enjoyable.

The concept of using the string is actually very simple. If you put a pin exactly in the vanishing point and then tie the string to it, you will know the exact angle of any vanishing line just by spinning the string around the paper or canvas. The idea is not that you use the string as a ruler by pressing the pencil or pen against it, because it is not sturdy enough and this would result in a curved and inexact line. You will just use it as a reference and draw your lines freehand following its direction in any given position. Many artists like Leonardo da Vinci and Vermeer have used this technique for hundreds of years to create perspective in their drawings and paintings. As a matter of fact, evidence has been found of prehistoric cave paintings made with strings trying to imitate perspective. How cool is that?!

I am going to use urban sketching to showcase the technique, but you can use it to draw anything you want. The reason it is perfect for urban sketching is the number of lines and details architectural drawings have. Many of those lines are parallels going to the vanishing point that you can draw very easily just by moving the string around. You will be able to see this very clearly once I start showing you examples. In this lesson, you will also learn how to create depth in windows, doors, openings and other objects. This is a concept that can also be applied to any other drawing.

The first thing I want to show you is how to set up your working space. I will start by fixing my corkboard to the table with masking tape (Picture 1). One piece in every corner is enough to keep it in place. I am using a 20 x 28-inch (51 x 71-cm) corkboard. This is rather large because I need to work with different formats, but you can choose a smaller size that is large enough to fit your preferred format. I also prepared a thumbtack and a string with a small loop on one end.

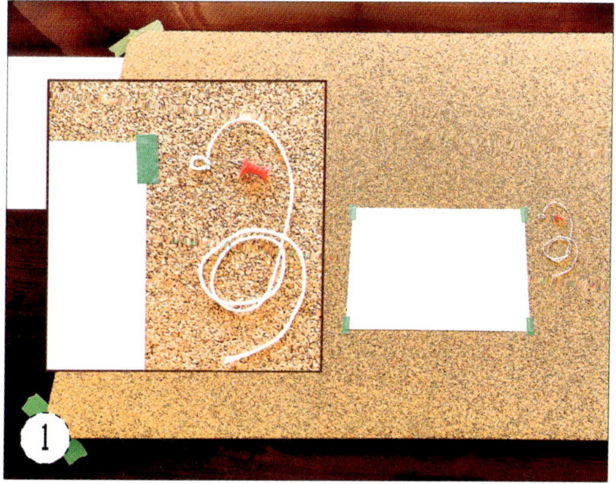

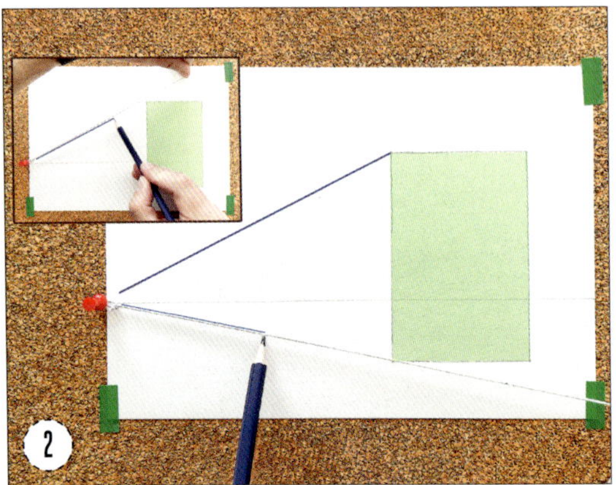

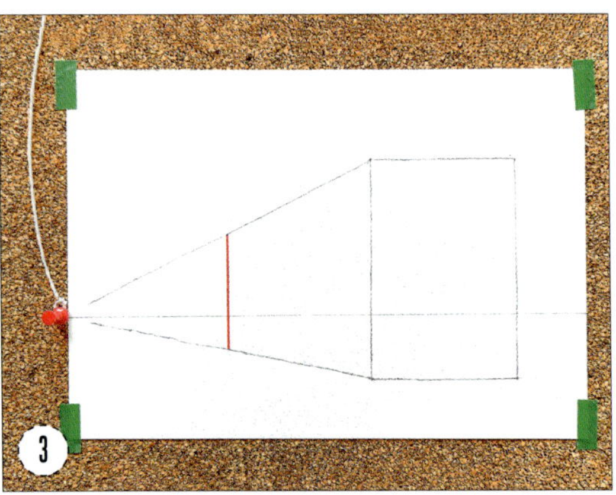

I will be drawing a small two-story building with doors, windows and balconies. I will be placing the horizon line low on the paper to achieve a view as if the observer was walking at street level, with the vanishing point (red thumbtack) to the left just outside the paper (Picture 2).

PRO TIP: The vanishing point can be placed as far outside the paper as you need, as long as it remains aligned with the horizon line.

The thumbtack is going through the string's loop so I can spin it around freely. You can see that I drew a front-facing plane (shaded in green in Picture 2) and I am using the string to draw lines (blue) from the vanishing point to the top left and right corners of the plane. I will then join those two lines with a vertical line (red in Picture 3).

So, I basically drew a rectangular box, but it was so much easier using the string.

When drawing buildings, it is always a good idea to divide the box into smaller sections. This ensures that all the details are well proportioned to the overall size of the building and that the design of the façade makes sense.

Let me show you what I mean. I will start with the horizontal divisions first. These are normally the height between floors. In this case, you just need one (blue in Picture 4). This line is a little bit above the middle of the box, because first floors are always a bit higher than the rest. Transfer that same line to the front face of the box (yellow) to unify the heights (check out Step 3 of the Sketching a Natural Landscape project on page 36 to remember how to transfer heights).

The vertical divisions (red) usually coincide with structural components like columns or walls and almost always determine the position of windows and balconies. In this case, I am drawing two pairs of equally distanced lines on the left side and two more on the front, but the one furthermost right is much closer together.

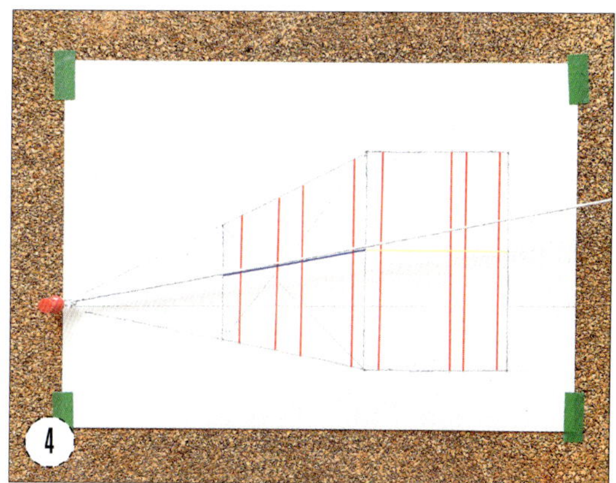

Now that there is a clearer view of the building's design, I can start adding architectural details. The first thing I want to show you is how to make a balcony. I am going to place it between the two blue lines in Picture 5, starting exactly where the second floor begins. A balcony's normal height is approximately one third of the total height of the floor. So, I need to draw another box (red) with that height and place its bottom right corner where I want it to start (green dot). You can see that the length of that box is exactly the distance between the two blue lines. As for its depth, you can make it as deep as you want, but balconies are normally rather shallow.

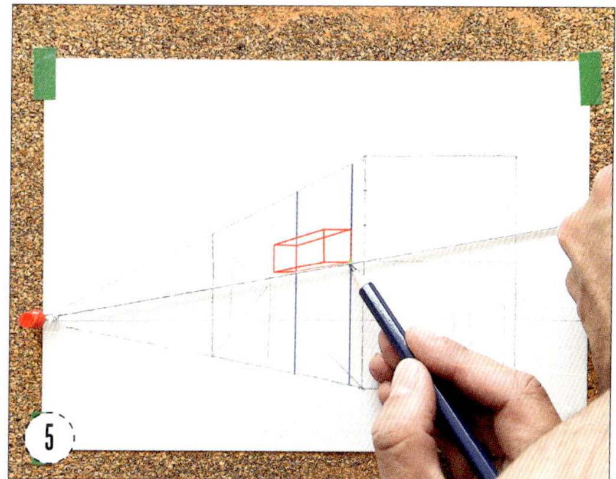

When you have the box in place, you can add detail. I am adding double lines at the bottom to mimic the slab and on the top to emulate the handrail (red in Picture 6). Then I will draw pairs of vertical lines (blue) between them as balusters.

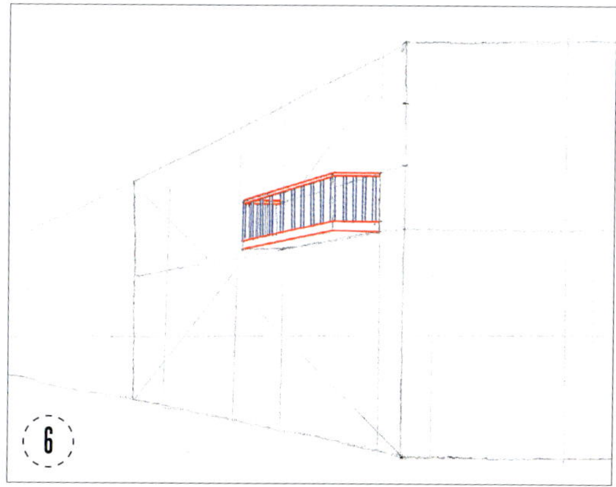

The next step is to draw the first-floor windows and doors. I am assuming that there are shops on the first floor, so there would be large windows facing the street and doors to enter.

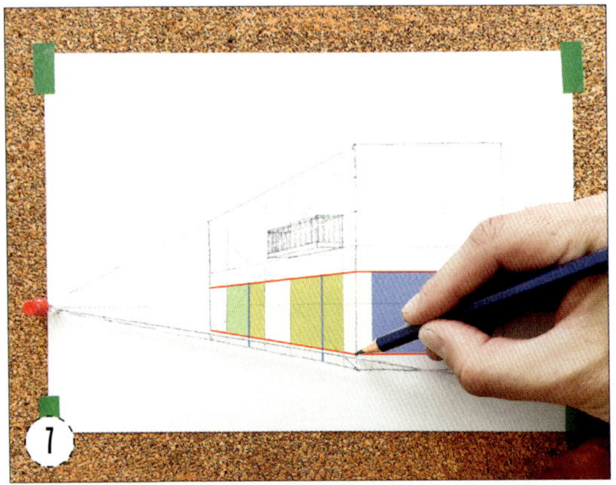

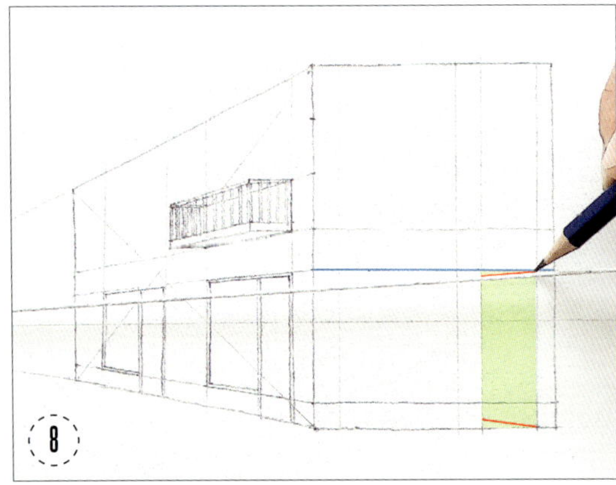

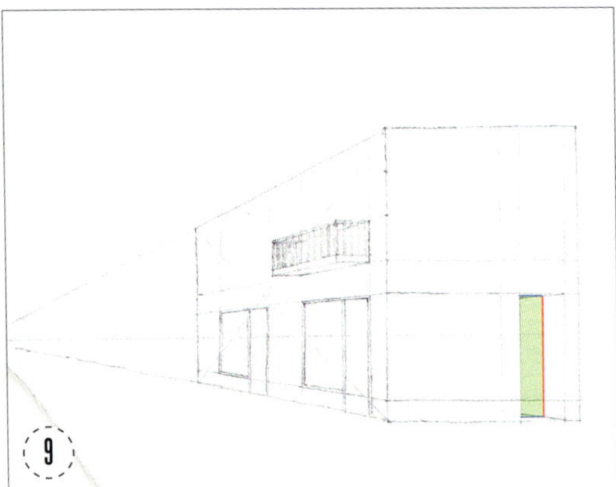

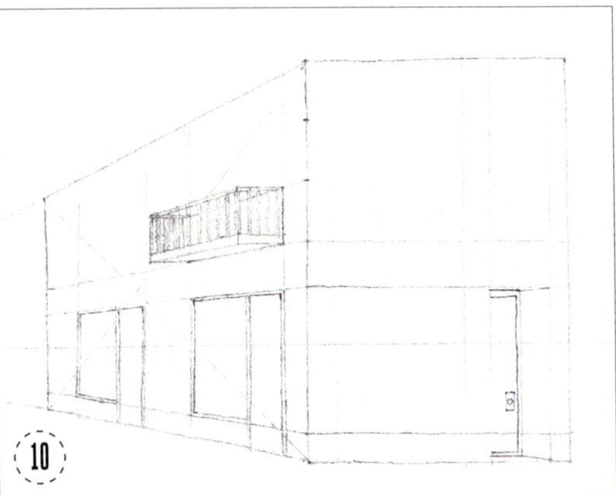

I drew two lines (red in Picture 7), using the string, that determine the height of the two windows on that side (shaded in green) and continued them in the front-facing plane so that the window on that side (shaded in blue) has the same height.

Then, I drew two vertical lines (blue) close to the right side of each one of the green windows. They are drawn approximately at one third of the total windows' length. Those lines go all the way to the floor and will become doors. The window on the right side has no door.

For now, I will keep things simple and just do double lines all around to create thickness in the frames (Picture 8). The main door opening of the building is on the far right (shaded in green). Its height is the same as the window's (blue line). But this door is going to be different because I will push it back a bit so that it looks like it is recessed. To do that, I draw a couple of lines (red) with the string from the right top and bottom corners of what will become the entryway until they hide behind the front wall.

Those two lines create the depth in the hall, at the end of which is the door. Now I just must decide how deep I want that hall to be. I do that by drawing a vertical line (red in Picture 9) that joins them. The farther to the left you draw the line, the deeper the hall is going to appear.

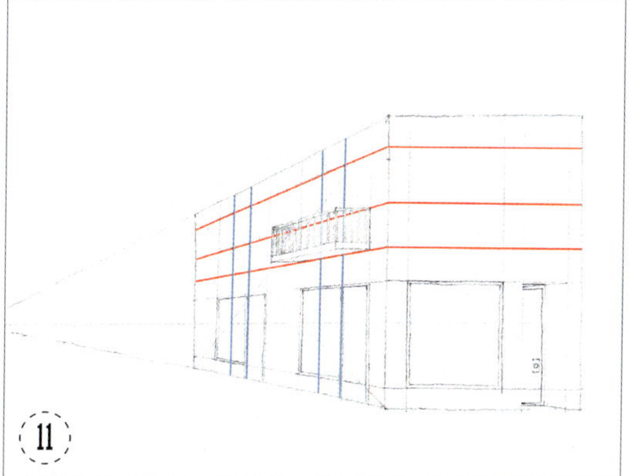

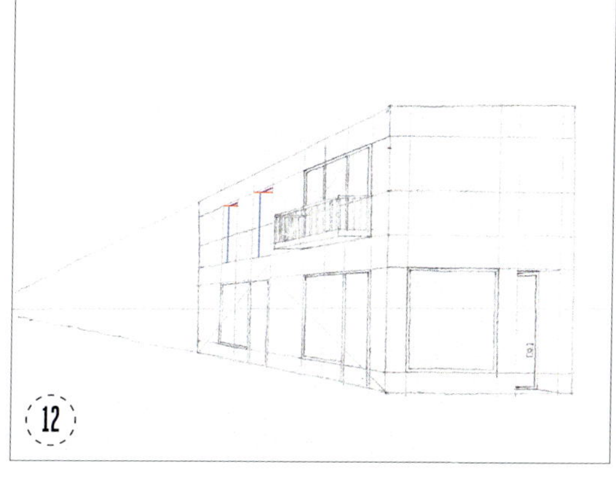

Then, draw a couple of horizontals (blue) from the new vertical's ends until they hide behind the wall. The plane shaded in green is the new position of the door. Picture 10 shows how you can only see the right side of the door, because the rest is hidden. I added double lines for the frame and a door handle to finish it up.

That wraps up the first floor. Now I will go upstairs and complete the façade using a very similar process. I start with three lines (red in Picture 11), drawn using the string, that determine the height of the windows and then transfer those lines to the other side, so the heights are unified. Note that the two bottom lines match exactly the lines of the balcony. I am eyeballing the height of the third line, using the windows on the first floor and the balcony itself as a reference, given that I want to have floor-to-ceiling doors and windows.

Next, I will draw the verticals (blue) that will help me figure out a design for the upper floor windows. I want them to match the ones on the first floor, so I will divide the ones on the left side into three sections using the doors below as reference, remembering that they were drawn at one third of the total window's length. I can find the other third by dividing the first-floor window into two equal sections. For the window on the front, I will just make the outer lines match so I do not need to make any additional lines.

In the balcony, I am just going to make a big window with doors that has three equal divisions and do double lines all around to simulate the thickness of the frame (Picture 12). On the left, I want to make a couple of vertical receded windows. To do that I will follow a very similar process to the one I used for the door on the first floor, starting with two horizontal lines (red) from the top left corners of the windows until they hide behind the wall. Then, I choose the depth of the windows and added two verticals (blue) until they hide behind the ledge. From that same point I draw two lines (purple) with the string until they hide behind the wall.

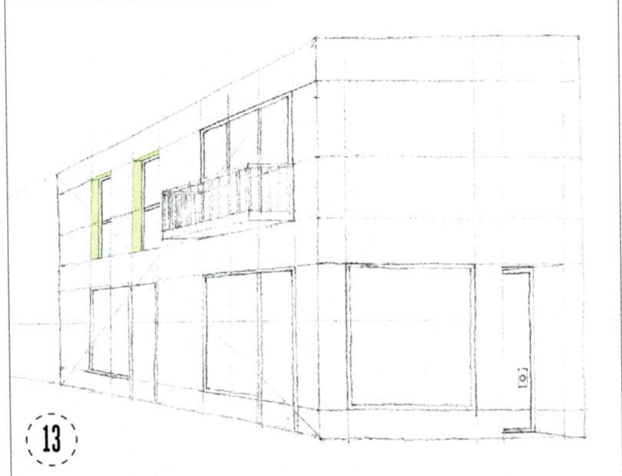

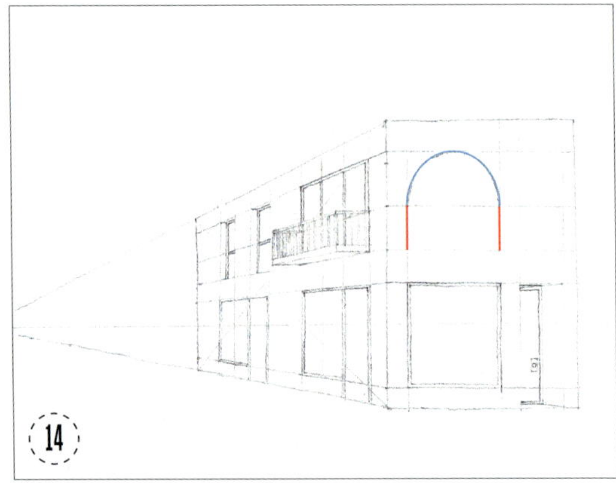

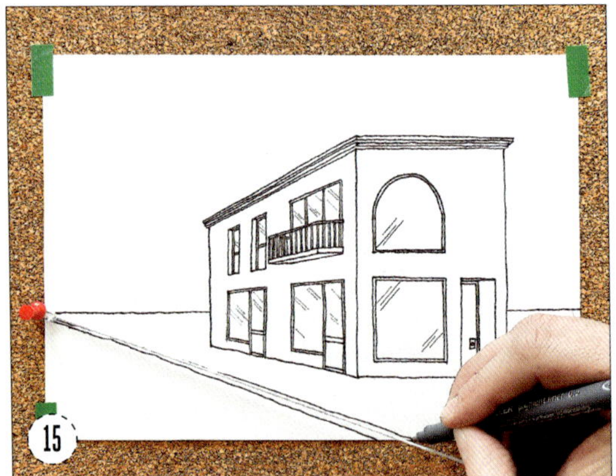

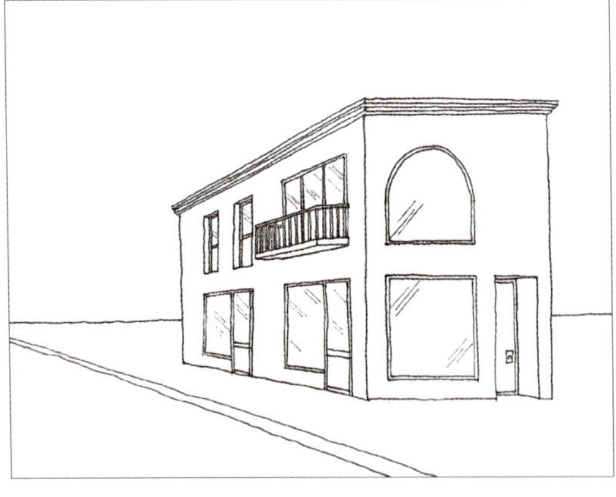

Picture 13 shows the windows drawn in that receded plane. These windows are above the horizon line, so you will only be able to see the depth on the left and top sides (shaded in green).

Okay, I am almost done! I only need to figure out the window on the top right side. How about doing a beautiful arched window? You will see in Picture 14 that I drew a couple of verticals (red) joining the two lower horizontals. From their upper ends I sketched an arch (blue) that reaches the top horizontal.

To finish up the sketch, I added some final details to help it feel complete and situated in space (Picture 15). I used some parallel lines at the top to draw a cornice. This is very typical of mid-twentieth-century architecture. I also drew the sidewalk in front of the first floor and added random diagonal lines in the windows to emulate reflections.

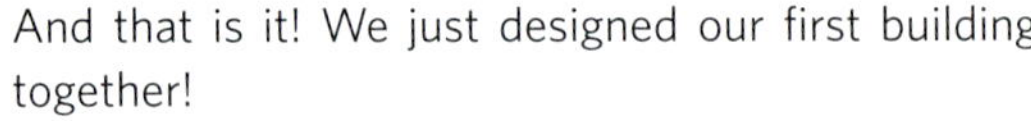

And that is it! We just designed our first building together!

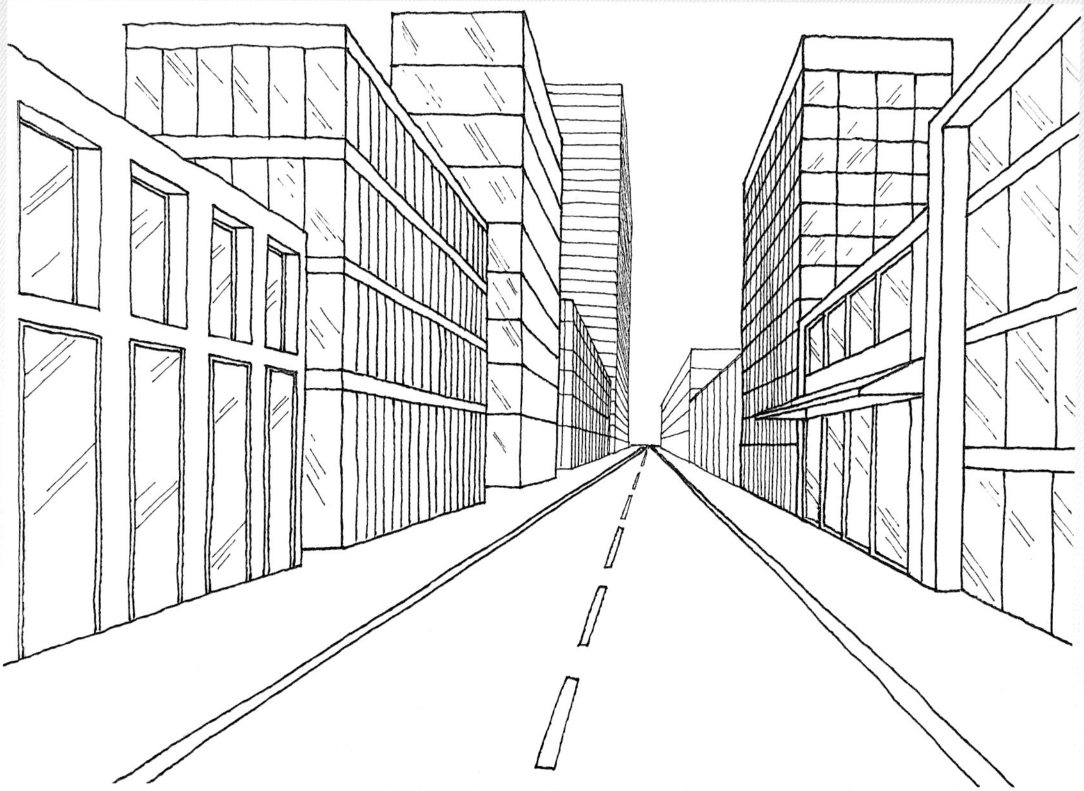

PROJECT: BEGINNER'S CITY LANDSCAPE

Drawing a city street is one of the most fun projects you can do using one-point perspective. It is ideal to generate the sense of depth that perspective is famous for. And doing it with a string is even better! You are going to be creating a series of buildings at either side of a street and experimenting with different façade and architectural designs. So, without further ado, start drawing!

Additional Materials

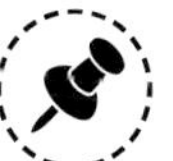
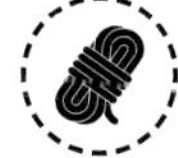

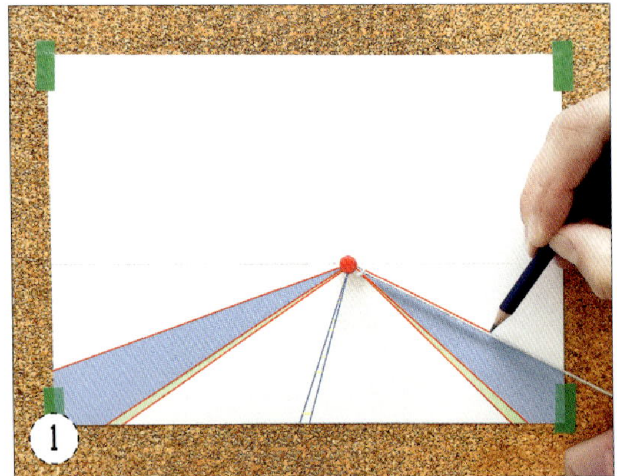

STEP 1: Draw the horizon line below the center of the paper and the vanishing point a little bit to the right. Pin the thumbtack with the string exactly in the vanishing point (see the Urban Sketching with String lesson, page 49). Now use the string to draw two sets of three lines (red) going to both corners of the paper. Two of them should be very close together (as the height of the sidewalk, shaded in green) and the third one a bit more separated (for the actual sidewalk, shaded in blue).

Again, using your string, draw two lines (blue) to the bottom middle edge of the paper. Then, make very short pairs of horizontals (yellow) between those two lines. They need to be closer together as they move away from the observer to give the illusion that they are getting smaller. Those are the division lines of the street.

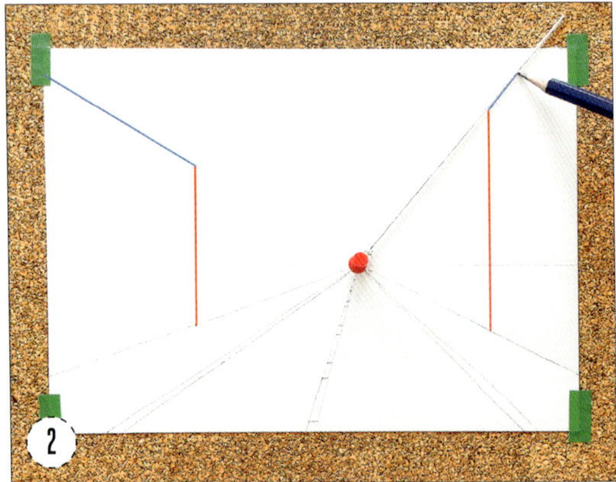

STEP 2: Now it is time to start with the buildings. Each one of them is going to be a box (or the visible part of one). It is best to draw all the boxes before doing any details. That way, you can make sure that you are satisfied with the overall composition first. You will build from the front to the back. Draw a couple of vertical planes by drawing two verticals (red) up from the sidewalk, and from their top ends, two vanishing lines (blue) using the string until they go off the paper. Those two planes are the front façades of the first two buildings.

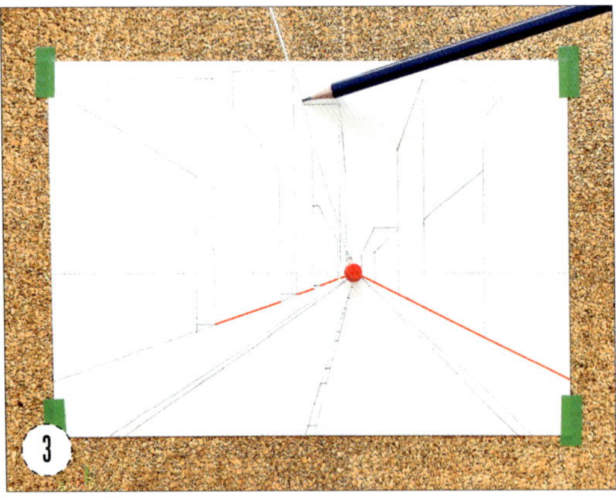

STEP 3: Draw boxes of different sizes all the way to the end of the street. The bottom line of all their front planes (red), must be aligned with the sidewalk just like the first two. You only need to draw the planes—or sections of the planes—that you would be able to see. You can draw them together stacked side by side, as I did on the right side, or leave a small gap between them as on the left side.

STEP 4: The boxes are done and it is already looking pretty cool! The next thing to do is define the horizontal floor divisions. I have decided that the first building on the left should be two stories high. So, draw two lines (both red in Picture 4a) using the string. Align the first one with its top edge. Then, draw an X on the front plane to find its center and draw the second one a bit above the center because first floors are usually higher than the rest of the floors. These two lines set the height for the first and second floor in every building on that side. If you use those two lines as reference, by comparison you could determine that the next building has four floors. So, you can draw another couple of lines (blue), that have roughly the same distance between them as the red ones.

This is a process that you can continue all the way to the end. It is a very important step to ensure that the floor heights are well scaled throughout. When visual comparison is too difficult, use the following method: Take the height that the floor lines have at that point (green) and repeat it all the way to the top of the following building (alternating light blue and pink lines). From those height marks, add new lines (yellow) to the vanishing point using the string. With those lines, the third building is ready too. And then, repeat for the tall one at the end (purple lines).

I have done the exact same thing on the right side (Picture 4b). Keep in mind that the heights need to be similar to the ones on the left. By comparison to the left side, the first building on the right is four stories so I drew an equal number of red lines. Because it is shorter than the first, the second building is done. And now, just repeat with the other buildings. The yellow lines show that process.

STEP 5: Draw horizontal lines on the other side of the boxes (red). They need to be aligned with the intersections of the vanishing lines for the stories and the closest verticals of each box (green dots in the second building on the left).

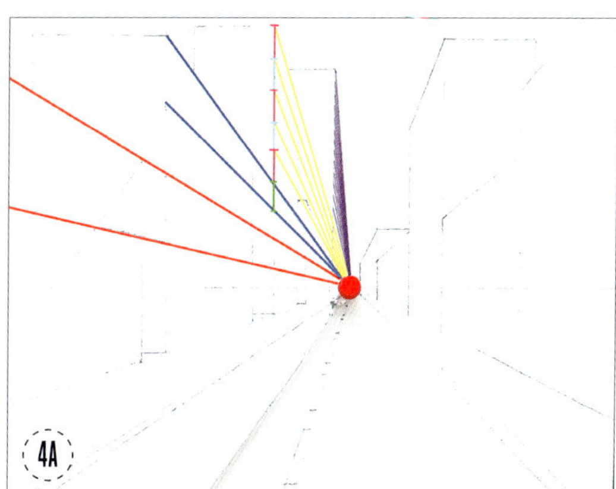
4A

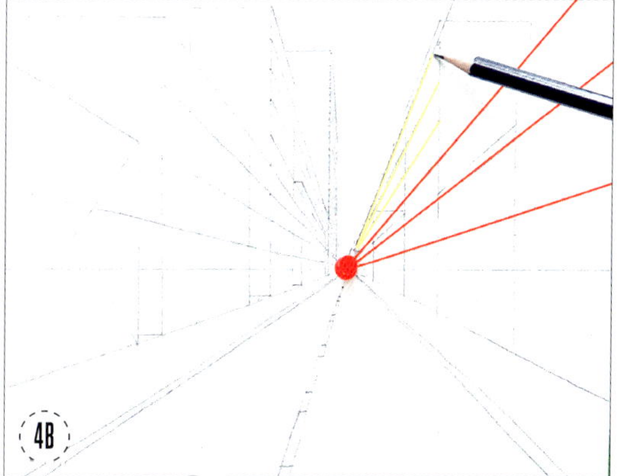
4B

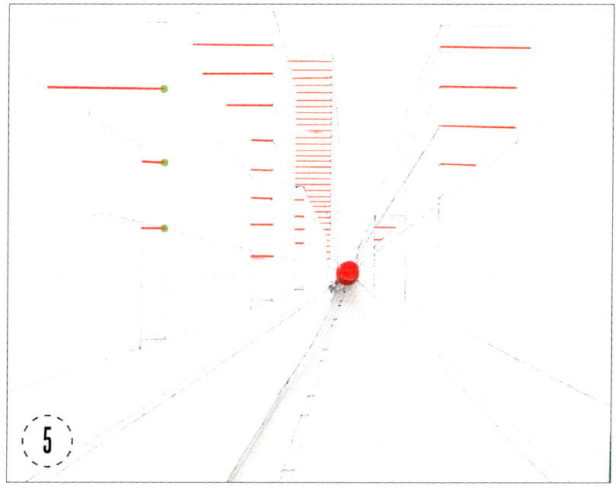
5

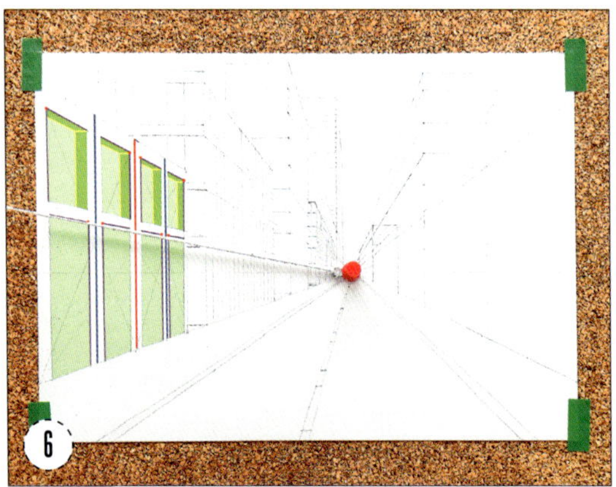

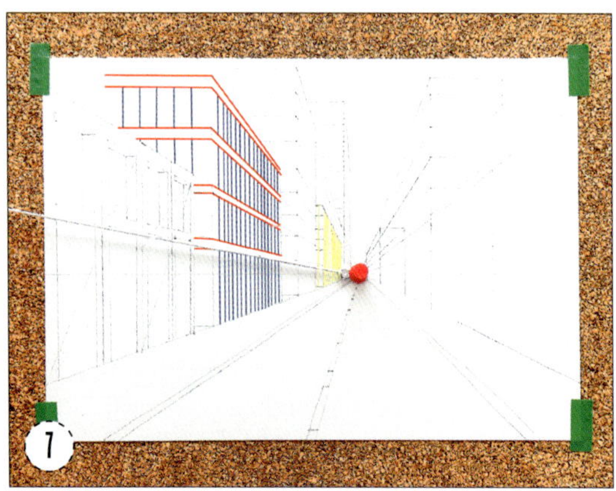

STEP 6: The horizontal floor height grid is ready. Now, you will start with the details, beginning with the first building on the left. Draw a vertical line (red) that passes through the center of the X. Then draw another X on either side and add two more verticals as you did before (blue). That divides the building into four equal parts.

Now draw planes (shaded in green), leaving columns between them using all those lines as guides. See how I am using the diagonals to know the exact size of those planes (red dots and purple lines). The string comes in handy to do this, because it helps you keep those top and bottom lines aligned at all times. Those planes are the windows. I want to add a little bit of character by doing receded windows on the second floor as you learned in the Urban Sketching with String lesson (page 49). The yellow lines and darker green shading show you how I did it here.

STEP 7: For the second building, you are going to do something very simple: Draw double lines in every floor division (red), and then vertical lines between them (blue). They will look closer on the side of the street because of the angle. The amount of lines depends entirely on what you want the building to look like. Try to draw them slightly closer together as they get farther away. In the third building, just leave the horizontals as is. The fourth building will be a grid of horizontals and verticals, so just add the verticals (yellow), in the same way you did with the second building but going from the floor to the roof unbroken. For the last building on the left side, which that is taller than the rest, you will do only horizontals again. The farther away the buildings are, the less detail they should have so the sketch does not feel overloaded.

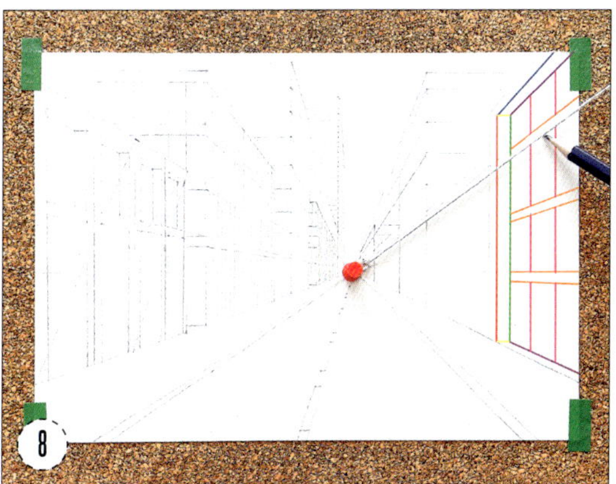

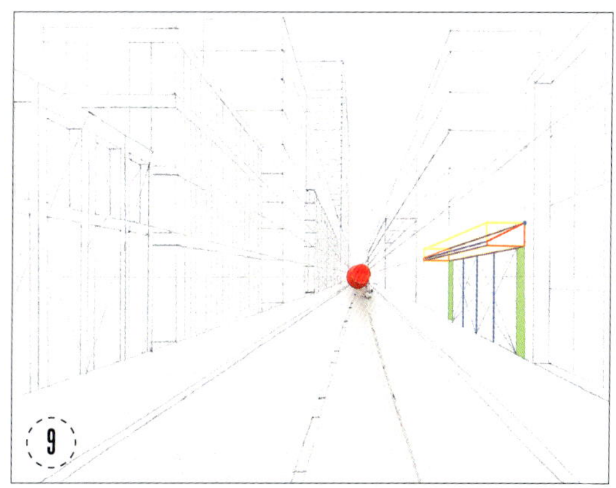

STEP 8: It is time to cross the street and work on the other side. The first building will have a frame all around and then a receded glass wall. Draw a vertical line close to the left edge (red) and join it with a string -drawn line near the top edge (blue). Then, draw the depth of that frame just as you did with the windows on the second floor on Step 6. Draw a couple of small horizontals (yellow) from the corners of the frame. Now join their ends with a vertical (green) and a couple of vanishing lines (purple). To finish, draw double floor division lines with the string (orange) in the receded plane and a couple verticals between them (pink) to give the illusion of glass divisions.

STEP 9: The second building on the right side will have a very cool canopy over the first floor like the ones you would see on a café or a shop. Draw a long, slim rectangular box (yellow) that covers the entire length of the building. Its top right corner (blue dot) should be aligned with the first-floor division line. In the closer plane of the box, draw the shape of the side of the canopy (red). Then use the string to draw lines (purple) from every corner of that shape to the opposite plane. Finally, join all the loose ends of the purples forming the same exact shape on the other end (orange lines). Your canopy is ready!

Below the canopy you will make a glass window from side to side leaving a small frame (shaded in green) on either side. Now divide the window into four equal parts (blue lines) repeating the process you did in the first building on the left (Step 6).

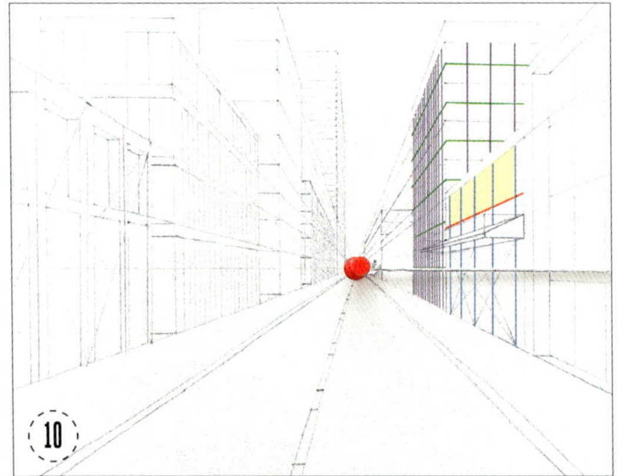

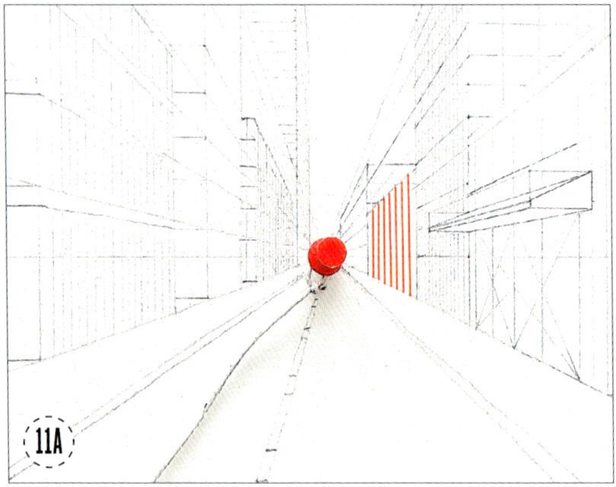

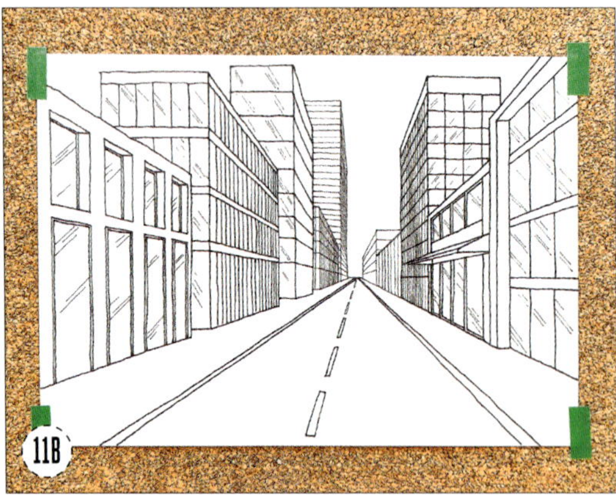

STEP 10: On the second floor of that building, draw a line with the string (red) that marks the lower edge of the window. Then sketch projections (blue) of the lines that make up the first-floor window. Now, use all those reference lines to draw a shorter replica of it (shaded in yellow) on the second floor.

The third building will have a glass grid. Draw lines with the string (green) that go to the middle point of each floor, except for the last one. Then, wrap them around to the front-facing plane. Next, add vertical lines (purple) on that plane up to the penultimate floor, forming a grid of rectangles. Now, draw a similar grid on the front of the building keeping in mind that the windows will look very narrow because of the angle.

STEP 11: You are almost done! Only two buildings to go. The fourth will be very simple. Erase the horizontal lines and just draw verticals (red) across the front. The last building will have only horizontal floor divisions.

The last thing to do is remove the pin. It will leave a small hole, but it has an easy fix. Rub the paper back to its place on both sides and draw something on top. I drew the horizon line at the end of the street and you can see it is barely noticeable. The finished result looks amazing. Congratulations!

LESSON: UPPING YOUR FLOOR PLANS

One-point perspective drawings often focus on an observer's view at eye level, with the viewer looking straight ahead with objects upright. But you can change the observer's position and have them look straight up or down, creating new and totally different views that use the exact same techniques you have studied so far. This is very useful for someone doing animation, cartoons or movie storyboards, because it gives the freedom to look at any scene from every angle. For this lesson, I want to show you how to create a bird's-eye view. That means that you will be looking at the objects from directly above. Architects use this all the time to do floor plans.

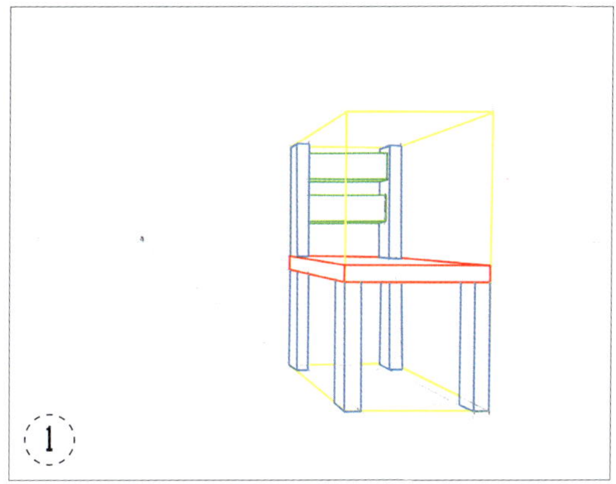

So first, let me explain how to shift the viewing angle. I will draw a very simple object in a normal view and then I am going to switch to bird's-eye view. A chair is always a good example, so let's go with that.

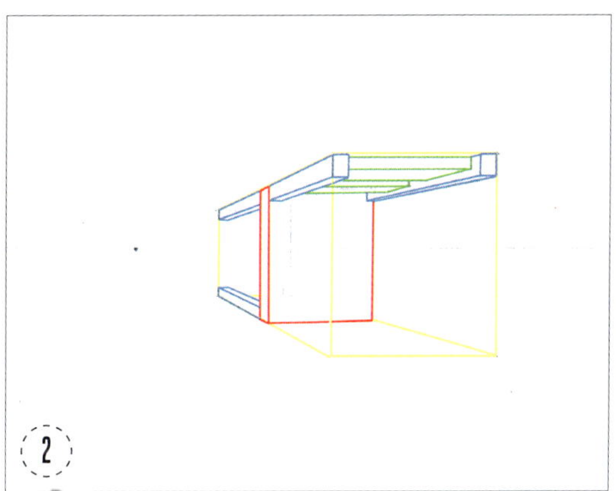

Picture 1 shows the regular view. I made a container box (yellow) with top and bottom rectangular planes that are just a little bit deeper than they are wide. Its height is approximately double its width. I am not going to describe the step-by-step process, but the colors show the way I built the chair. I drew the red box for the seat first, starting from the center of the box down. The four tall and thin blue boxes are the legs, and you can see that the ones in the back continue above the seat to become the back's support. The two thin horizontal green boxes make up the back. The order in which I described them is the same in which I drew them.

Now I am going to place the observer above the chair looking down. Imagine you are glued to the roof and the vanishing point is directly below. The horizon line and the vanishing point are in the same place (Picture 2). I am also drawing the chair in pretty much the same spot within the paper, which is a bit to the right of the vanishing point and using the exact same technique. But now the closest plane to the observer is not the front one but the one on top, so I have to think differently to construct the chair with the same elements.

Pretty cool, right? A bird's-eye view is simply the exercise of imagining how things look from a different position: from above. Note that when the observer is looking down, all lines that would be vertical in real life go to the vanishing point.

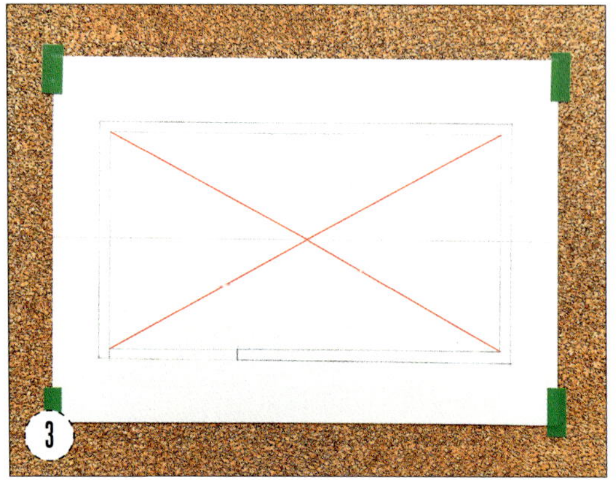

3

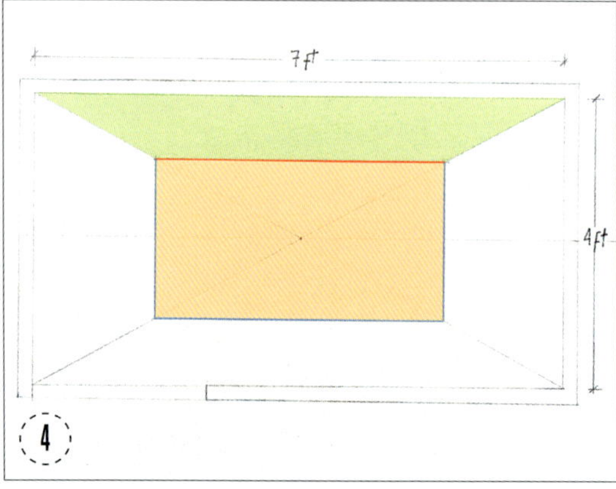

4

Next, I want to show you how to put the objects inside a room and scale them according to the space. Of course, I need to start with the room. I am placing the horizon line and vanishing point in the middle of the paper and drawing a rectangle with double lines all around except for an opening in the lower left corner (Picture 3). This is a bathroom seen from above. The double lines represent the width of the walls from the top and the opening is where the door will be. You will see this much more clearly in a minute.

Next, I will add lines to the vanishing point from every corner (red). Those lines are the vertical corners of the bathroom and will help me determine its height. They also form its four inner walls (planes), but I need to decide how high I want them to be.

I am assuming the bathroom is 7 feet (2.1 m) long, 4 feet (1.2 m) wide and 8 feet (2.4 m) high. That means the upper plane (shaded in green in Picture 4) should be a bit taller than a square (7 x 8 feet [2.1 x 2.4 m]). Knowing its size, I can eyeball the length of the upper plane and draw a line (red) to define it. Then, I need to transfer that same height all around by joining the vanishing lines with two verticals and another horizontal (all in blue). This forms a rectangle in the center (shaded in orange) that is the floor of the bathroom.

PRO TIP: Eyeballing the size of planes in perspective takes time and practice to develop. I always recommend drawing at least three very light lines and trying to determine which one feels and looks more like the size you need.

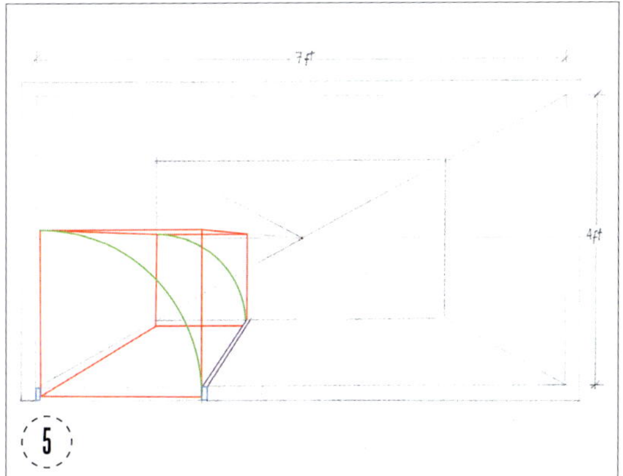

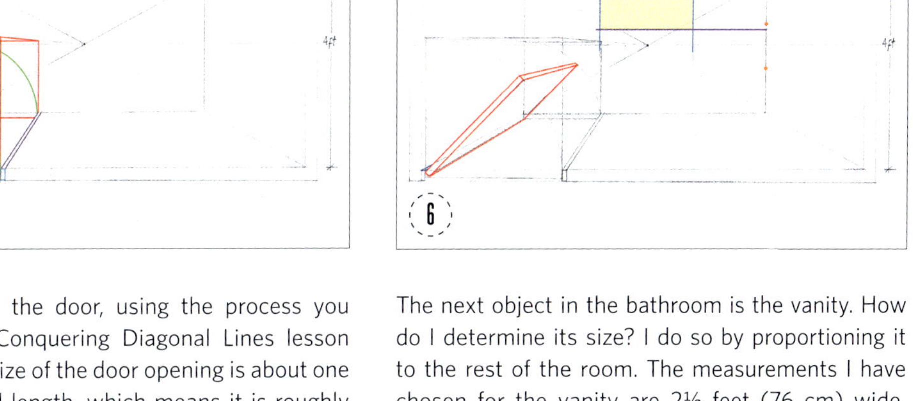

I will start with the door, using the process you learned in the Conquering Diagonal Lines lesson (page 40). The size of the door opening is about one third of the total length, which means it is roughly 2⅓ feet (70 cm). First, I made a couple of small rectangular planes (blue in Picture 5) on either side of the gap that represents the frame of the door. Then I added lines (purple) to the vanishing point from the corner of the right one and the wall corner to the floor. Then, I drew a container box (red) with squared top and base planes that fits perfectly in the door opening. Its height is the same as the wall's. On both the top and bottom, I drew a couple of arcs (green) that define the door's path.

Using all those reference lines, I can now draw the door as a very long and thin box (red in Picture 6) with the chosen opening angle. After that, I can add the verticals (blue) from the left side frame and wall corner to the floor where they are visible. I really love how doors look in any kind of perspective. This is just a small room with a door and it looks awesome already.

The next object in the bathroom is the vanity. How do I determine its size? I do so by proportioning it to the rest of the room. The measurements I have chosen for the vanity are 2½ feet (76 cm) wide, 1½ feet (46 cm) deep and 3 feet (91 cm) high. I will start by defining the bottom plane of the vanity, which would be on the floor, starting with its length. So, I know that the long wall is 7 feet (2.1 m) long and if I divide that length into three equal parts (green dots), I get three segments of 2⅓ feet (70 cm).

That means that the vanity would be a little bit longer than one third of the total bathroom's length. I want it to be centered in that wall, so I drew two lines (blue) to position it. I will do a similar process to find out the depth of the vanity and divide the short wall into three parts (orange dots). Four feet (1.2 m) divided into three parts is 1⅓ feet (41 cm), meaning the vanity should be a little bit deeper than one third of the width of the bathroom. I can then add a line (purple) to define that and complete the bottom plane (shaded in yellow).

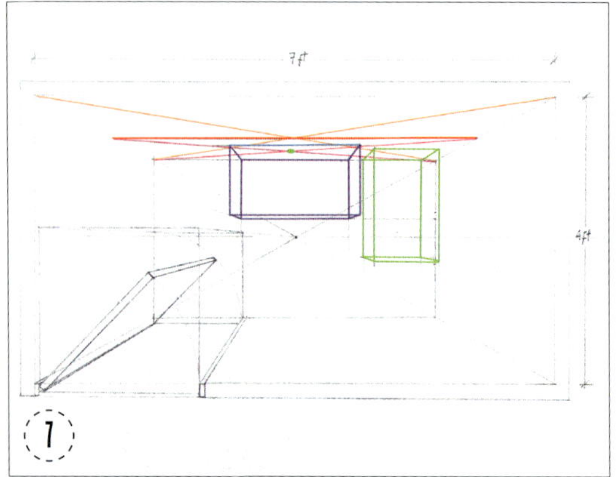

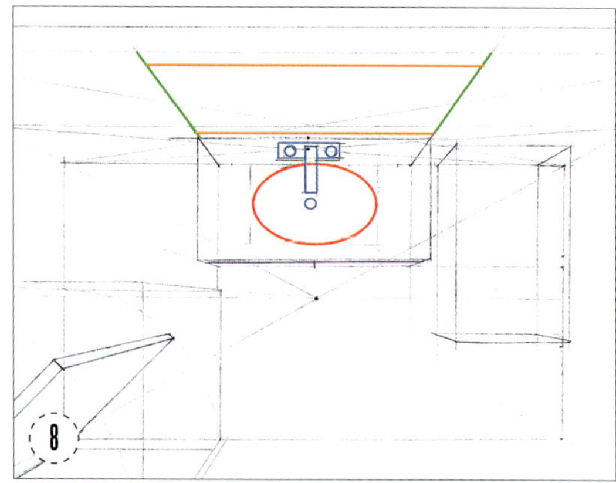

The following step would be to define the vanity's height. I will sketch an X in the upper wall from opposite corners (orange in Picture 7), and a horizontal line (red) that goes through the middle point. That line is 4 feet (1.2 m) high. Then I will sketch another X (pink) on the lower half and the intersection point (green dot) is 2 feet (61 cm) high. That means the height of the vanity is the middle point between the red line and the green dot (blue line). Now, using the bottom plane and the blue line, I can build the vanity (purple).

The more objects you have in the drawing, the easier it becomes to calculate the size of the next ones, because there is more information to compare. Let me give you an example: The toilet that will be placed in the right corner beside the vanity is 2½ feet (76 cm) long (and high) and 1½ feet (46 cm) wide. If you remember, the space between the vanity and the wall is close to 2 feet (61 cm), so if I leave a small space on either side of the box, I will have a very good approximate measure. The vanity is 3 feet (91 cm) high, so the toilet is a little bit shorter. And, the side wall is 4 feet (1.2 m) long so the toilet's length would be approximately two thirds of that. With all this information I can safely build the box representing the toilet (green).

I know this looks more like math than art, but it is very important for well-proportioned and well-scaled drawings. Using a reference picture, you could eyeball this; but again, it is nice to know the technical way of doing this.

Now I can add some details. I will start with the vanity. How about an oval-shaped sink? I will draw it centered horizontally on the top plane (red in Picture 8), but a bit toward the front, to make space for the faucet. The faucet will be as simple as a rectangular plane (blue), and a couple of circles with another plane in the other direction beneath them (all in blue). An additional circle will represent a drain.

The vanity itself will only have a double line near the top edge of the front plane to mimic its top counter and a vertical down the middle as if it had two doors (all in purple). A mirror above it would make a great addition, and it would be perfect if it had the same width as the vanity. So, I am going to extend the back edges of the vanity's box upward (green lines) and draw two horizontals (orange) to determine its height.

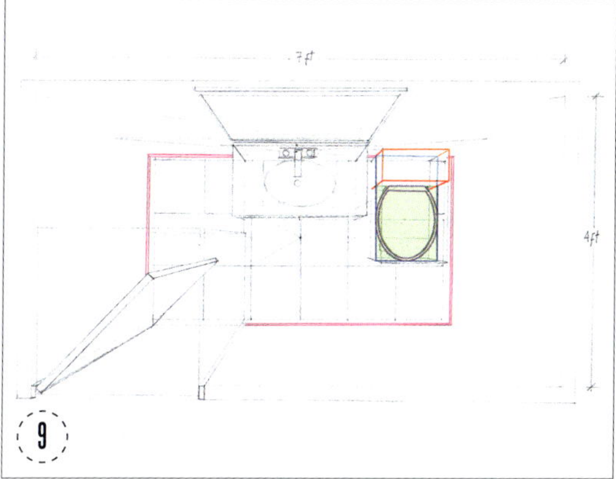

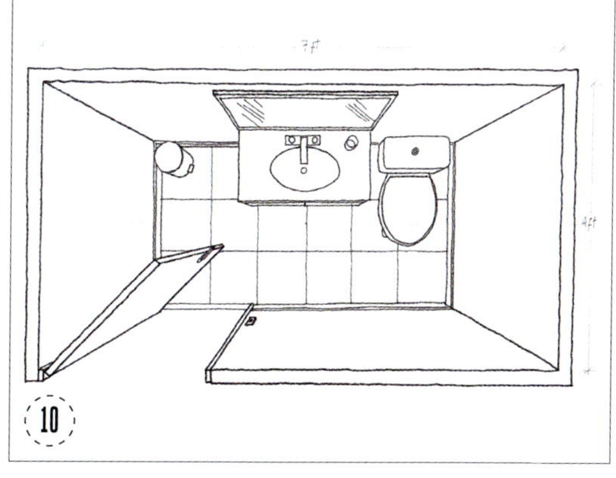

The toilet is normally divided in two parts: the tank and the bowl. The tank makes about one quarter of the total length of the box so I will make that division (red lines in Picture 9). The bowl is approximately half the height of the box so I will divide it in two vertically (blue lines). Now I draw a couple of ovals with their top cut straight (purple) on the green plane and I have the lid of the bowl. I add a box (orange) from the middle blue division to the top for the tank.

Finally, on the floor I made a grid of equally distanced horizontals and verticals to create tiles. A double line near the bottom edge of the floor (pink lines) will work perfectly as a baseboard.

Picture 10 shows the finished result. This top-down view is a thousand times more interesting and fun than a normal floor plan, which many people struggle to understand. I added a couple more details like a light switch near the door, a door handle, a trash can in the corner and a glass on the counter. Now, get ready to apply all this new knowledge to draw a cool little bedroom in the next project.

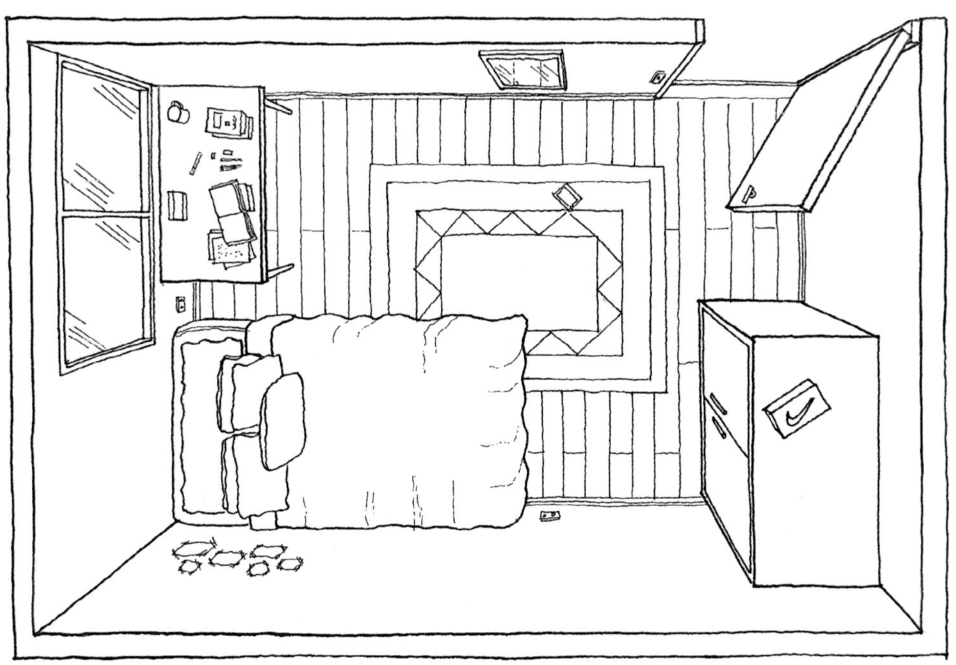

PROJECT: 3D FLOOR PLAN WITH STRING

I love drawing bedrooms! Bedrooms are very relatable. Though they're so common, they can be personalized in any number of ways. In this project, you will create a small bedroom with three main features: a bed, a closet and a desk. But this time I want you to start adding your own personal style and details. Change something, add objects that you have or would like to have in your own bedroom—anything that makes it your own and not an exact replica of the one shown in this project. It is time to allow your own style to kick in.

Additional Materials

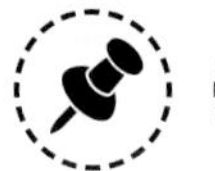

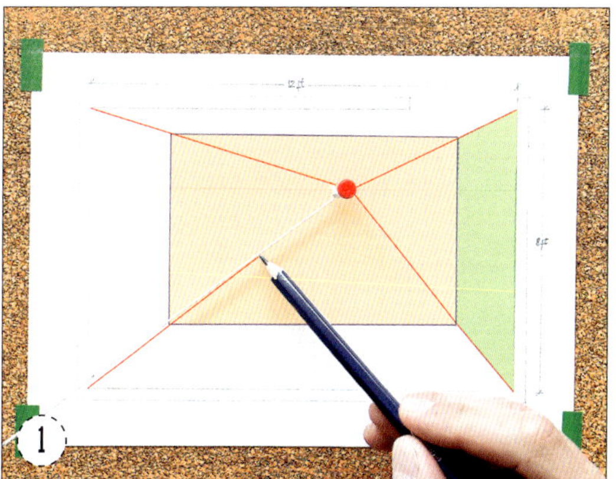

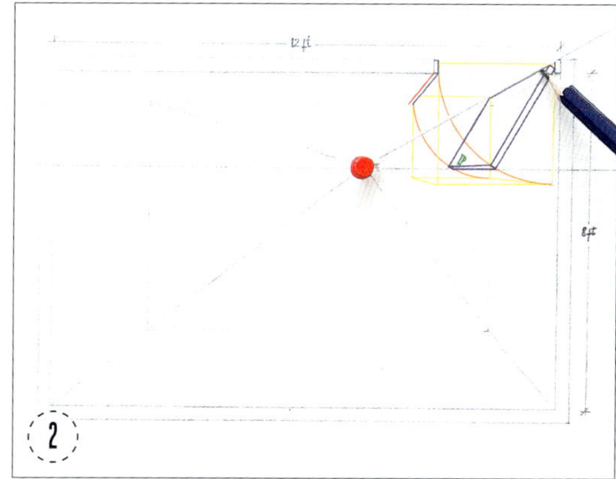

STEP 1: Draw the horizon line slightly above the center of the page and the vanishing point a bit off center to the right. Next, draw a horizontal rectangle (pink) with a 2:3 ratio that will become the top edge of the walls shaping the room. It should be about 8 feet (2.4 m) wide by 12 feet (3.6 m) long. The rectangle should have double lines representing the thickness of the wall and an opening on the top right corner where the door will be.

To make sure the door is proportional to the size of the space, it needs to be approximately one fourth of the total length, or 3 feet (91 cm). Now add lines (red) from the corners of the rectangle to the vanishing point using the string. This room is going to be 8 feet (2.4 m) high, so draw a squared plane (shaded in green), using a vertical line (blue) to build it. Then, transfer that same height all around by drawing lines (purple) joining the diagonals. That gives shape to the floor (shaded in orange). The basic shape of the room is now ready.

STEP 2: The first thing I will add is the door. Draw a vertical (red) from the left edge of the door to the floor. Then do the exact same process described in the Upping Your Floor Plans lesson (page 61). Start with both sides of the doorframe and lines to the vanishing point in the left one (all blue). Then draw the container box (yellow) fitting the door gap with squared top and bottom planes, and arcs on both of them (orange).

Choose the opening angle and draw the door (purple). I drew it about half open and added a door handle by drawing a small circular plane (green) at about one third of the height going up and a rectangular plane parallel to the direction of the door.

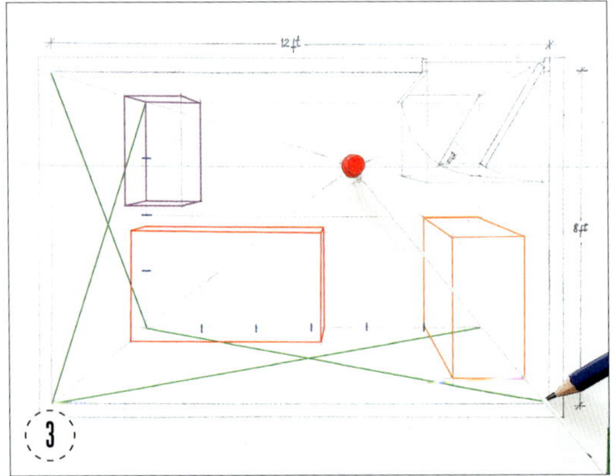

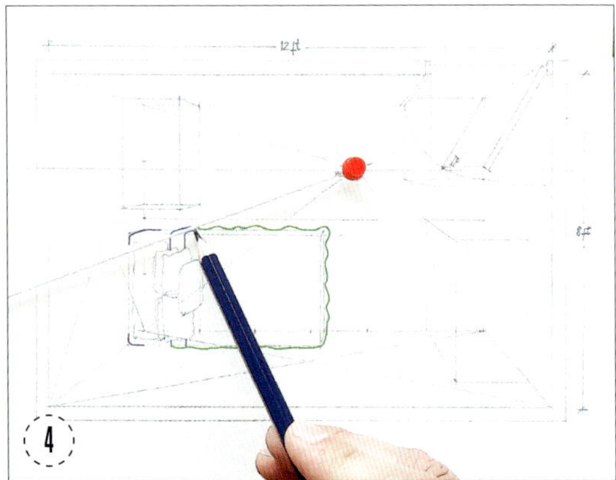

STEP 3: It is always a good idea to have the general layout of the drawing outlined before doing any details, so go ahead and create the boxes for the three main objects. Divide the width and the length of the room in 2-feet (61 cm) modules, by drawing small lines (blue). Draw an X on each one of those two same walls (green). These measurements will allow you to scale the objects correctly.

The bed will go in the left bottom corner. It is 6½ feet (1.9 m) long, 3½ feet (1.1 m) wide and 2 feet (61 cm) high, which is a bit more than three modules long, a bit less than two modules wide and its height will be half the distance between the floor and the middle of the wall (the center of the X). The red box shows the bed.

Proceed to drawing the other two boxes using the same process. The desk is in the top left corner (purple box), and its measurements are 3½ feet (1.1 m) long, 2 feet (61 cm) wide and 2½ feet (76 cm) high. The closet is in the right bottom corner (orange box) and is 4 feet (1.2 m) long, 2 feet (61 cm) wide and 6 feet (1.8 m) high.

STEP 4: Now you can add the details for each object separately. For the bed, draw some pillows near the top (Picture 4). Just do random, squiggly rectangles and squares with rounded corners stacked on top of each other, and the main pillow underneath at the top of the bed. Then, draw a couple of lines beneath them (blue) that mimic the fold of the bedspread and wrap them down around the mattress. The string will help you figure out the angle of the vertical lines going down the side of the bed, so just join the two lines in both directions with a small, curved corner. Next, draw a wavy line all around the bottom edge of the bed (green) and wrap it around the side that is against the wall.

Keep in mind this is fabric so draw it very loose. You also need to soften the corners of the mattress that are exposed so it looks more natural (purple).

STEP 5: For the desk, draw a line (red) parallel to the top right edge of the box and just below it to define the desktop's width. Then, use the string to do a couple of cylindrical legs (blue) near its corners. To do this, create two lines and join them at the bottom with a semicircle. Add some details on the desk, like books, pens, cups, papers and so on. I made all of mine with simple shapes like planes, boxes and cylinders.

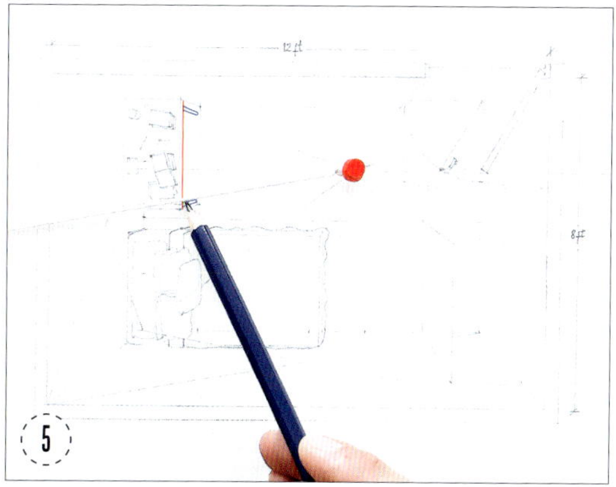

STEP 6: The closet will be very simple. Make a frame all around the front by drawing double lines (red). Then, draw a vertical (blue) down the center of the same plane to create two doors. Add a couple of thin, long rectangular planes (green) below the center of the doors that represent the door handles. I am also going to put a shoe box on top. You can draw this box at any angle you want as long as the verticals go to the vanishing point and the bottom lines are parallel to the top ones.

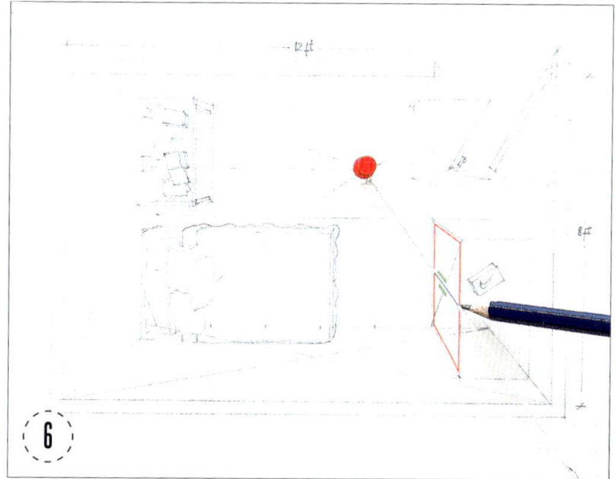

STEP 7: This room needs a window and no place would be better than above the desk. Draw a rectangular plane (red) with double lines all around. Make it as big as you want and draw another vertical double line (also red) that goes right through the middle. The depth in windows and openings is very important. Draw small horizontal lines (blue) from the two bottom corners, and then join their ends with parallels to the bottom frame (green) and verticals (purple) until they disappear behind the upper frame.

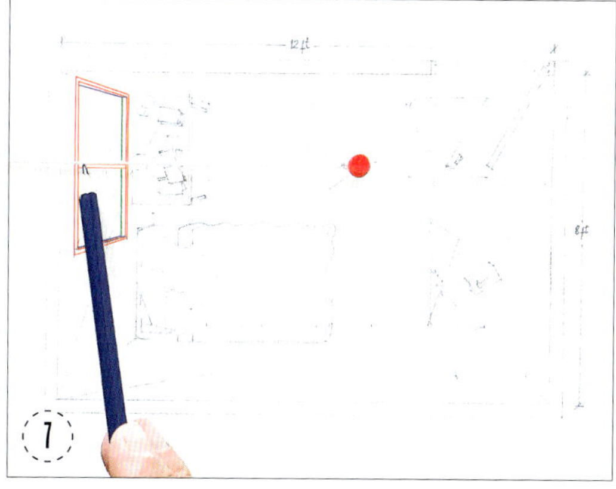

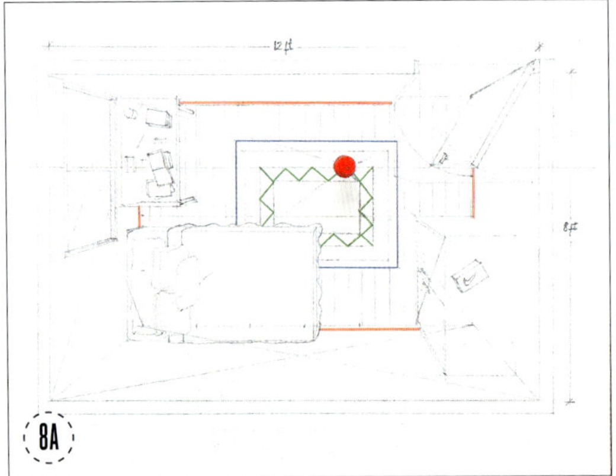

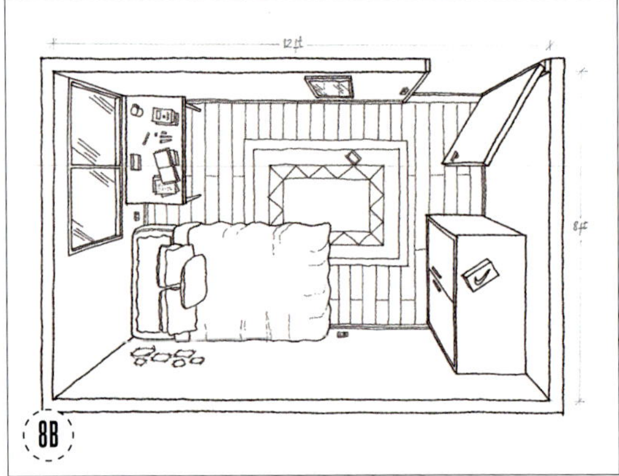

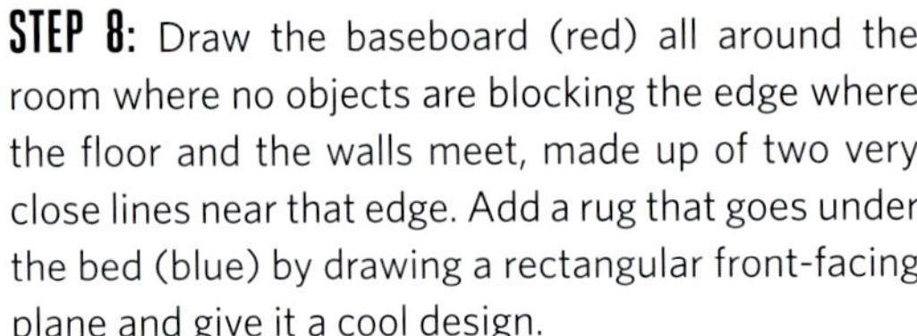

STEP 8: Draw the baseboard (red) all around the room where no objects are blocking the edge where the floor and the walls meet, made up of two very close lines near that edge. Add a rug that goes under the bed (blue) by drawing a rectangular front-facing plane and give it a cool design.

I am going to make proportional rectangles that get smaller near the center and a string of triangles (green) in one of the resulting stripes. To wrap up the floor, draw vertical lines at the same distance from each other that imitate wooden floorboards.

Take a look at this beautiful room that you just created. My final touches include: light switches and power outlets, some pictures on the wall near the bed and a hanging mirror near the door. They were all drawn using planes. I also added some small horizontals on the floor here and there to mimic where the boards meet. Have fun including all the details that you want.

Now that you've become somewhat of an expert in one-point perspective, I think you are ready to jump to the next technique.

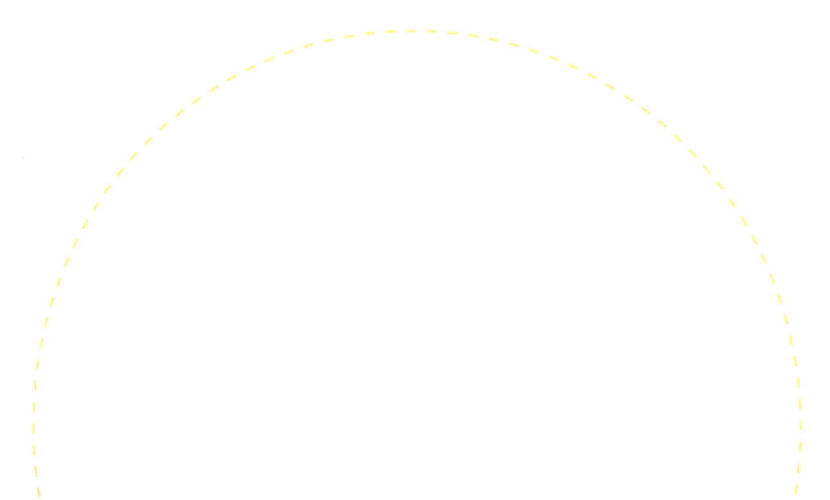

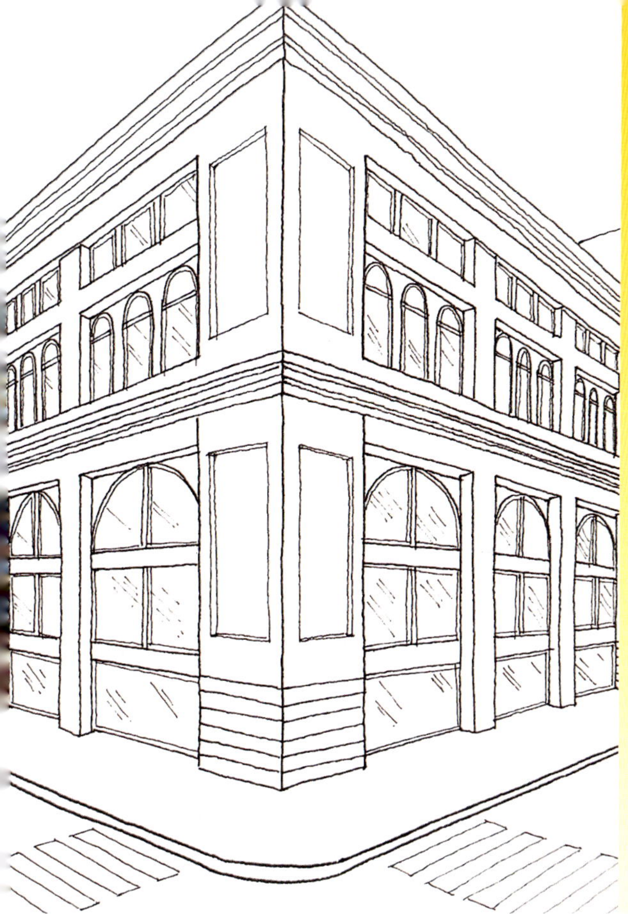

2

UNDERSTANDING TWO-POINT PERSPECTIVE

Welcome to the second big technique that you will be studying in this book. It is very similar to one-point perspective so you will be able to understand it very easily after you study the differences. Once you learn and master one-point and two-point perspectives, you will not have any trouble studying every other perspective technique.

In this chapter, you will explore the basic rules of two-point perspective, its components and how to use it. I will show you how to apply it using an elastic string just as you drew one-point perspective with a string. If you are an architect or urban sketcher you will be using two-point perspective a lot!

I also want to show you a little bit about how to draw inclined surfaces and roofs, which is another super useful skill for architecture sketching. And you will apply some of that knowledge to draft a U-shaped staircase, which will be super fun.

Finally, you will see how there are different ways of placing the vanishing points and creating different views. One of those ways is to place them vertically instead of horizontally and we will design a city landscape like that on page 106. By the end of this chapter, I hope to have made you fall as much in love with two-point perspective as I have.

LESSON: TWO-POINT PERSPECTIVE BASICS

Two-point perspective is made up of the same three elements as one-point: horizon line, vanishing points and lines. First, just as in one-point perspective, the horizon represents the height of the observer's eyes.

The second element, vanishing points, is the first big difference from one-point perspective. As its plural name indicates, now you do not have a single vanishing point, but two. The best way to describe this is that in one-point perspective the objects portrayed are positioned in 90-degree angles, so that one of their sides is always facing the observer, and the lines on the other sides go to a single vanishing point, but in two-point perspective the objects are shifted into a different angle so that none of their sides face the observer directly, but instead go to separate vanishing points.

Picture 1 shows the difference between the two techniques. The cube above the horizon line is drawn in one-point perspective and the vanishing point is right in the middle (red). Its closest side (orange) is facing the observer directly and the left (green) and bottom (yellow) sides are planes going to a single vanishing point (vanishing lines marked in red).

The cube below the horizon line is drawn in two-point perspective and the vanishing points are on either side of the paper (blue and green). In this case, the closest thing to the observer is not one of its sides but one of its edges because its angle is now shifted, and the sides go to different vanishing points. The top is made up with lines going to both vanishing points. This means that the angle formed when lines coming from different vanishing points meet or cross is 90 degrees.

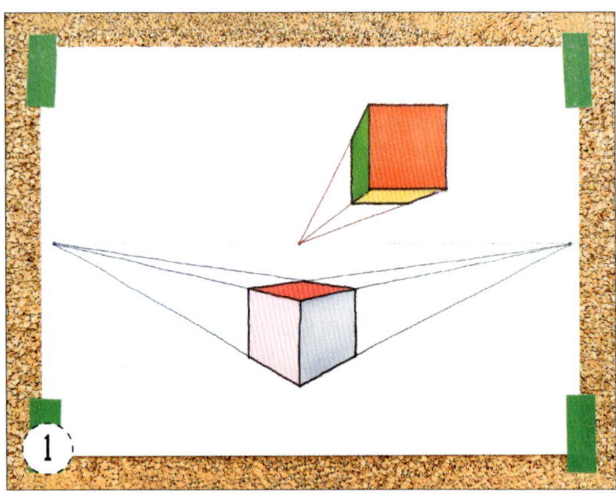

You could move the cube anywhere in the paper and that would continue to be true. In two-point perspective front-facing planes cease to exist. You will understand this better when I show you how to build different shapes using this technique.

Finally, there are lines. As in one-point perspective, they are the basic construction blocks of the drawings and can be classified in two types:

1. **Verticals:** Lines that go straight up and down.
2. **Vanishing lines (or lines going to the vanishing points):** These are horizontal lines that have the same direction as the observer's eyesight when looking at either vanishing point. If continued, they will always join at one of the vanishing points depending on their direction.

Let me clarify all this by showing you step by step how to construct some basic shapes. I will start with the horizon line in the middle of the paper and the vanishing points as far as possible on either side of the paper without going off the edge (Picture 2). As with one-point perspective, I suggest drawing your horizon line, vanishing points and all other construction lines lightly in pencil.

PRO TIP: The distance between the vanishing points is arbitrary and depends on the kind of view that you want to create. The closer they are, the more forced and skewed the perspective is going to look; the farther away, the more relaxed it will look and the softer the angles will appear.

First, I will draw a vertical line in the middle of the paper, above the horizon line (red). From its two ends, I will draw lines to two vanishing points. Now, I will add another vertical (blue) between the two vanishing lines on the right, and a couple of horizontals closing the shape (also in blue) to create a squared vertical plane (shaded in green). Next, I created another squared vertical plane (shaded in orange) going to the other vanishing point following the same steps (purple lines).

You can see the two front faces of a cube, but you need to figure out the bottom one. To do that, I am going to draw a line (red in Picture 3) from the bottom left corner of the left-side plane to the right vanishing point. Remember that lines coming from opposite vanishing points meet in 90-degree angles and that is exactly what is needed here.

Next, I drew the opposite from the other corner (blue line). Those two lines are going to meet and the resulting plane (shaded in green) is the bottom of the cube. And that is the way you draw a cube or rectangular box in any position in two-point perspective.

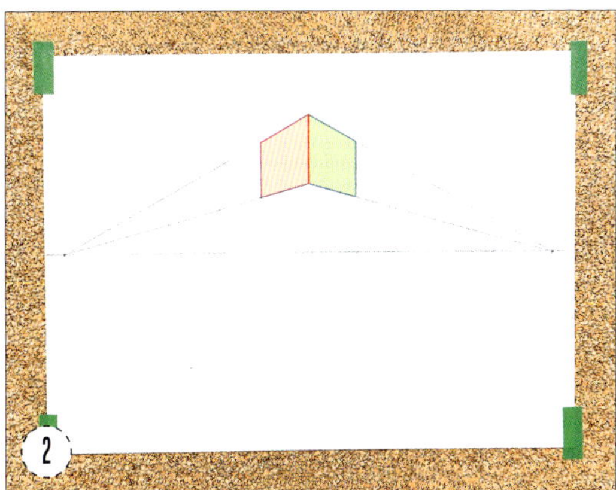

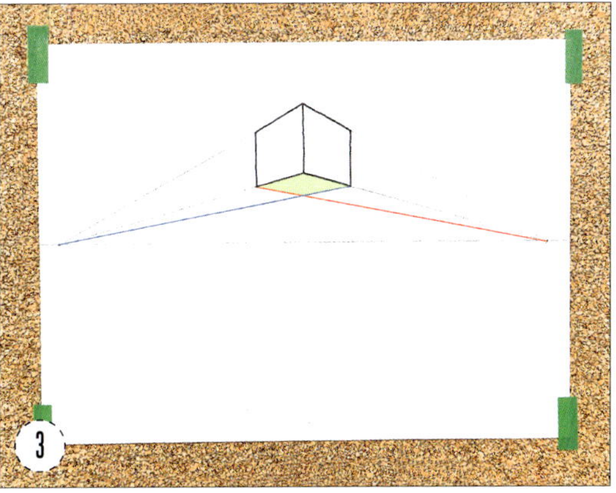

Once you know how to draw a cube, you can build all the same shapes that you learned for one-point perspective to create a container box. Let me show you an example of that. I am going to draw a cylinder and place it to the right of the cube. The first step of course is to draw a box. Specifically, a vertical rectangular container box (yellow in Picture 4).

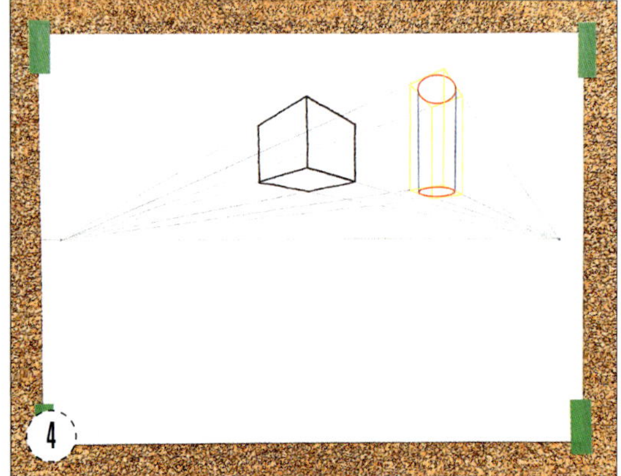

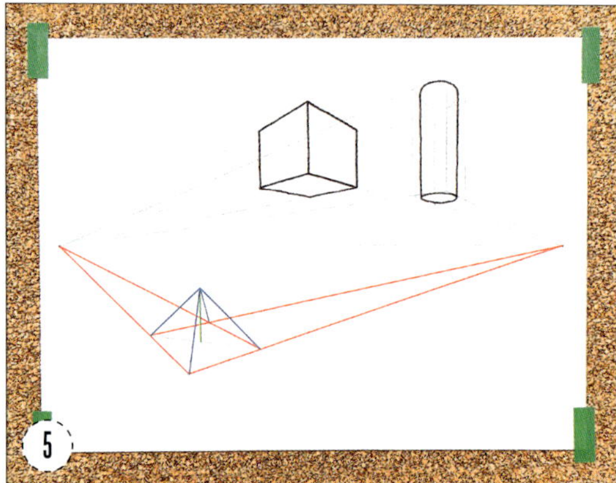

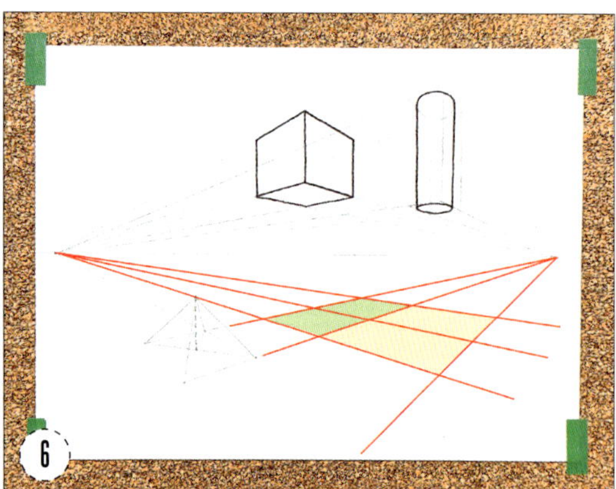

Notice that the right side of that yellow box looks smaller and its top and bottom edges have steeper angles than the left side—even though both sides are supposed to have the exact same measure. This is because the box is much closer to the right vanishing point than to the left. I am eyeballing the size difference between the two sides and that is something that you will learn to do with practice. The angles are just the result of the lines going to either vanishing point. Now I will draw ellipses inscribed in both the bottom and top planes (red) and join their outermost edges with a couple of vertical lines (blue).

Next, I will draw a pyramid, starting with a horizontal plane that is the result of the crossing of two pairs of lines coming from either vanishing point (red in Picture 5), just like the base of the first cube. I then draw an X from opposite corners of that plane to find its center. From that point, I sketch a vertical line (green) to determine the height of the figure. Now I just need to join its tip with all four corners of the base (blue lines).

I want to make sure that you understand how different directions work in two-point perspective so I am going to draw an L-shaped box. I do want to let you know that there is not only one valid way of building any of these figures. You could have started the first cube, for example, by drawing the base instead of the vertical line and the end result would have been exactly the same. I am doing them in the way I think they will be easiest to understand and remember but you will figure out your own methods as you practice. That being said, I will start this box with its top.

First, I will draw three lines (red in Picture 6) coming from each vanishing point and make them cross at the right side of the pyramid. You can see that the third line coming from the right vanishing point is a little bit more separated. That one will be the long side of the L.

The crossing of those lines created a grid of two squared horizontal planes (shaded in green) and two rectangular horizontal planes (shaded in orange).

Now I will join the two squared horizontal planes and the farthest rectangular plane in a single L-shaped plane (red in Picture 7). I will begin figuring out the body of the box from its left side, so I will draw a couple of verticals (blue) from the leftmost vertices. That side's bottom edge will be defined by a line (green) coming from the left vanishing point, because it must be parallel to the top one.

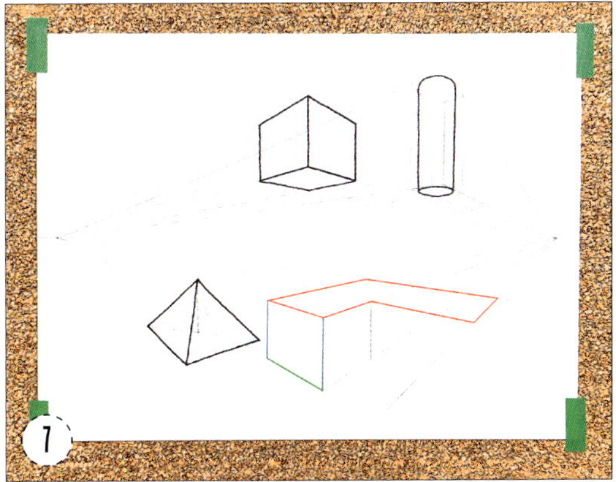

Once you have defined the height of one of the sides of the box, all you need to do is transfer it to the rest using verticals and vanishing lines parallel to the top edge of each side. Let me show you what I mean. From the bottom right corner of the side just completed, add a line (red in Picture 8) going to the right vanishing point. From the middle vertex of the L, add a vertical (blue) until it meets the red one. The resulting plane (shaded in green) is the second face of this shape.

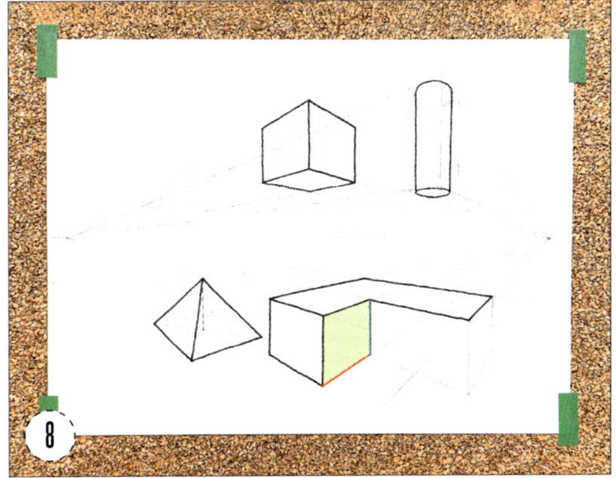

Picture 9 shows how I finished the other two sides following the same steps. I used the red lines to figure out the green side and the blue lines for the orange side. This shape could have had many more right and left turns and you would have been able to figure all of them out by repeating this over and over.

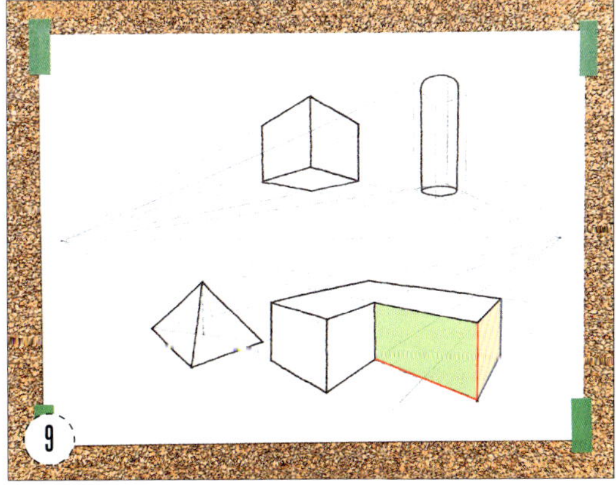

As you can see, two-point perspective has a unique sense of volume that makes it perfect for things like urban landscapes, interior views, product design, architecture showcasing and so on.

In the next project, you will draft an interior perspective, so if you are ready, dive right in.

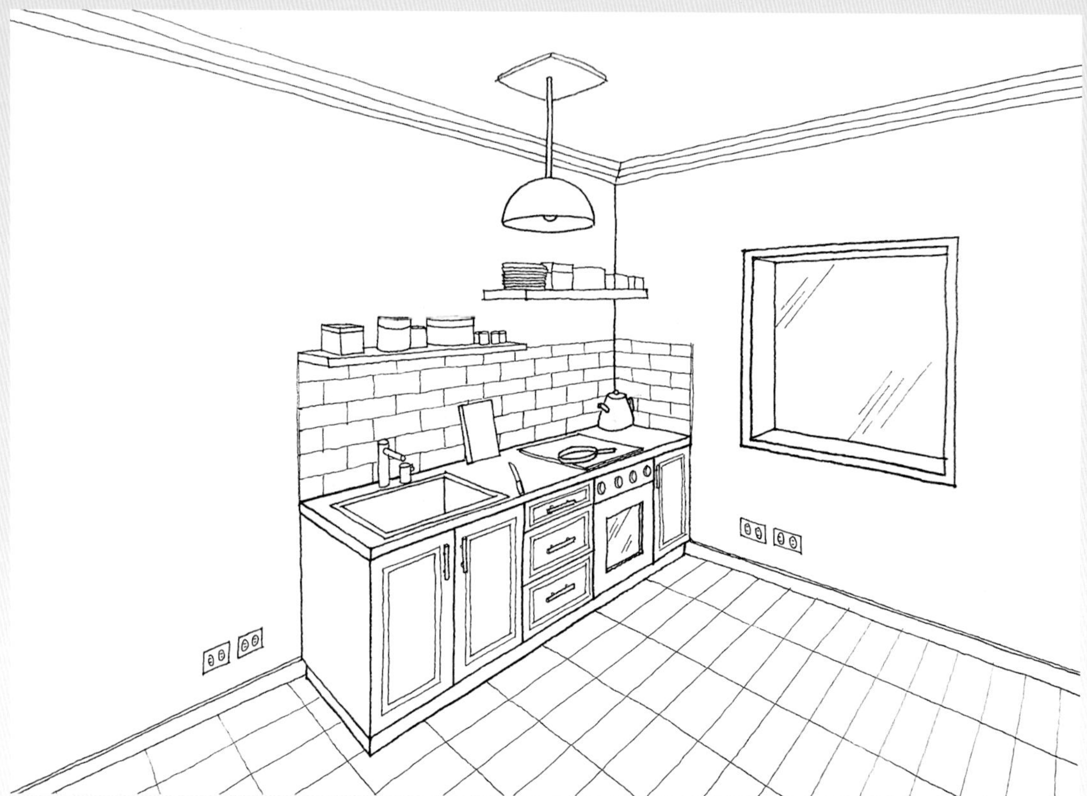

PROJECT: PLACING OBJECTS IN SPACE

In this project, you will learn how to draw a small corner kitchen. Corners are two-point perspective's specialty, so whenever you have to draw one, whether interior or exterior, you know that this is the technique you need to use. This is a valuable skill, because corners are particularly appealing to the eye and many focal points will be placed in one. So, it does not matter if it is a staircase, a chimney or a reading nook; you will be able to portray all of those spaces using the two-point perspective technique.

This project is also designed to let you practice placing different objects within a space, which is another key concept of perspective drawing.

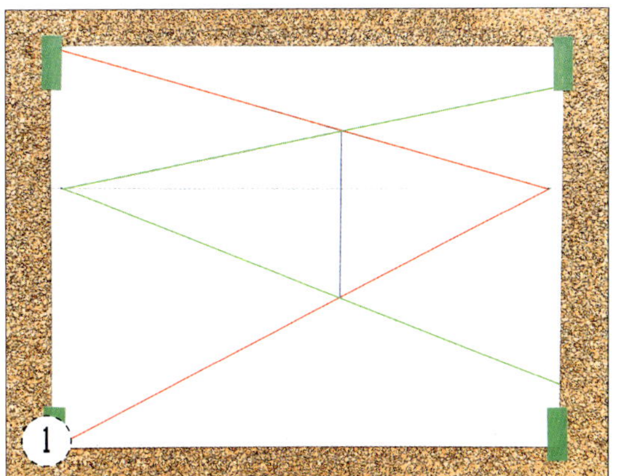

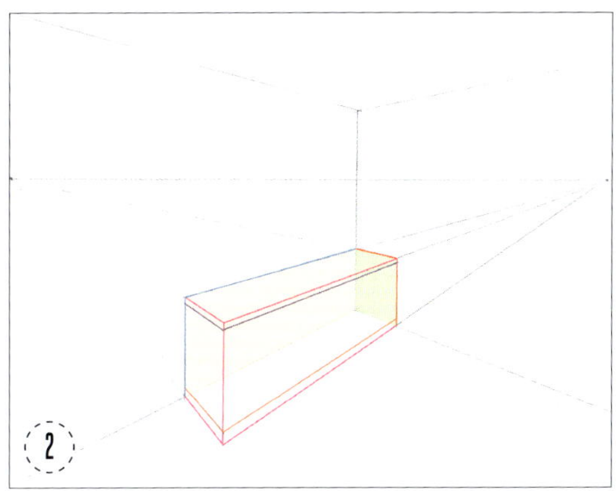

STEP 1: Draw the horizon line slightly above the center of the paper and place the vanishing points as far away from each other as possible without going off the page. Now, sketch out a couple of lines from the left corners of the paper to the right vanishing point (red), and a vertical (blue) joining them a little bit off center to the right. Then add another couple of lines (green) from the left vanishing point passing through both ends of the vertical line. As simple as that, you have created a corner.

STEP 2: In my sample, I am going to erase the sections of the vanishing lines that go from the vanishing points to the vertical line so you can have a clearer view. Now, draw a rectangular plane (shaded in green) on the bottom left corner of the right-side wall with a vanishing line and a vertical (both in red). It has one third of the room's total height and is a little bit taller than it is wide.

Do the exact same thing on the opposite side with the same height but this time the plane (shaded in orange) must be much longer (blue lines). Using those two planes as reference, draw a rectangular box (pink lines). That is the main body of the base cabinet. I will draw two additional lines. One of the lines is very close to the bottom of the box (orange) and that is going to be the recessed base, and the other one (purple) close to the top will be the countertop.

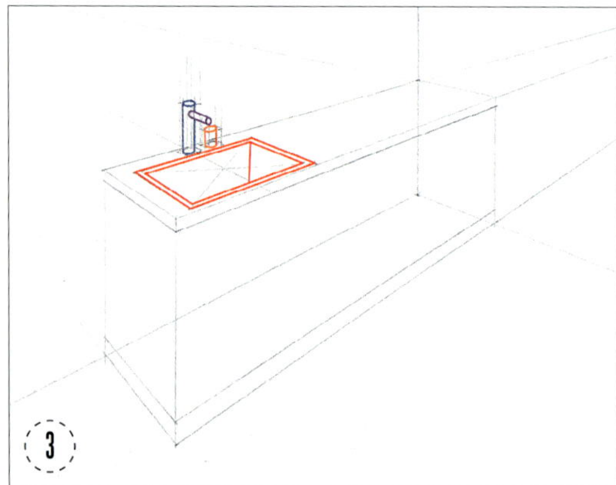

STEP 3: Draw the sink and faucet next. Draw a horizontal rectangular plane with double lines all around (red) near the left end of the countertop and add a vertical (also red) going down from its top-right corner until it reaches the front edge.

The faucet is made up of three cylinders. The first one (blue) is centered behind the sink. I drew an X in it and drew a line back to the left vanishing point to find that center. Draw the second one (purple) using the left vanishing point as if it were inserted near the top of the first one. This one should be thinner. And the third one (orange) is very similar to the first, but smaller.

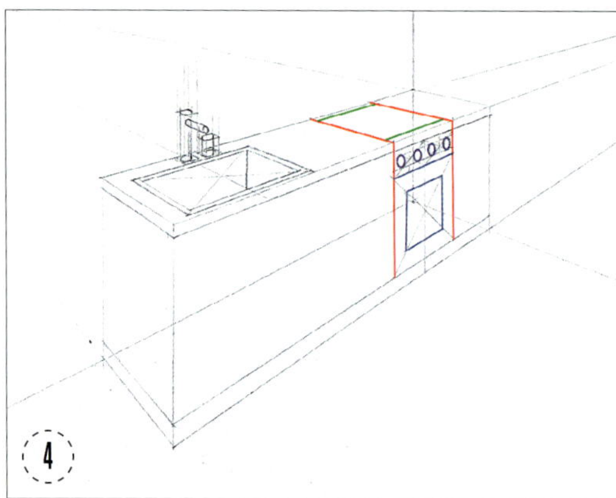

STEP 4: Next, draw the oven and cooktop. Draw two verticals (red) from the cabinet's base to the countertop. Leave enough space against the wall for a cabinet door that you will create later. From their top, join them with two more lines (also red) coming from the left vanishing point. The oven will have the following design: Draw a vanishing line (blue) near the top of the cabinet and a squared plane (also blue) beneath it. Above the first line, draw four circular planes (purple).

For the cooktop, just draw a couple of lines (green) going to the right vanishing point very close to the counter's edges. That plane represents a glass top induction stove.

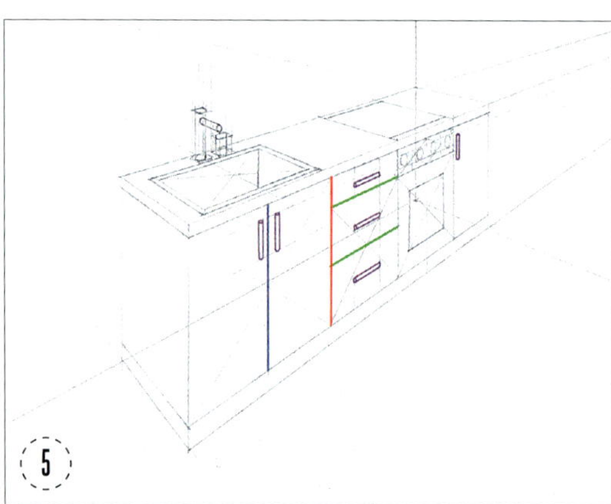

STEP 5: Now go ahead and design the drawers and doors in the cabinet. Draw a vertical line (red) to the right of the sink's corner. Find the center of the leftmost section with the X method (page 18) and draw another vertical (blue) passing through it. Next, add two vanishing lines (green) in the section to the left of the oven, dividing it into a smaller drawer on the top and two equal ones on the bottom.

For door handles, draw very slim and long vertical cylinders in the doors (purple) and horizontal ones centered in the drawers. Note how I used a couple of vanishing lines (pink) to make sure all vertical cylinders have the exact same measure.

STEP 6: A couple of open shelves on the wall above this cabinet would look great. Draw a couple of long, slim rectangular boxes (red) that have half the depth of the base cabinet and about half its length each. The first one is aligned with the left side and you can see I drew a couple of vertical lines to define its starting point and depth. The second one is higher and starts where the other finishes and goes all the way to the corner. I used another couple of verticals to transfer the depth of one to the other.

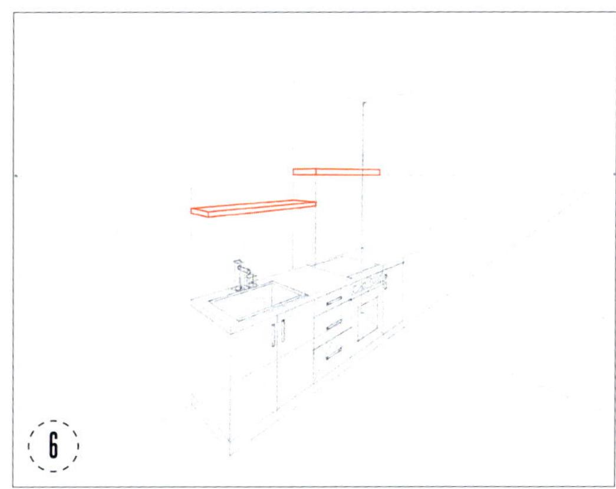

STEP 7: Now I want to teach you how to do a tiled backsplash. First, define the area that will be tiled with a couple of planes (both red). In the left plane do equally distanced parallel lines (blue) using the right vanishing point and the exact opposite on the right one (lines in purple). Next, draw equally distanced vertical lines (orange) in the top line. In the second line also draw equally distanced verticals (green) but now, they should begin in the middle of each tile in the top line. Repeat the same pattern of those first two lines all the way to the countertop.

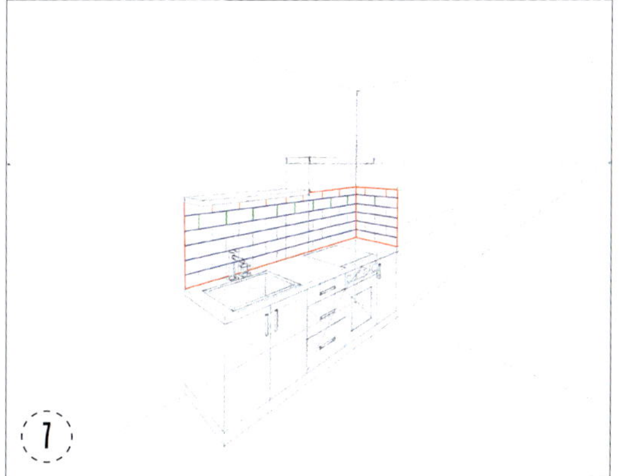

STEP 8: Of course, there should be a lamp in the ceiling. Draw a vertical rectangular box (yellow) with squared top and bottom planes hanging from the ceiling. You can see that I added a division near the bottom. Find the center of the top and middle planes and join them with a couple of verticals (blue). Draw an oval (purple) in the bottom plane and from its edges an arc (green) that goes a little bit higher than the center point of the plane just above.

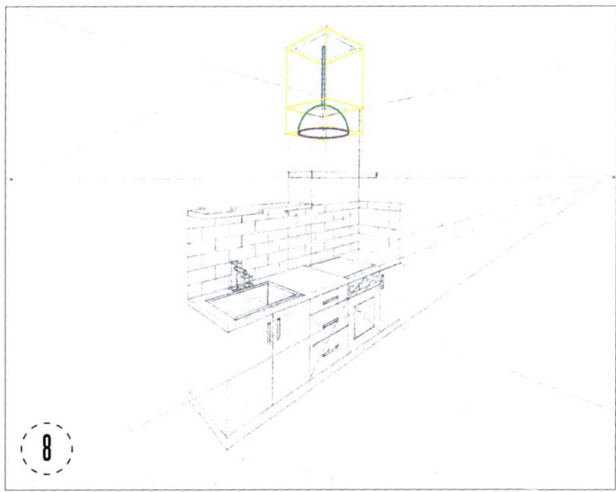

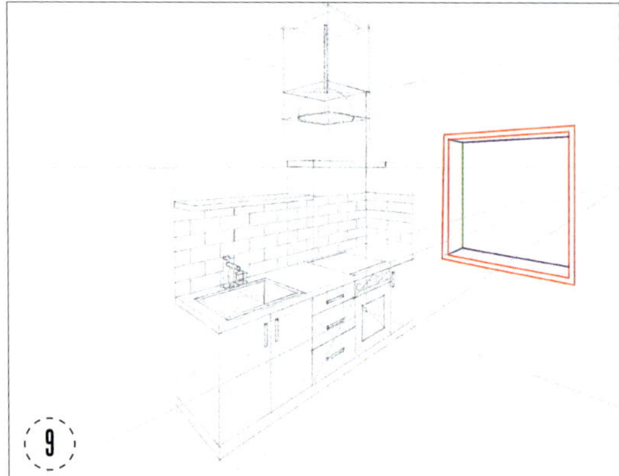

STEP 9: Add a plane (red in Picture 9) on the right wall with double lines all around. This is going to be a window, so you need to add depth to the frame. Do that with a couple of lines (blue) going to the right vanishing point from both left corners and then joining their ends with a vertical (green). And, from their ends, draw two lines (purple) going to the left vanishing point until they disappear behind the vertical frame.

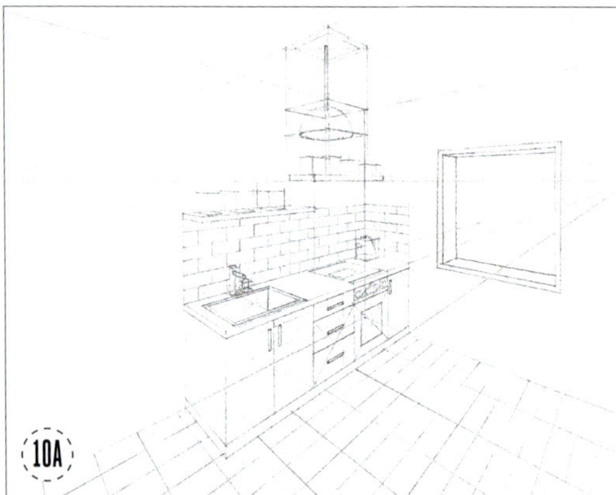

STEP 10: Now you need to fill those shelves with glasses, pots, containers, jars, plants and so on. Draw cylinders and boxes on top of the shelves and on the counter. The more details you add, the better it is going to look. See how I inserted a kettle in the corner?

Finally, I want you to learn how to do tiles on the floor. Draw a grid of equally distanced lines going to both vanishing points on the floor plane. Notice that the ones going to the left are farther apart from each other resulting in horizontal tiles.

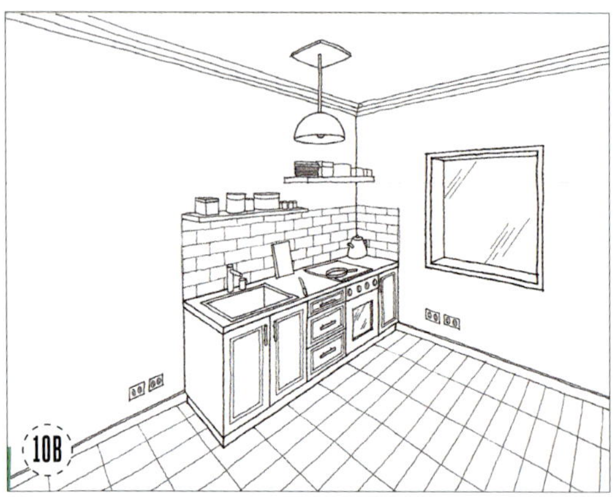

And this is exactly what I was telling you at the beginning of the project. See how appealing and approachable this kitchen looks? Final details can include a decorative design on the fronts of doors and drawers. I did this by tracing double lines all around, close to their edges. I turned all the boxes and cylinders in the shelves and countertop into different objects.

I also added crown molding on the ceiling and the baseboard at the bottom of the walls. The fridge would probably go at the left side of the cabinet, but you can leave that for a future project. I did create the power outlet for it though.

LESSON: THE ELASTIC STRING TECHNIQUE

One day I found a video of an artist using an elastic string to draw a two-point perspective of a building. I was absolutely and immediately blown away—not just because of how cool it looked, but for the simple reason that it was so incredibly easy to understand. It was so intuitive that I thought it would be a great way of teaching total beginners how to use two-point perspective.

A lot of people struggle to figure out which lines go where. And many, if not all of us, find it a bit annoying having to use rulers or reference lines back and forth from the vanishing points to figure out the angle of every line. A simple elastic string gets rid of all those problems.

The way this technique works is straightforward. All you have to do is fix the elastic string in the vanishing points of the drawing. There are many ways of doing this. I have seen it done with masking tape, with a cardboard under the paper that has little indentations where you can put the elastic string and keep it in place, perforating small holes in a table so you can introduce it and secure it in the back and so on. I have tried all these techniques and they all have their pros and cons. However, there is one for which I have not been able to find any cons, and that of course is the one I will be teaching you.

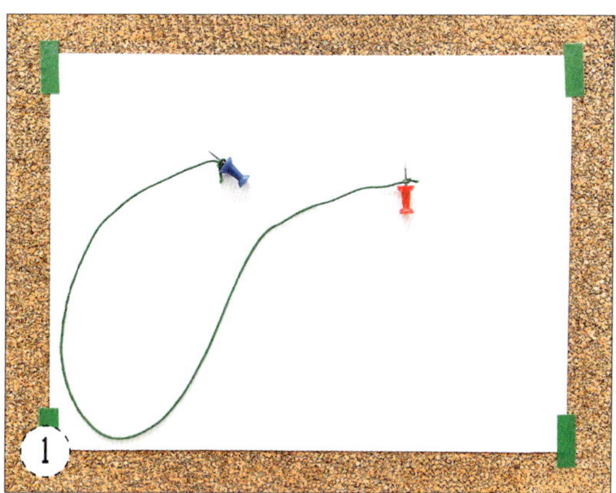

1

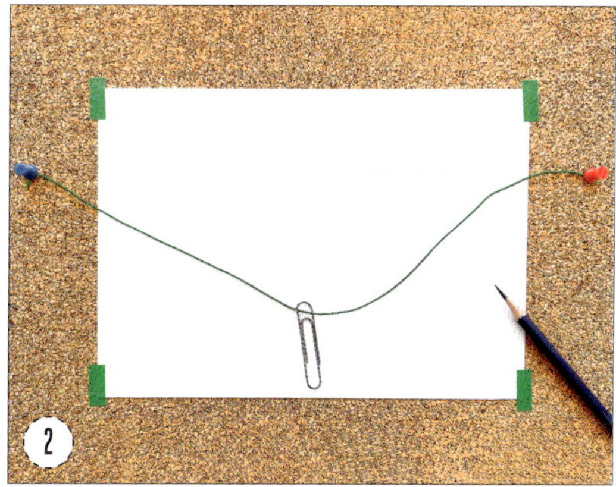

2

You will need the same corkboard you have been using so far, and a couple of pins or thumbtacks. I cut the elastic string at least 2 inches (5 cm) longer than the paper on both sides to allow room for handling. I then make loopholes on either end so I can insert the pins through them as shown in Picture 1.

Pin the elastic to the corkboard, making sure that it is not fully stretched (Picture 2). The pins can be as far from each other as you want them to be, but they need to be at the same height as the horizon line. When everything is in place, insert a paper clip through the elastic string so you can move the elastic freely in any direction with the help of the paper clip.

There is no better way to learn a new technique than drawing something with it, so that is exactly what you are going to do. This time I want to show you how to do a small study room. As you can see in Picture 2, I placed the horizon line halfway between the center and the top of the paper. The first object I will draw is the desk, starting with its top.

Picture 3 shows the way I use the elastic string to draw two pairs of lines (red) going to either vanishing point. The ones coming from the left are a bit more separated from each other so that the desk top becomes a rectangular plane (shaded in green) instead of a squared one. Then I give thickness to that plane by turning it into a very thin rectangular box (blue lines).

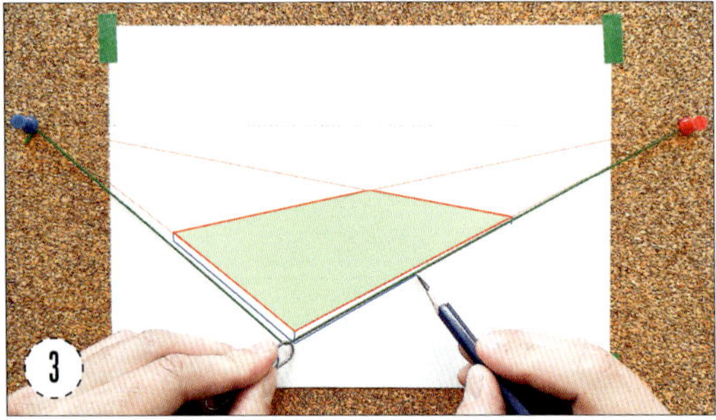

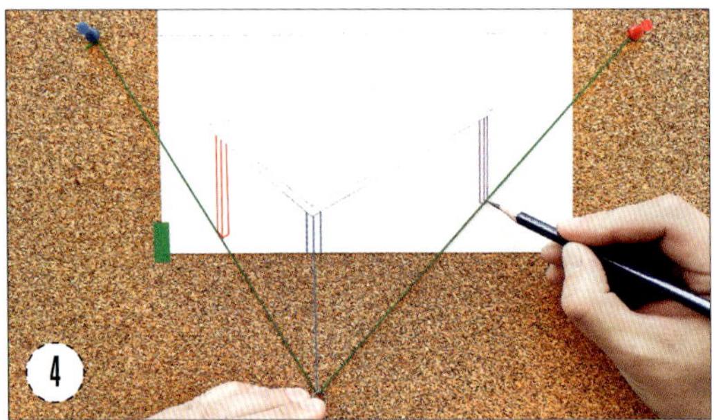

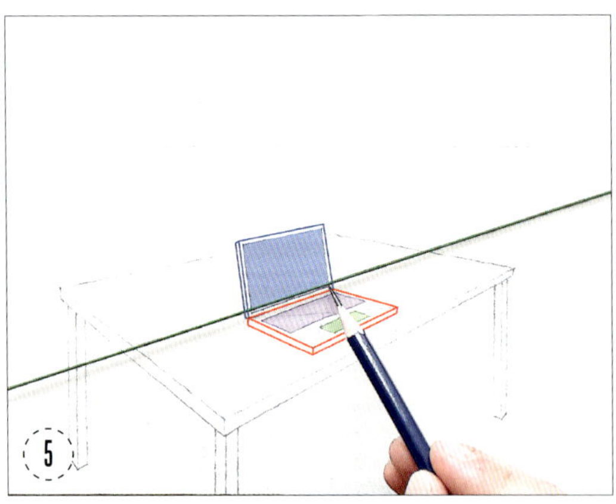

The elastic is super useful when you have to transfer heights from one object to the other. In this case, I drew the first leg on the left (red in Picture 4) with a very long and thin rectangular box near the table corner. Now I need to draw the other two visible legs with the same height, but the closer one (blue) goes off the paper, so I cannot draw a line to transfer the height. I can use the string by aligning its left side with the bottom of the red leg and placing the paper clip just below the corner of the table where the bottom of the second leg would be. The right side will let me know the height of the last one on the right (purple).

Next, I will draw a laptop on top of the table. A thin rectangular box (red in Picture 5), drawn in the same way as the table top will be its base panel. I will draw a small plane (green) in the center near the front of its top plane as a touchpad, and a longer one in the back (purple) that will be the keyboard. These two planes are oriented in the same way as the boxes we have drawn so far, so you can pretty much repeat the same process used to draw those boxes to make the touchpad and keyboard. Another even thinner and vertical box (blue), will be the top panel where the screen is. I will not make its verticals perfectly straight; instead, I drew them a little bit slanted so it looks more natural. Then, I drew a plane inside of the front face (also blue) of the box to mimic the screen. The horizontal lines of this vertical box and plane are going to the right vanishing point.

The more details, the better, so I will put some more objects on the desk. First, I will add a book just behind the laptop to the left. Start with a container box (red in Picture 6) that has the size of the book when it is open and find its center line. You can then use that box as reference to draw the cover and pages of the book, giving them their natural curvature.

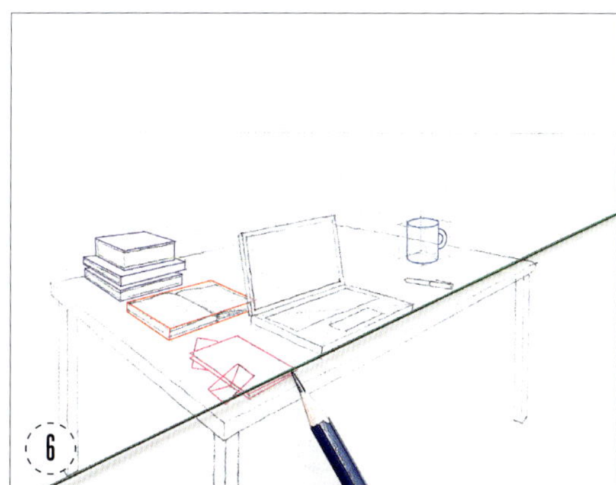

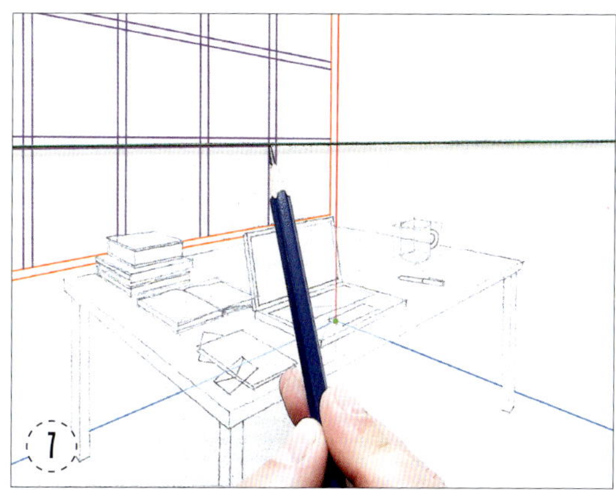

A coffee mug would also look great, and I will place it to the right of the laptop. Just draw a cylinder (blue) and add a couple of semicircles, one inside the other (also blue) as a handle. Behind the open book, I will draw rectangular boxes (purple) stacked upon each other. These are more books, and you can see I added double lines on the sides and fronts according to their position to imitate the covers and the spine.

In the left corner I will draw some rectangular planes (pink) that will look like papers or envelopes on top of each other. Some of them I can do with the string because they go to the vanishing points, but some have slightly different angles so that it looks more real. I will also add a pen or a pencil by the mug, giving it a different angle as well. Small objects are perfect for this because they are much easier to eyeball.

PRO TIP: Sometimes you start drawing the space and then you fill it with objects in different positions. Other times, as in this case, you can start with an object, then draw the space around it and continue adding more things afterward. There is not a single correct way of doing this. You will figure out your own methods as you practice.

Now that the focal point is ready, it is time to create the space around it. I would like this desk to be in a corner, so drawing a vertical (red in Picture 7) that starts close to the farthest corner of the desk will do just that. Then, I will add a couple of lines (blue), each one going to a different vanishing point, and passing right behind the lower ends of the table legs. You can see that if continued, those three lines meet in a single point (green).

Wouldn't it be lovely if there were a window in front of that desk? Yes, it would! A horizontal, elastic-string-drawn line (orange) going to the right vanishing point just above the top of the table will mark the place where it begins. Another horizontal joined with a vertical (also orange) will determine the thickness of its frame. The window will have a squared grid design, so it needs to be made up of horizontal and vertical pairs of lines (purple). Note that the vertical divisions seem a little wider the closer they are and I am using the horizontals as a reference to know how much. The wider the distance between the horizontals, the more separated the verticals also need to be in order to maintain the squared proportion of the grid.

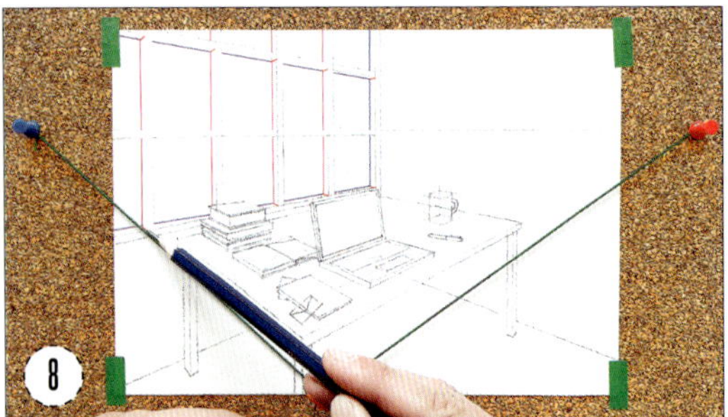

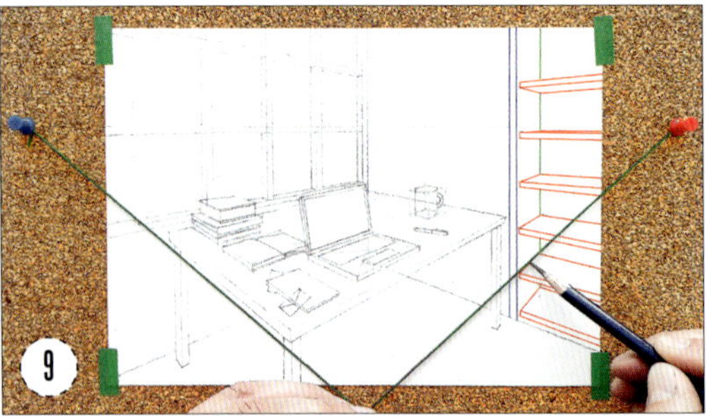

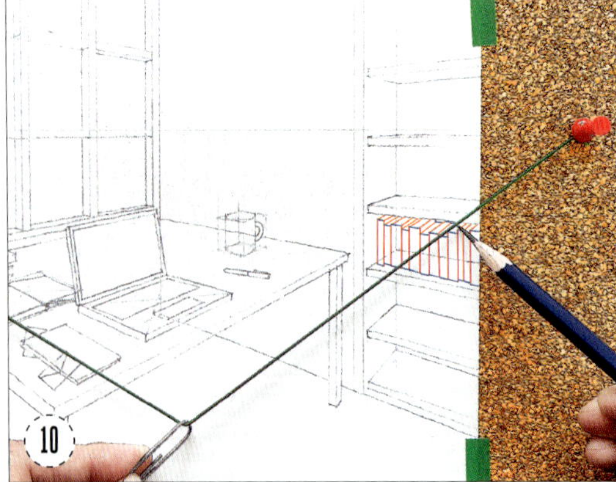

As always, you need to add depth to the frames. That is achieved by drawing very small lines (red in Picture 8) going to the left vanishing point from every corner of the window's frame grid where they would be visible. Note that in the middle horizontal frame, the depth is not visible because it is perfectly aligned with the vanishing points.

Next, I will draw a vertical (blue) joining the ends of the first two red lines on the right that jumps the horizontal frames until it goes off the paper. From the points where the reds meet the blues, I will add vanishing lines (purple) that jump over the vertical frames and reconnect with the red ones. Last, vertical lines (pink) will join the points where the reds meet the purples. These too, must jump the horizontal frames and continue.

What would a study room be without a library, right? The rightmost section of the drawing seems a perfect place to put one. Double vertical lines (blue in Picture 9) will define its starting point. The shelves are next, and I will create them by drawing slim rectangular boxes (red). I would like there to be two to three shelves below the tabletop so I will use that to figure out the height between them and place them at equal distances. Note that I drew a reference line (green) to know how deep those boxes should be so that all their back left corners match perfectly. That line is the beginning of the back of the shelves.

All that is left to do is fill the shelves with books. I will begin with the third shelf by drawing vertical lines (red in Picture 10) with random heights and separation between them that start a little bit above its front edge. Then, using the left side of the string, I will join those lines by their ends according to their height (blue lines). Next, I will create depth for the spines with lines going to the right vanishing point (orange). Now all I need to do is close those boxes with more lines going to the left vanishing point and verticals as needed (purple).

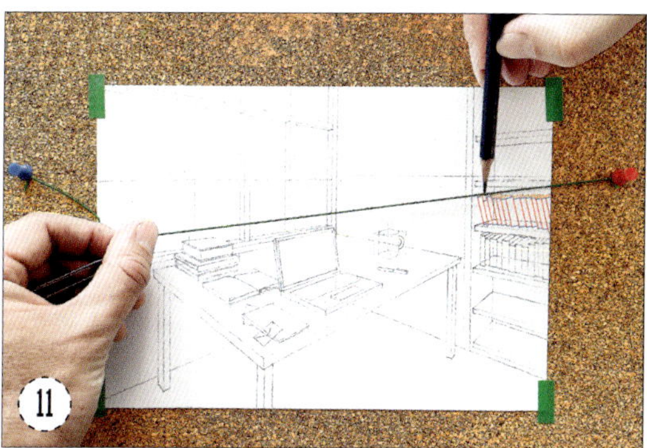

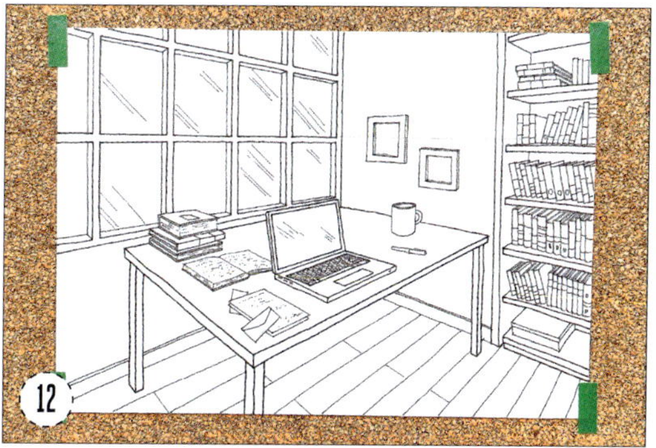

But everyone knows that not everyone keeps their books so tidy; you can also draw them with different angles. So, I will repeat the same process as in the shelf above, but this time the verticals (red in Picture 11) are a bit slanted to the left. The small lines (blue) that make up the spines need to be perpendicular to the red ones. The depth lines (orange) keep going to the right vanishing point because that direction is unchanged. The closing lines when needed should be parallel to the front ones.

The inked version (Picture 12) shows how I added more books in other angles and positions so you could see some other possibilities. Hardwood floors and a baseboard make a huge difference to the scene. I drew them exactly as I did the tile floor in the previous project (page 76). I just changed the proportions between the lines. In this case, I drew lines going to the right vanishing point and added lines that create a brick pattern going to the left vanishing point to mimic where the floor boards meet. A few small frames on the right wall are also a nice touch. I also drew the keyboard with super small squared and rectangular planes.

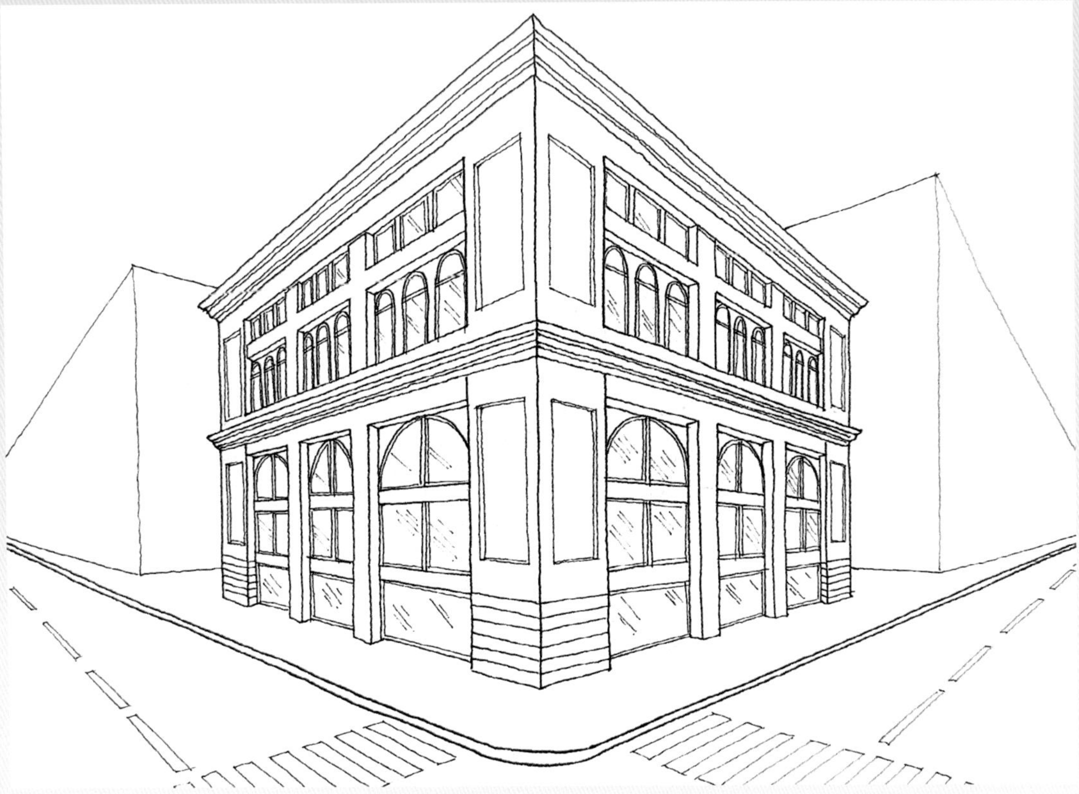

PROJECT: CORNER BUILDING SKETCH

Using an elastic string to draw perspective changed my whole perspective on perspective! I know it will change yours, too. When sketching out in the street, it is easy to carry a small corkboard and some pins and this technique will allow you to take your urban drawings to a whole new level. You will spend a fraction of the time creating them. Plus, it is going to be a lot more fun.

In this project, you will be drawing another corner building like the one in the Urban Sketching with String lesson (page 49), but because this is two-point perspective, you will be able to see the differences clearly. This type of perspective is huge in urban sketching, because it is perfect to showcase the volumetry and design of buildings.

Additional Materials

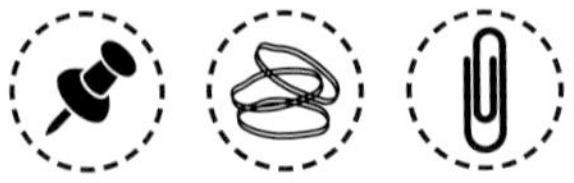

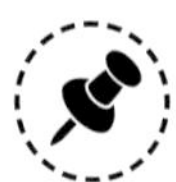
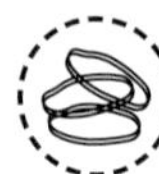

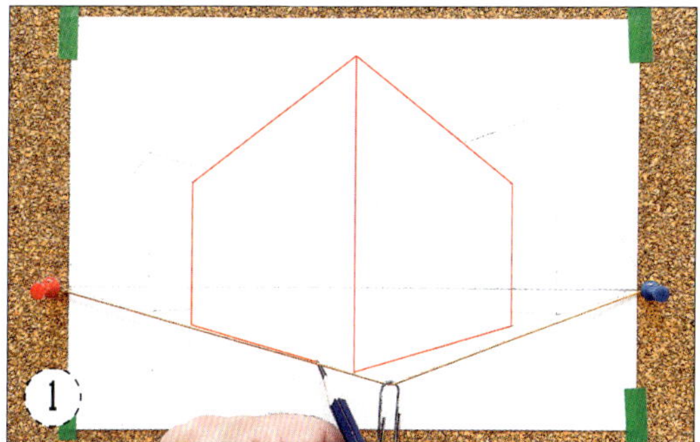

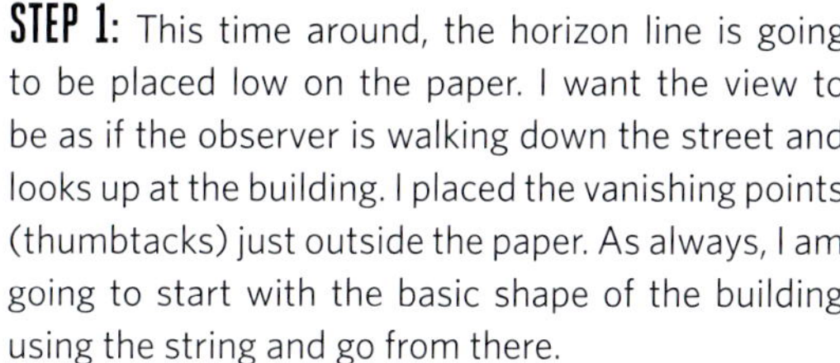

STEP 1: This time around, the horizon line is going to be placed low on the paper. I want the view to be as if the observer is walking down the street and looks up at the building. I placed the vanishing points (thumbtacks) just outside the paper. As always, I am going to start with the basic shape of the building using the string and go from there.

Draw a cube (red) with the closest edge right in the middle of the paper. If you compare this cube with the rectangle used in the Urban Sketching with String lesson (page 49), you will see that in one-point perspective one of the sides of the building was directly facing the observer. Now, each side goes to a different vanishing point. I am also going to draw two additional cubes, one on either side, representing nearby buildings. Their bottom edge needs to be aligned and I am leaving a space between them.

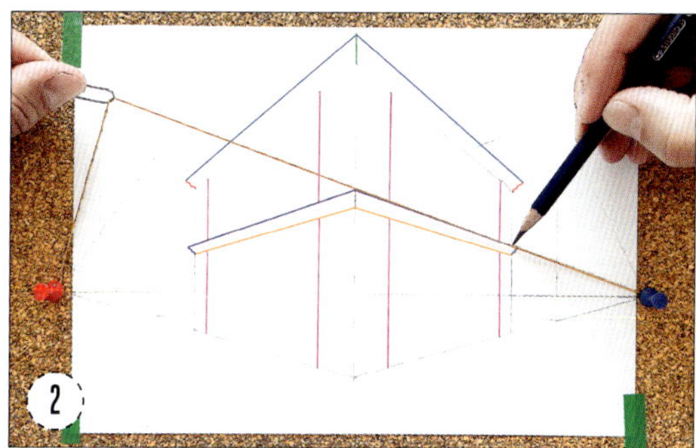

STEP 2: Now, divide the box in the main sections of the building and start adding details. Draw the cornice by tracing a couple of wavy bracket-like lines (red) in both top outermost corners and then join their ends with vanishing lines (blue) going in both directions until they meet in the center. From there, add a small vertical (green) to the corner.

There is another very similar structure a little bit above the center of the box. So, start with a couple of vanishing lines (orange), and repeat the same process, but do the wavy lines a bit smaller (all in purple).

Next, build thick columns on the corners using vertical lines (pink).

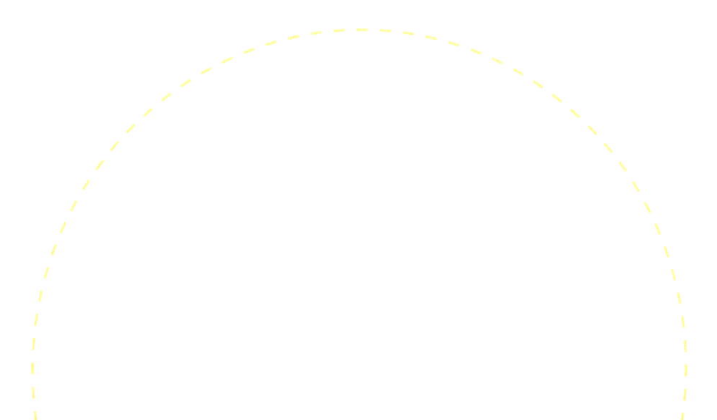

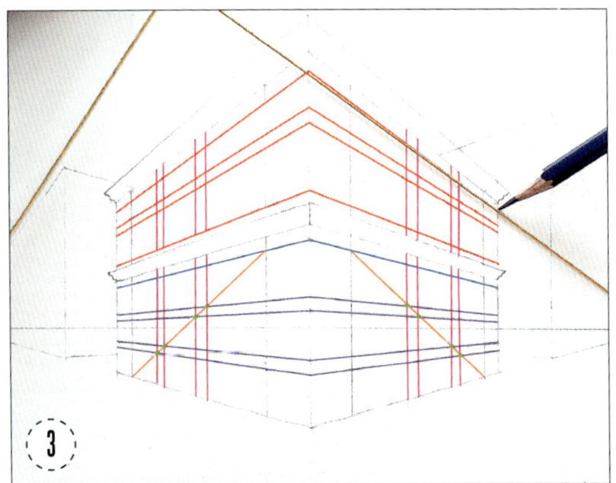

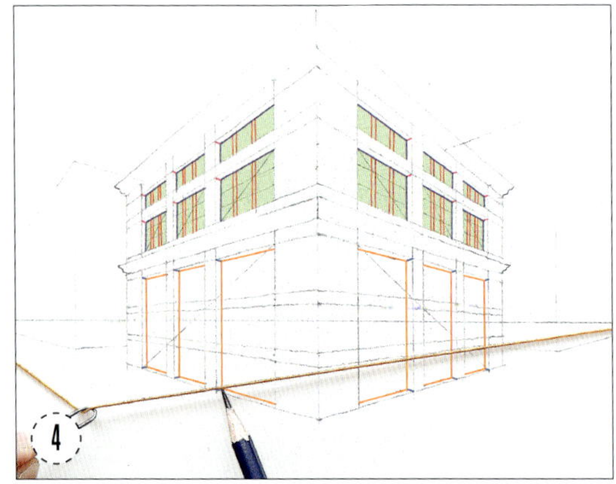

STEP 3: In the top section, use the elastic to draw four vanishing lines (red) that will determine the height of the windows. In the bottom section, draw a vanishing line (blue) beneath the cornice. Then divide the remaining space into three equal parts with double lines (purple).

PRO TIP: The diagonal trick is used to divide a squared or horizontal plane into perfectly proportioned sections when the horizontal divisions have already been defined. Draw a diagonal from corner to corner of the plane, and wherever it crosses the horizontal divisions, add a vertical line.

Each one of the sides between the columns will be divided into three equal vertical parts as well. To do that accurately, use the diagonal trick in the Pro Tip above. Draw two diagonals (orange) that join both corners of the bottom sections. Using the points where those diagonals cross the purple lines (green dots), draw verticals (pink) all the way to the top jumping the middle cornice.

STEP 4: You need to put depth in the grid of the top section, so repeat the process used for the window in The Elastic String Technique lesson (page 81). Draw very small vanishing lines (pink) from every farthest top corner in that grid. The ones on the left go to the right vanishing point and vice versa. From their ends draw verticals and vanishing lines (purple). Next, divide each one of those receded planes (shaded in green) in three equal vertical parts using the diagonal trick you used in Step 3 (red lines).

In the bottom, you also need to create depth in some parts. Draw small lines (blue) from the farthest corners of the six first-floor window sections to their opposite vanishing point. From their ends draw verticals and vanishing lines (orange).

STEP 5: The windows in the bottom section are going to be arched at their top. To draw the arches, you must find each one of their centers. So, I drew an X in each of the windows. Notice that each X is a little bit off center and they seem not to arrive exactly at the corners on one side. That is because I have to take into account that a part of each window is hidden behind the column and they are actually a bit wider than they look. I then added lines (yellow), from the center of each X to the top of the window. Now draw semicircles (red) in the top section (shaded in green) of each window.

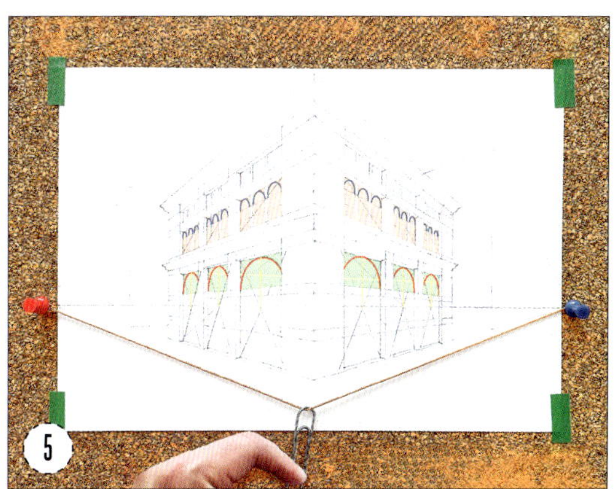

The six groups of three small windows on the first floor of the top section (shaded in orange) are also going to be arched. This time they are much smaller so it is possible to eyeball them. Draw semicircles (blue) at their tops.

STEP 6: Just a couple more details are needed to wrap up the windows. Draw double vertical lines (red) in the center of the top two sections of the grand arched windows. Use the X as a reference again. Now add double lines (blue) at the base of the arches of the small windows.

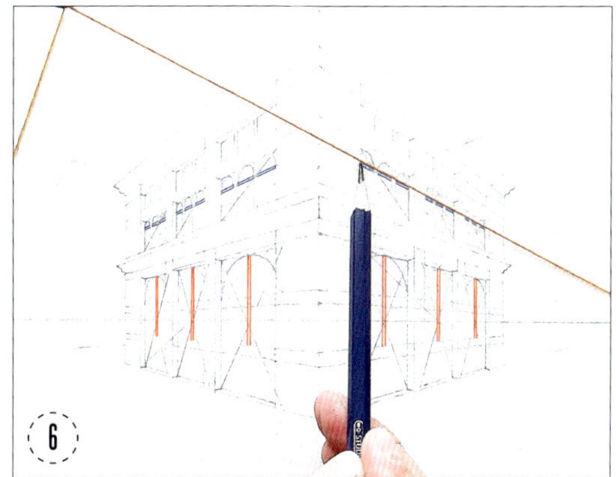

STEP 7: Now add some architectural details. Draw rectangular planes (red) on the corner columns. Add depth for those planes (blue lines), but they need to be very shallow, because they are just decoration. Next, draw parallel horizontal lines (green) in the base of the columns and wrap them around the corner (purple) where they are visible. Add parallel vanishing lines (pink) in the cornices indicating their volumetry. Make sure they match perfectly in the corners.

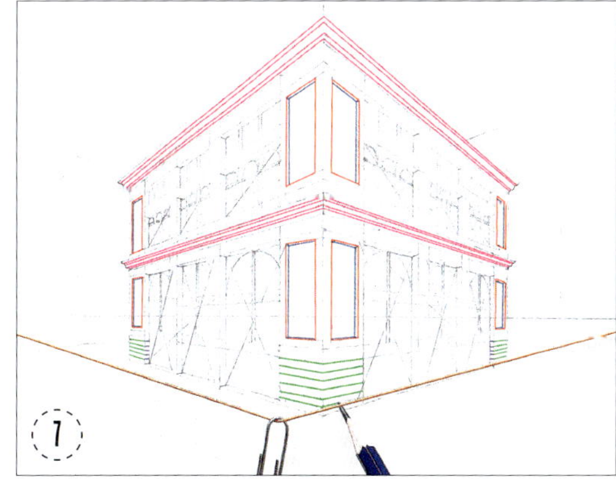

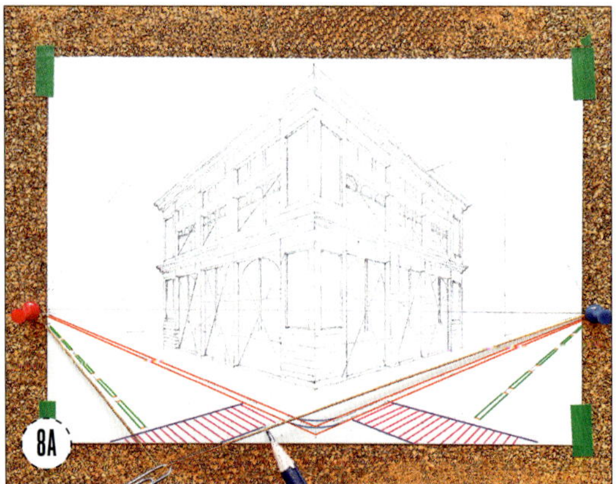

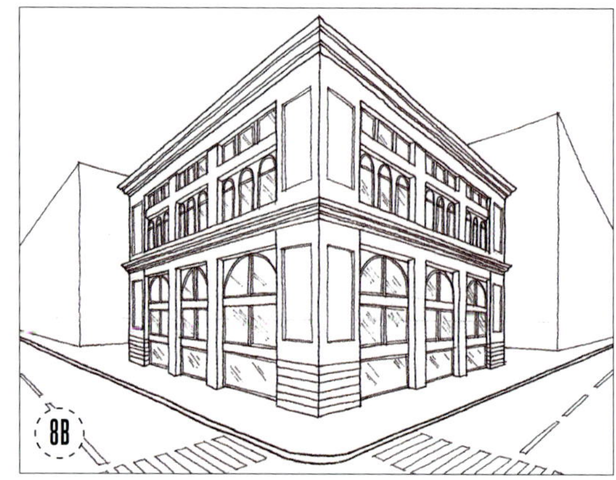

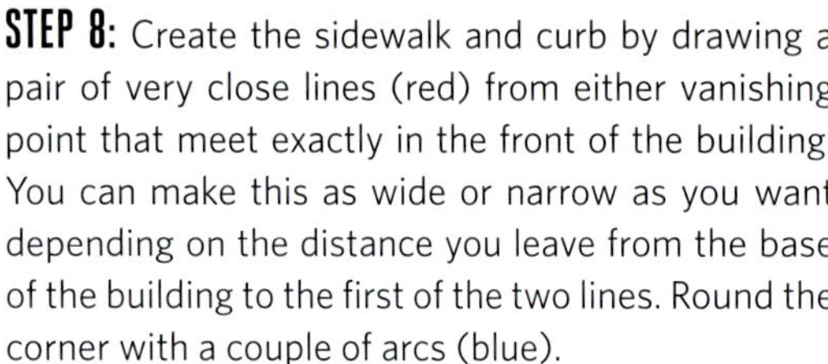

STEP 8: Create the sidewalk and curb by drawing a pair of very close lines (red) from either vanishing point that meet exactly in the front of the building. You can make this as wide or narrow as you want depending on the distance you leave from the base of the building to the first of the two lines. Round the corner with a couple of arcs (blue).

Some street lines would add a lot of interest. So, draw the crosswalk on both sides of the corner. Add a couple of lines (purple) from each vanishing point starting near the corner of the sidewalk and continuing off the paper. The distance between them is the length of the crosswalk lines. Then draw a series of pairs of lines (pink) in the opposite direction between the two first ones.

Adding lane division lines uses a similar process. First, draw pairs of lines (green) from the vanishing points and then a series of pairs (orange) in the other direction.

The amount of depth and spatial awareness that these corner perspectives create never ceases to amaze me and I understand why people are obsessed with them. Note that I drew frames with double lines around every window to give them depth. I also used different line weights to avoid having a drawing that looks flat. The main and closer lines are drawn with a wider tip, while details and farther lines use a thinner one.

As you experienced in this project, and in the lesson, drawing two-point perspective with an elastic string is not only easier but much more practical and cleaner. I hope you enjoyed it.

LESSON: DIAGONALS IN TWO-POINT PERSPECTIVE

I just love diagonals in perspective. They add a new layer of information that enriches your drawings and they are super useful for a lot of things, as you saw when you studied diagonals in one-point perspective. Everything you learned in the Conquering Diagonal Lines lesson (page 40) and Drawing a Simple Staircase project (page 44) is applicable here. If you remember, you started with a container box and used it as a reference to draw the diagonals. It works the same for two-point perspective.

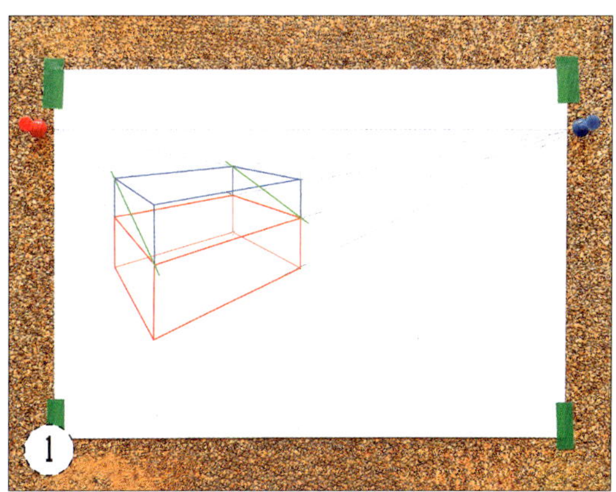

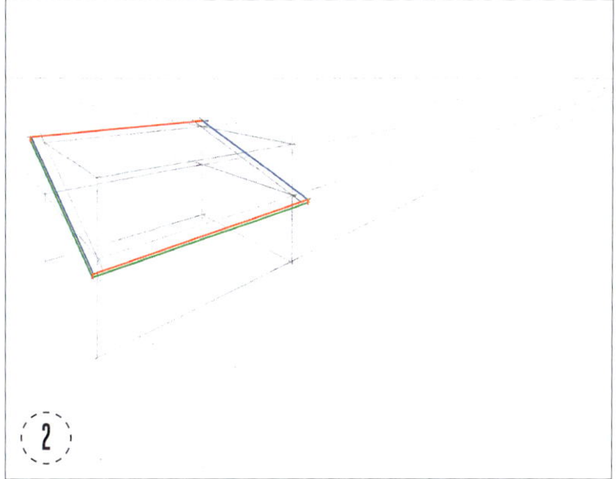

Drawing roofs is undoubtedly one of the most important uses for diagonals. I want to focus this lesson on drawing some of the most popular types of roofs. Note that all the drawings in this lesson are going to have a very high horizon line, because I want you to be able to have a very good look at all the roofs from an elevated position.

The first roof I want to draw is the skillion or shed roof. Its inclination goes in one direction only. In Picture 1 you can see that I built a rectangular box (red). That will be the body of the house. I then drew another box (blue) on top. The height of that box is going to be the inclination of the roof. You can make it as high or low as you want. In this case, I drew it a little bit shorter that the first box. Next, I added a couple of diagonals (green) from the back, top corners of the blue box to its front, bottom ones. Note that I extended them a little bit on both ends. This is to create the front and back overhang.

Then, I need to join those two loose ends with lines (red in Picture 2) coming from the right vanishing point. Those too need to be extended a little bit on their ends to create the lateral overhangs. To close the roof, just draw a pair of lines (blue) parallel to the initial diagonals. Finally, I want to give it thickness by adding double lines (green) to the visible sides and small verticals (orange) in the corners.

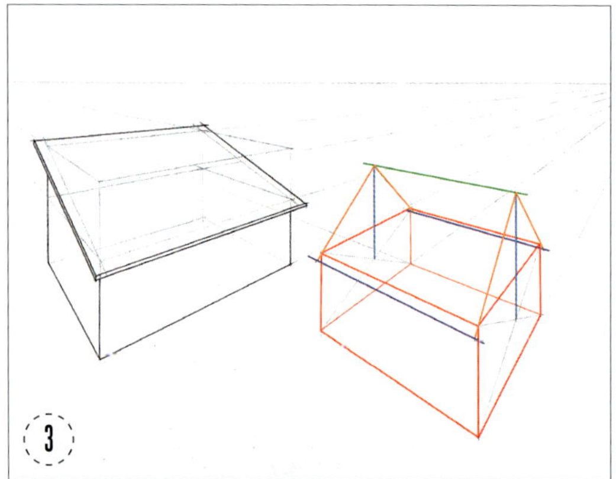

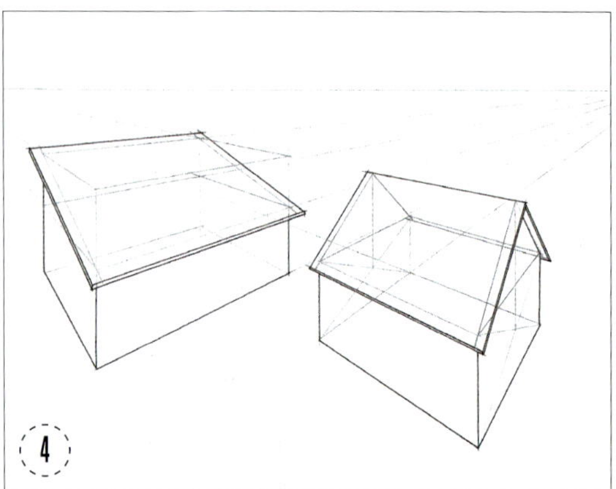

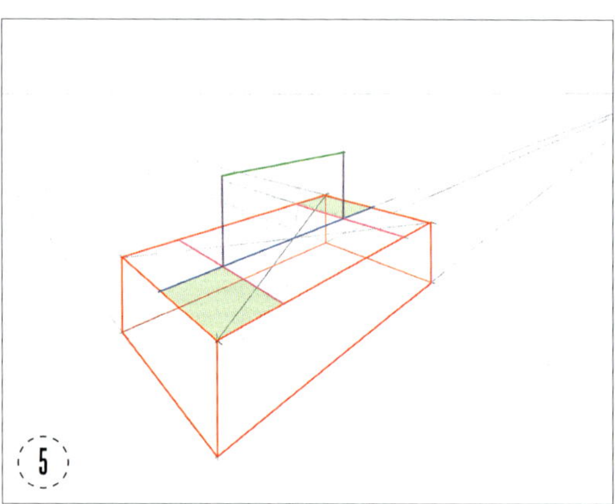

The next example is the quintessential double slope, which is called a gable roof. I drew another rectangular box (red in Picture 3). Then I found the center point of the right front side and back left one by drawing Xs on them (learn more about the X method on page 18). From the center point of the Xs I added a couple of verticals (blue), which will be the height of the roof. Again, those lines can be as high or low as you want your roof to be.

Next, I joined their ends with a line (green) coming from the left vanishing point and I extended it on both ends. That is going to be the ridge. From the points where the blues meet the green, I drew lines (orange) going to the top corners of the box on that same side and extended their ends a bit. Then, I joined those loose ends with lines (purple) coming from the vanishing point and extended their ends on both sides.

Picture 4 shows how I closed the roof by drawing four parallel diagonals joining the extended loose ends. I added thickness to all visible edges with double lines and small verticals in the corners. You can see very clearly that the overhang goes all the way around the house.

The next example has four different slopes and is called a hip roof. With this roof, I am going to include a dormer, which is a lot of fun to draw and looks incredibly cool.

Start with the base box (red in Picture 5). An X on its top plane will help determine the middle line (blue). Then I drew a couple of lines (pink) coming from the left vanishing point that have the same distance from the front and back faces of the box. I will try to draw squared planes (shaded in green) near the edges to have a reference but this is not necessarily a fixed distance for every hip roof. From the points where the pinks cross the blue, I need to draw a couple of verticals (purple) to determine the height of the roof. A line (green) joining their ends will be the ridge of the roof.

Now that the ridge is defined, you can close it. I added four diagonal lines (red in Picture 6), two on either end of the ridge, going to the four corners of the box. Again, I extended them just a bit to create the overhang. By joining those four loose ends with vanishing lines (blue), I will complete the roof. Don't forget to add thickness to the visible edges (green lines).

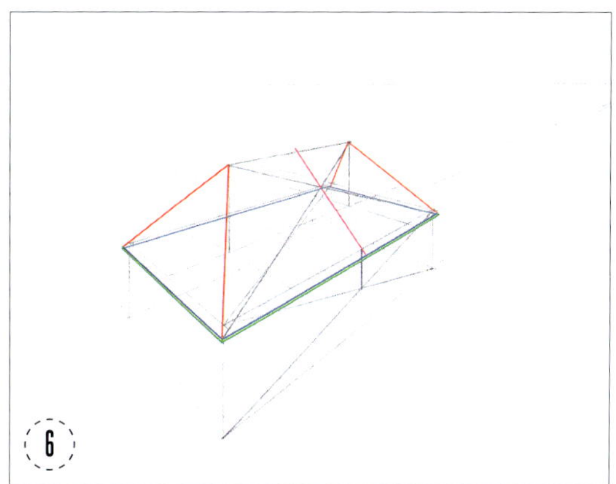

The dormer will be centered on the front right slope. To find that center I drew Xs on the slope and on the wall of the house. Then, I drew a line (purple) from the center point of the wall to its upper edge. Finally, I joined its top end with the center point of the sloped plane (pink line) dividing it in two equal parts.

Using that middle line as a reference, I drew a centered squared vertical plane (red in Picture 7) with a triangle-shaped plane (also red) on top. The bottom edge of the squared plane coincides with the top edge of the box (yellow). Also note that I extended the sides of the triangle.

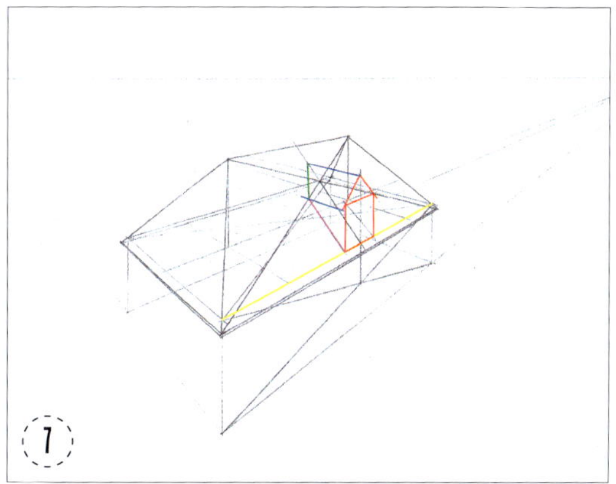

Next, I added two vanishing lines (blue) coming from the ends of the left side of the triangle. The top one goes all the way to the center line of the roof and the other I left loose for now. From the bottom left corner of the squared plane, I drew a diagonal line (pink) parallel to the center one until it finds the blue line that was left loose. Finally, from that point a green line joins the two blue ones and that completes the dormer.

Picture 8 shows the result. For this drawing I added details like the tile lines that let you know how they would look in real life. On the triangle-shaped sides, the tile lines are parallel to the line (red) that joins the tip of the triangle with the middle point of the opposite edge (red). The ones on the other side are parallel to the middle line (blue). Also, note that in the ridge and hips I put an additional line on either side that represents the pieces that are used in those joints to avoid water filtration.

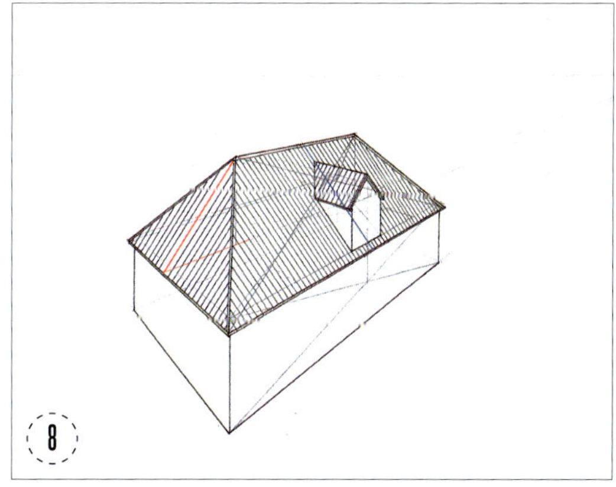

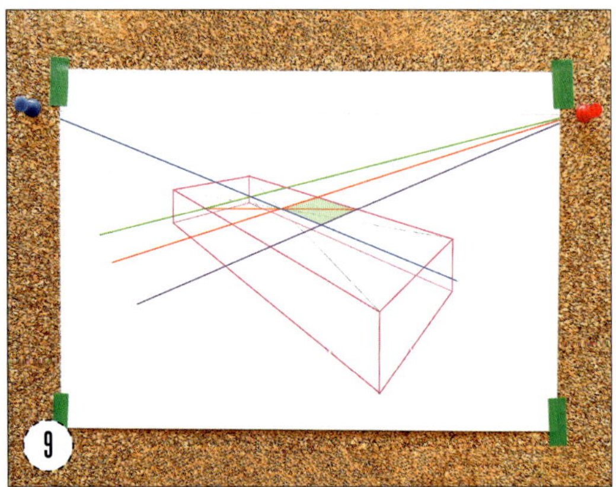

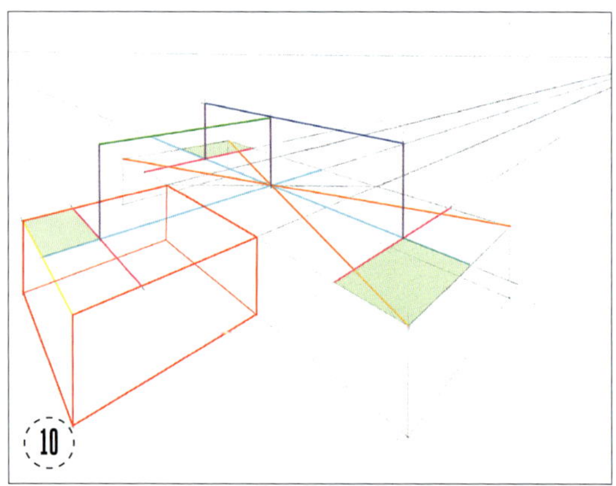

The last type of roof I want to show you is the hip and valley. It is basically a hip roof that covers a T-shaped structure. This will also allow me to teach you how to draw that house shape.

First, I drew a rectangular box (pink) that is longer than the ones I have done so far. An X on its top plane will reveal the center point and I drew lines (red and blue in Picture 9) coming from both vanishing points passing through it. Then I drew a line (purple) from the right vanishing point to the right of the red one, which creates a squared plane (shaded in green). From the top right corner of that squared plane I drew a line (orange) that passes through the intersection of the red and the blue and reaches the other edge of the box. I used that point where the orange meets the edge as a reference and drew another line (green) coming from the right vanishing point.

As you can see, the top T-shaped plane is almost finished. I just need to close it with a line coming from the left vanishing point (yellow in Picture 10). Now I just have to give it volume by turning it into a box (red lines) that is attached to the main one.

The process to build the actual roof is very similar to the one used with the hip roof. Add vanishing lines (pink) close to all three ends of the T, to create semi-squared planes (shaded in green). From the points where pinks cross with the center lines (light blue) and the two diagonals (orange) cross each other, draw four verticals (purple) that will determine the height of the roof. Next, join their ends with two vanishing lines (green and blue) that also form a T. That is the ridge.

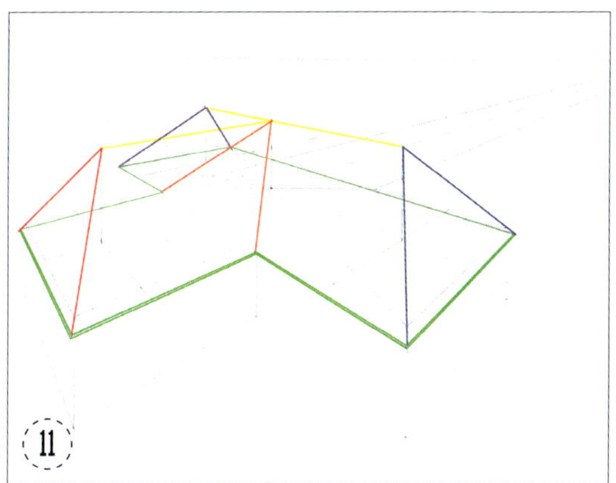

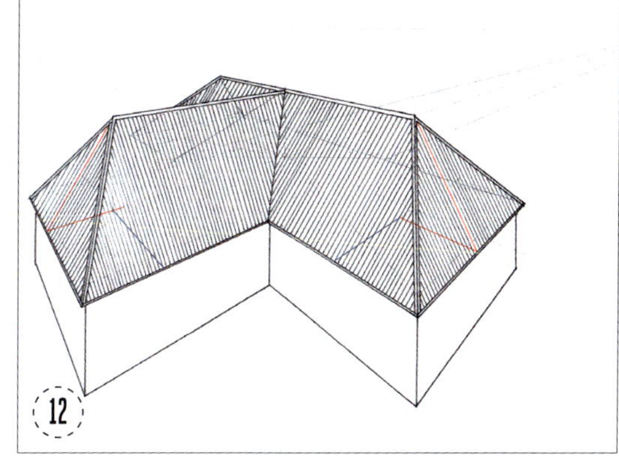

By now, you know where this is going. You are only a couple steps away from completing this beautiful roof. Draw pairs of diagonals (red, purple, orange and blue in Picture 11) from the tip of the four verticals that make up the ridge (yellow), to their corresponding corners and extend them a little bit to create the overhang. Then join all the visible ends with lines (green) going to the corresponding vanishing point and give thickness to the visible edges of the sloped planes with double lines (also in green).

The triangle-shaped sides will have tile lines parallel to the line (red in Picture 12) that joins the tip of the triangle with the middle point of the opposite edge. On the other sides the tiles are parallel to the line that joins that same tip with the reference line used to find it (all in blue).

Learning how to draw roofs is crucial for architecture sketching and you can see why here. If you are traveling around Europe, Latin America or anywhere in the world and want to draw a landscape of an old historic town, now you will be more than able.

There are so many more roof types but, in some way, they are all small variations of the ones studied here, so you should be ready to handle anything that comes your way.

In the next project, you will tackle a U-shaped staircase, which is another popular use of diagonals in perspective drawing.

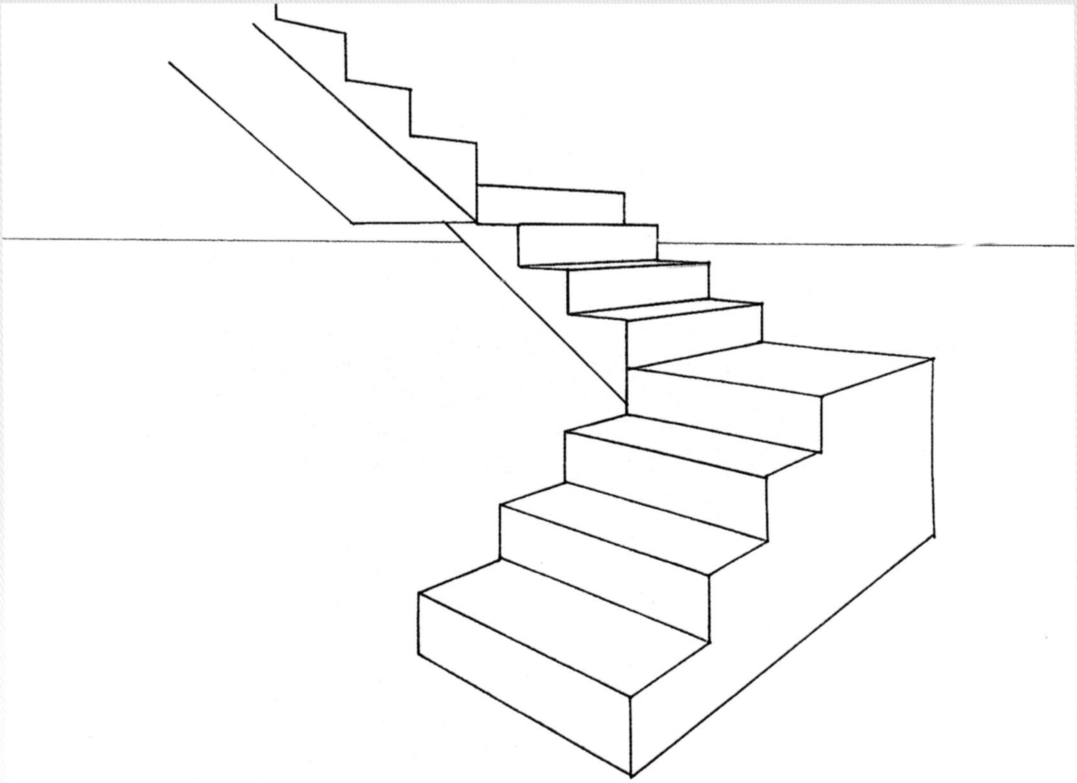

PROJECT: U-SHAPED STAIRCASE

The dreaded and absolutely gorgeous U-shaped staircase: This project is the perfect marriage between drawing and a puzzle. Staircases are made up of different parts that make sense once you join them and that is particularly true for this one. The sense of fulfillment they produce when you are done is totally worth the effort. Some of the skills you will be using in this project are drawing container boxes and making horizontal and vertical divisions of container boxes and diagonals, so this project is going to be great practice, too.

Additional Materials

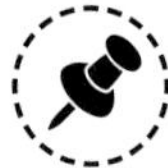

STEP 1: Place the horizon line slightly above the center of the paper. The vanishing points are represented by the two thumbtacks on either side. Start with a container box with an approximate ratio of 3:3:1—three units high, three units long and one unit wide. Draw a squared plane (purple lines in Picture 1a), and then I will show you how to give it a depth that is one third of its length. Use the diagonal trick you learned about in the Pro Tip on page 88 (orange lines) to find its third part and match it on the other side (orange shaded planes). Use the width of the plane on the right side to build the rest of the box (pink lines).

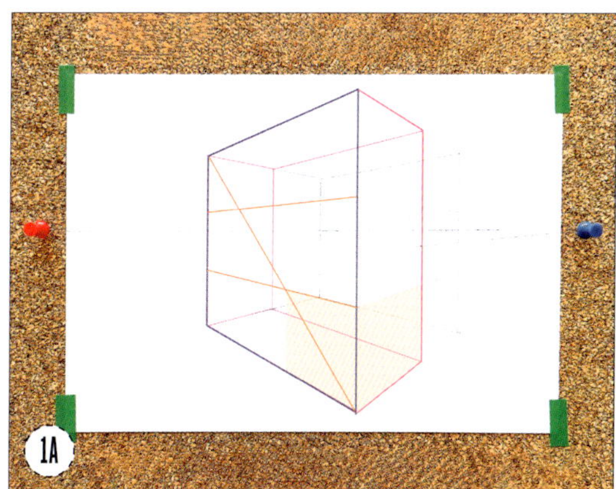

Double the depth of that box (pink in Picture 1b) to get the exact size needed for the staircase. So, draw a line (red) from the middle point of the closest edge going to the right vanishing point. Then draw a diagonal (blue) that starts at the top left corner of that plane and passes through the intersection (yellow dot) of the red line and its back edge, until it meets the projection of the bottom edge. That point marks the correct distance to build a 3:3:2 box, so now use it as a reference to build the box (green lines).

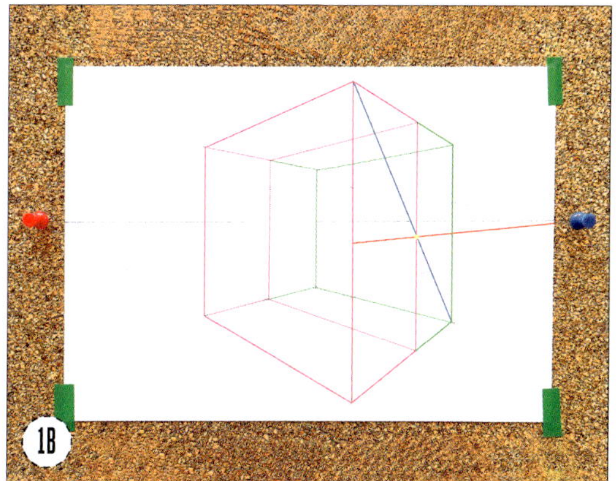

STEP 2: Different parts will be needed to build the staircase. You will be creating a grid of 1:1:1 boxes. Divide the front planes in three equal-sized stripes (red lines). That divides the front right plane in 1 x 1 squares (shaded in orange and green). Now do the same on the left side. Repeat the diagonal trick (blue line). The points where the red lines meet the blue lines (yellow dots) mark the perfect size for 1 x 1 squares on the front left plane. So, draw verticals (green) passing through those points and you are all set.

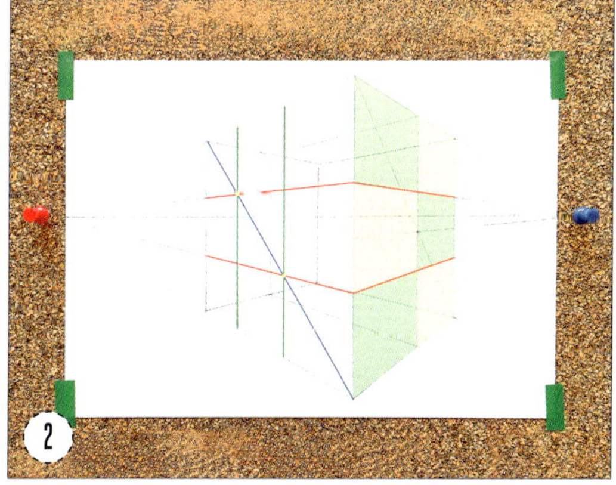

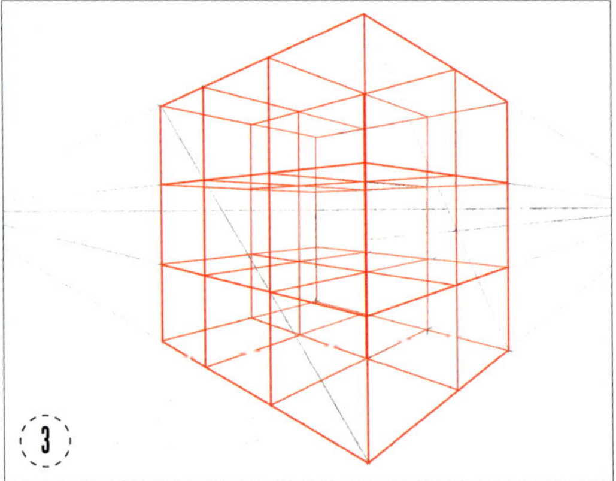

STEP 3: Now you need to transfer the grid from the front faces to the whole box. To do that, wrap every line around the box on the outside and also transfer the lines to the intermediate tiers. Red lines in Picture 3 show how that looks.

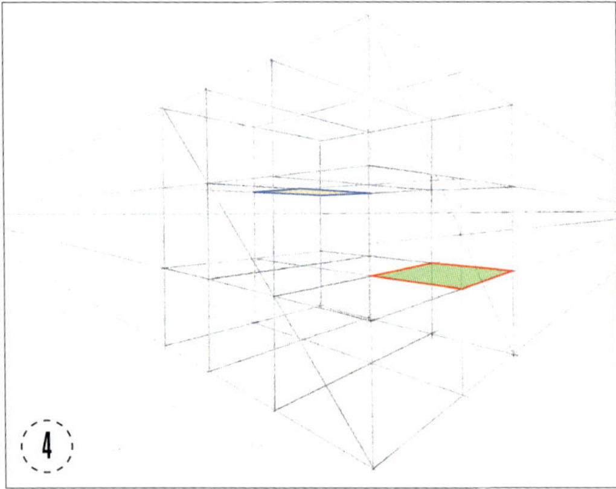

STEP 4: A U-shaped staircase has two landings at one third and two thirds of its height, and normally, an equal number of steps between them. For this staircase that number will be three and you need to define the position of those landings. The first one will be located at the back right corner of the second tier (shaded in green), so draw lines (red) that define it. Draw the second one (blue lines) in the back left corner of the third tier (shaded in orange).

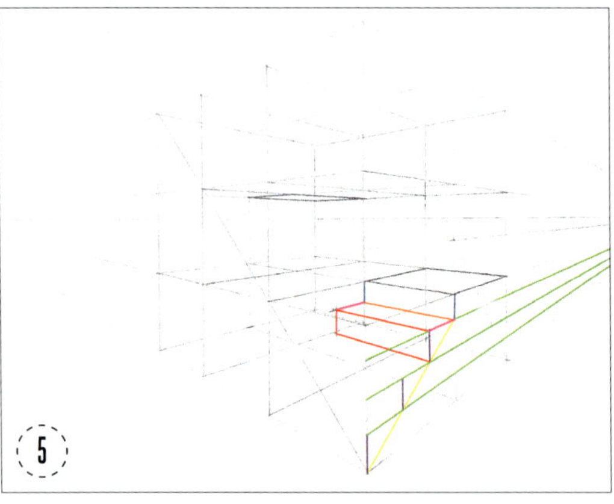

STEP 5: With the landings ready, go ahead and start drawing steps. To do that, draw three lines (green) going to the right vanishing point that divide the bottom strip of the front right face of the box in four equal parts. Those will be the heights of the steps. Now, draw two verticals (blue) from both corners of the staircase's front left edge of the landing until the right one meets the second green going down, and from that point join their ends with a line (orange) going to the left vanishing point. Starting in that same point, add a diagonal (yellow) going to the bottom front corner of the box. That diagonal represents the inclination of the steps.

Draw verticals (purple) between the green lines where they meet with the yellow diagonal, descending in steps until you get to the corner. This is the coolest part, because it is when you watch the first section of the staircase appear. Use the orange, blue and purple lines as reference to build it.

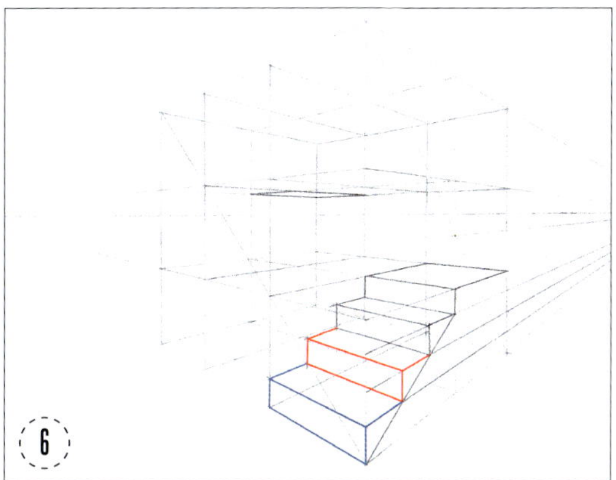

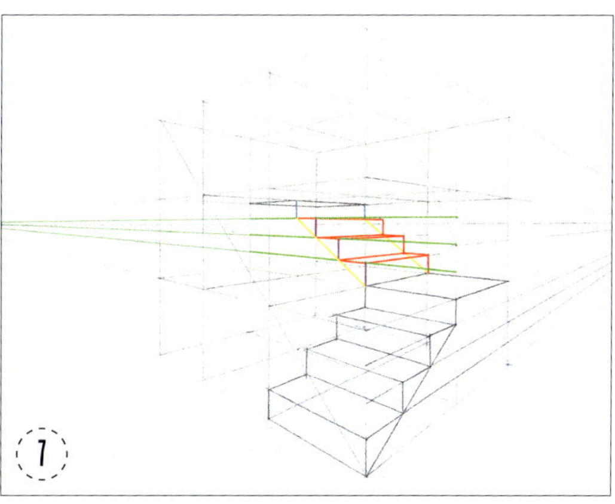

Draw a line (pink) going to the right vanishing point between the lower end of the right blue line and the top end of the purple. Then replicate that same length with another line (also pink) from the lower end of the left blue line. Now join them with a line (red) going to the left vanishing point. From that left corner of the tread, add a vertical and join it with a line coming from the bottom of the purple going to the left vanishing point again (all in red). This is why I said this was going to be like a puzzle, and it is great to see how everything starts falling into place. You just drew the first step coming down from the landing.

STEP 6: Repeat the same process described in the last paragraph of Step 5 for every new step until you get to the floor (red lines are for the second step and blue lines for the first step).

STEP 7: Next, build the section between the two landings. This time start from the second landing going down and use the same process you used for the steps coming from the first landing. Divide the second floor of the box in four equal parts with three lines (green) going to the left vanishing point. These division lines should always be drawn in front of the steps and not behind, so that is why I did not draw them in the back plane of the box but rather in the middle division (shaded in yellow).

From both ends of the front right edge of the landing draw a couple of verticals (blue) until the left one meets the first green. From that point add a diagonal (yellow) that lands in the front left corner of the first landing. For this section, I also drew a yellow diagonal from the end of the other blue to the other corner of the landing. That one is not necessary but sometimes having both helps construct the steps. Draw the vertical lines (purple) that join the green lines at the points where they meet the yellow diagonal. With all those reference lines you can build all the steps going down (all in red). Note that in this example, the first tread going down is almost aligned with the horizon line, so it looks like a line rather than a plane.

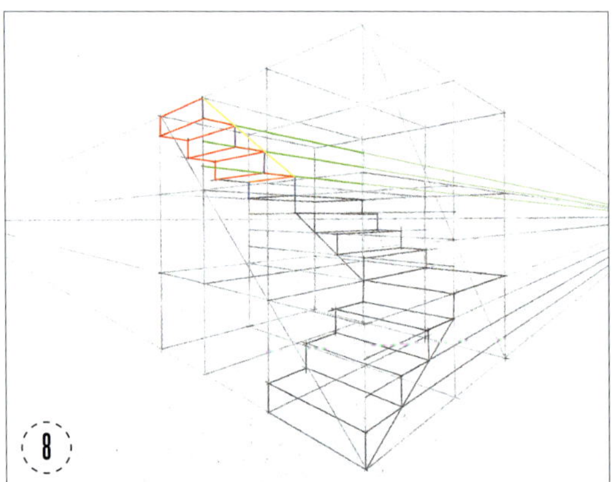

STEP 8: Again, repeat a similar process for the last section, which starts at the second landing and ends on the next floor. This time work from the landing going up and be careful because now you are looking at the bottom of the staircase instead of its top.

The green lines going to the right vanishing point divide the third floor of the box into four equal parts. I put them on the wall that is in front of where the steps are going to be. From both ends of the front left edge of that landing, add verticals (blue) until the right one meets the first green, and from that point join their ends with a line (orange) going to the left vanishing point. From that same point draw a diagonal (yellow) that reaches the end of the staircase. Next, draw the verticals (purple) that join the greens at the points where they meet the yellow. Use those lines as reference to draw the rest of the steps (all in red).

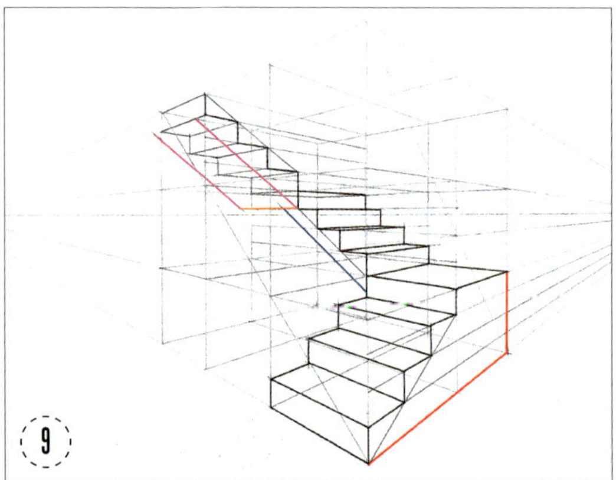

STEP 9: You can see that I drew the thickness of the staircases' slab so that it does not look like it was made in origami. The first section is easy, because you just draw the whole bottom (red) following the shape of the box, under the landing and the steps. For the second section, draw a parallel (blue) to the steps' inclination line, and the last section needs two of those parallels (pink) because you are seeing the whole bottom of that slab. I joined them at the end with a line (orange) going to the left vanishing point.

You could add a lot more details like handrails, pictures on the wall, hardwood steps and so on. However, I think that because this is the first U-shaped staircase you may have done, you can call it a day.

LESSON: VERTICAL VANISHING POINTS

The most common way of working in two-point perspective is with horizontal vanishing points, one on the right and another on the left. But that is not the only way. You can also place your vanishing points in a vertical position, and the results are incredible. Vertical two-point perspective achieves a quasi-three-point perspective look, combined with a bird's-eye view effect.

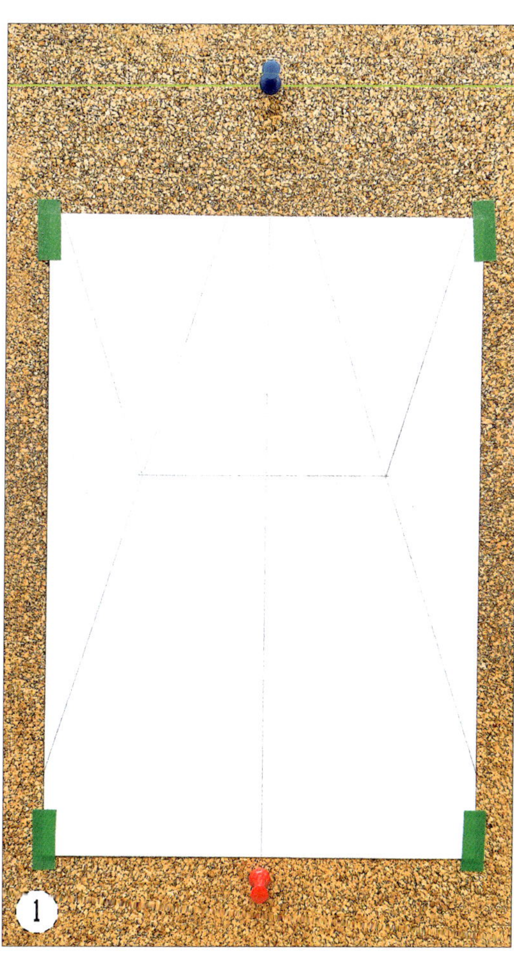

PRO TIP: The format you work in is intimately tied to the technique you use. Some techniques are better suited for horizontal formats and some for vertical ones. Always choose accordingly before deciding the orientation of your paper. One-point perspective is the most versatile and can be used in either a horizontal or vertical format. Two-point perspective is best suited for horizontal formats when used with horizontal vanishing points, but when the vanishing points are shifted to a vertical position, a vertical format will work best. For three-point perspective, page orientation depends on the position of the third vanishing point. If it is close to the horizon line, a vertical format will work best to avoid perspective distortion as much as possible. As you move the third vanishing point farther away, you can widen the format accordingly. You will learn more about this when we study this technique (page 112). When in doubt, a square format will work well most of the time.

As always, the best way of explaining is by showing you an example. I will use a vertical paper format, which is something I haven't done so far but works best for this type of drawing. The vertical line joining the two vanishing points is going to pass exactly through the center of the paper. The vanishing points will be represented by the two thumbtacks (Picture 1). For vertical two-point perspective, the top vanishing point is placed on the horizon line (green), which, being so high, will produce a semi-bird's-eye view.

If you remember, with horizontal vanishing points, the vertical lines were drawn straight vertically and horizontal lines went to either vanishing point depending on their direction relative to the observers' eyes. When you change their position, this changes too. Now, the bottom vanishing point will be used for all verticals. The horizontals will be drawn going to the top vanishing point or straight horizontally, depending on their direction.

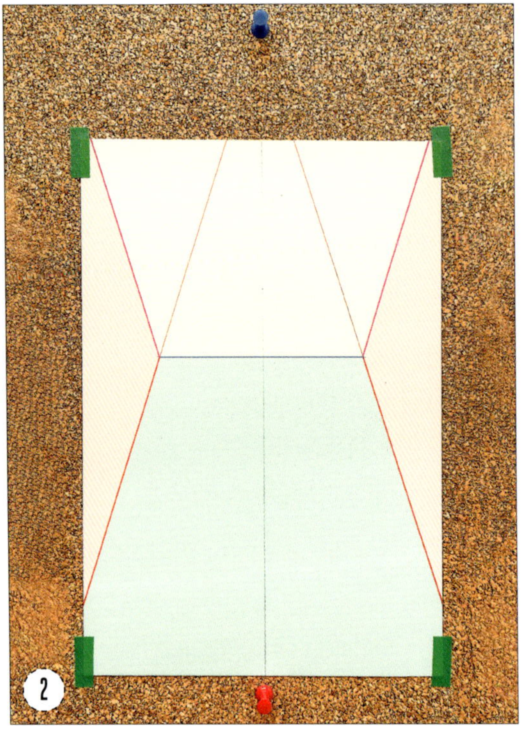

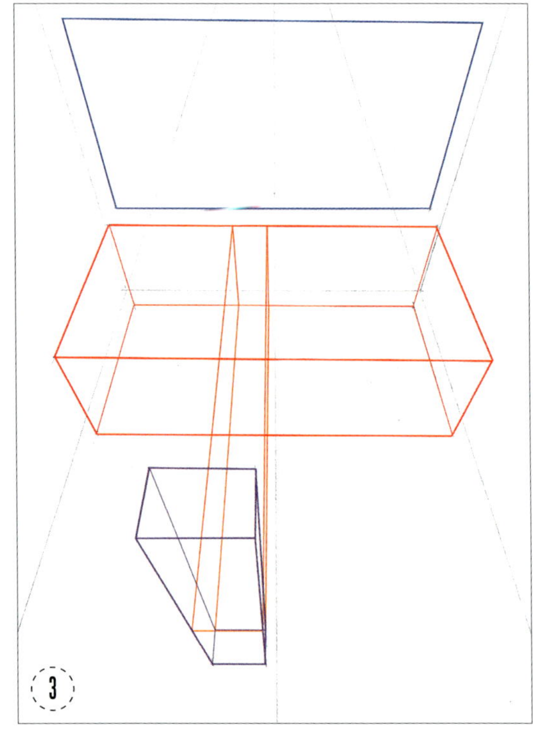

Let me show you how it works. I am going to draw a small room with a window, a sofa and a woman. I start by defining the space, so I will draw two lines (red in Picture 2) going to the top vanishing point that start a little bit above the bottom corners of the paper on either side. Then I will join those two lines with a horizontal (blue) just above the center of the paper and, from its ends, draw two verticals (pink) going to the bottom vanishing point until they go off the paper. With those lines you just defined the floor (shaded in green), the walls on either side (shaded in orange) and the wall at the end of the room (shaded in yellow).

The sofa will occupy the entire width of the room and will be placed against the back wall. So, I will build a container box (red in Picture 3) with its dimensions. Note that the box is wider than it is tall according to the normal proportions of a sofa. Next, I define the position and size of the window with a horizontal plane (blue) above the sofa's box in the back wall.

Another box (purple) near the bottom of the paper will represent the woman. The proportions of the boxes for humans depend on the pose in which you are going to draw them. In this case, she will be standing up, so it is going to be a tall rectangular box. My main concern is to keep it scaled with the sofa, so I want it to be at least twice as tall (orange lines for reference).

Now I can start working individually on each of the objects. First, for the sofa, I am going to draw a C shape (red in Picture 4) on the top plane using an X to determine how far back I need to go. Choose the arm-width you want and go all the way back, using the top vanishing point, until you find the diagonal of the X. Join the end of those two red lines to complete the C and it will become the arms and back of the sofa. You will also need to transfer the width you want of the arms to the front plane with lines (blue) going to the bottom vanishing point that meet with the ends of the red ones.

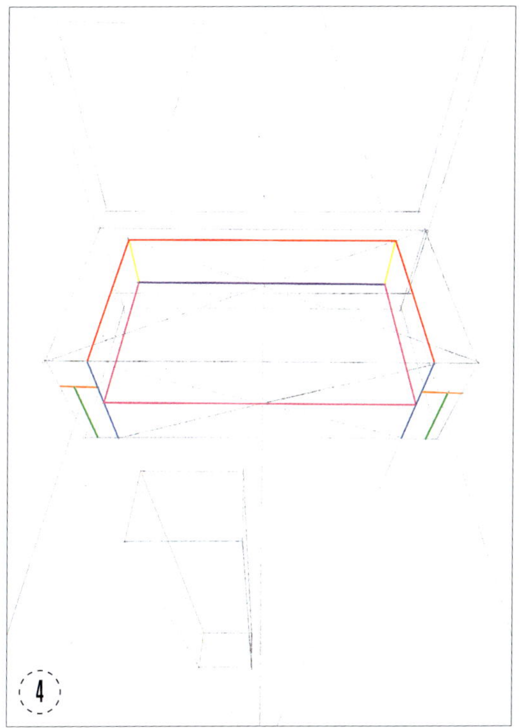

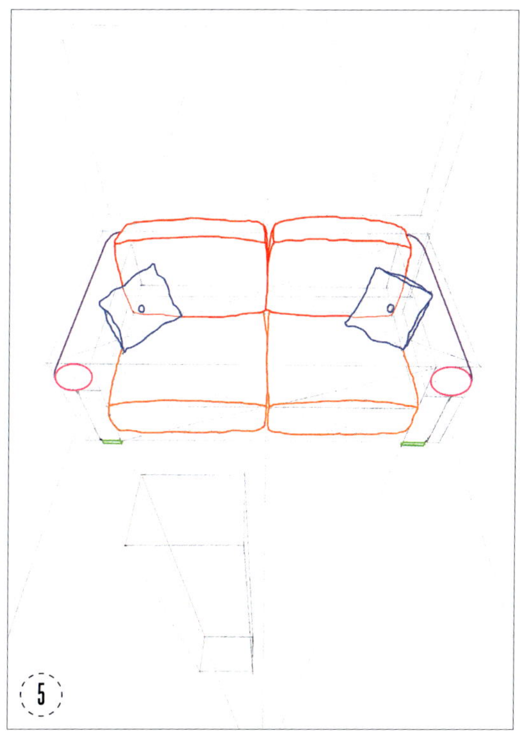

Then, I divide the front plane between the arms with a horizontal (pink) passing through its middle to represent the height of the seat. From the ends of that line, draw horizontals (also pink) going to the top vanishing point, until they meet with verticals (yellow) coming down from the corners of the C; join them with another horizontal (purple). Next, I draw a couple of small horizontals (orange) creating squared planes at the top of the arms and divide the bottom plane with two verticals (green).

With the geometry of the sofa figured out, I can turn it into a soft-edged, pillowy object. I will start with the back cushions. I drew a pair of round-edged boxes (red in Picture 5) against the back a bit taller than the back of the sofa. Next, against the corner of the arms and those cushions on both sides, I drew a couple of curvy-lined squared planes (blue). These are decorative pillows and their angle is totally random and not drawn using perspective.

I drew the seat cushions by rounding the lines and corners (orange) so that they look like upholstery. And of course, I need to do the same with the arms and back. I drew ellipses (pink) inside the squared boxes at the top of the arms first, and from their outer edges, horizontals (purple) closing the arms on both sides. I also need to slightly curve and soften all other corners and edges. A couple of small boxes (green) under the arms serve as legs.

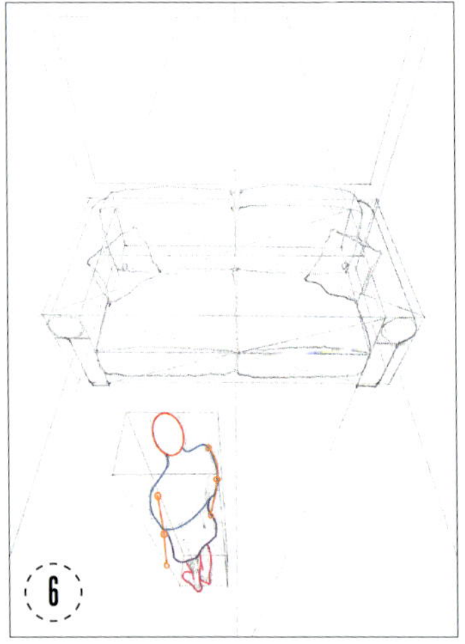

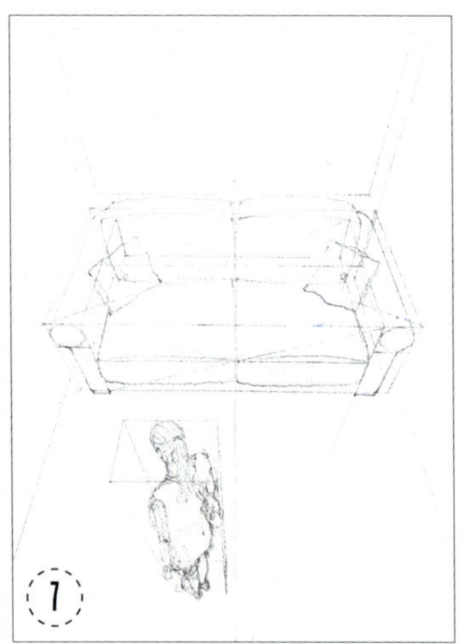

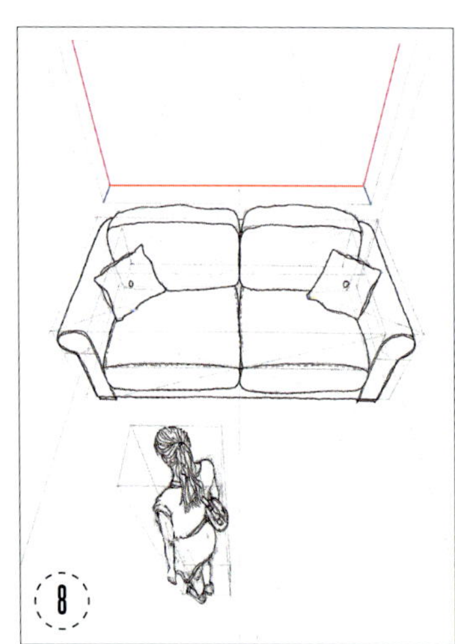

Next up, to draw the woman—using the container box as a guide—I insert the basic shapes (in various colors in Picture 6) that make up her body. I used the normal proportions for humans, with the hip joints, wrists and crotch at half her height and the head one-eighth of her total height. The shoulder width for a woman is about 2½ head widths (for a man, it would be a bit more). I suggest using a reference picture to make sure everything looks right. With those basic shapes as a foundation, I can draw all the details (Picture 7). Note that the box forces you to draw her head and torso bigger than her lower body.

The window is the easiest of the three objects in our drawing but I will use it as an opportunity to teach you how to create the depth of the wall and then the depth of the window frame itself. This is something that you will be using over and over in architectural sketching. The depth of the wall is generated by two lines (blue in Picture 8) going to the top vanishing point, from the bottom corners of the window plane. The length of those lines depends on the width you want for your walls. Then, join their ends with a horizontal (red) and add two lines (pink) going to the bottom vanishing point until they hide behind the opening frame.

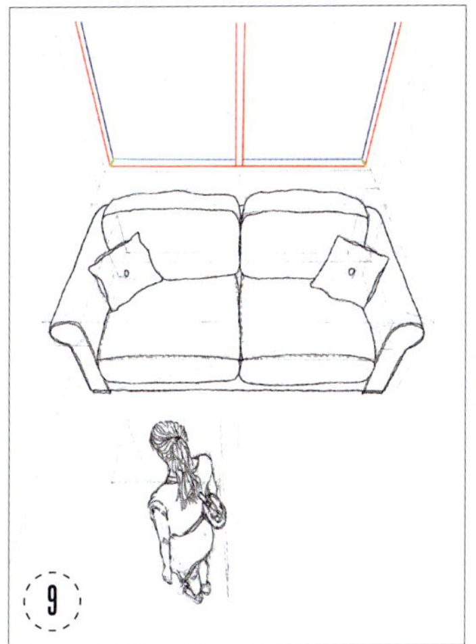

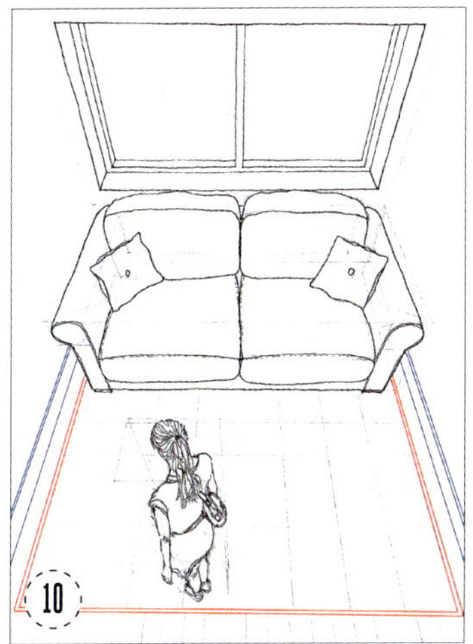

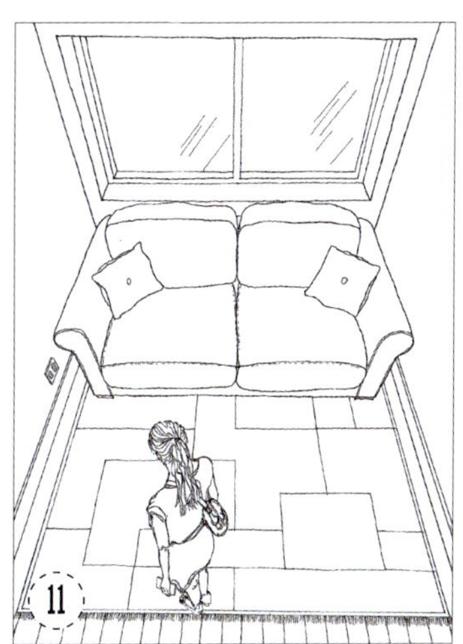

Next, to create the thickness of the window frame I made a vertical division in the middle, starting with a longer horizontal line across the base of the windows (red in Picture 9) and four verticals (also red). Two of those verticals are close to the side edges and the other two are on either side of the middle point that I found using the X method (page 18). Make sure the thickness of the frame is the same in all sections.

To define the window's depth, start again with two small lines (green) from the corners going to the top vanishing point. Note that in the center division you will not be able to see the depth of the frame because it is aligned with the vanishing points. Then I join their ends with a horizontal (blue) that skips the center division and finally two verticals (purple), until they hide behind the opening frame.

To finish up this little sketch, I added a carpet by drawing a horizontal plane in the floor with double lines (red in Picture 10) all around. I also traced a squared grid inside to work a cool design afterward. I also added a flooring design, in this case, hardwood floors with equally distanced horizontal lines going to the top vanishing point. And you cannot do hardwood floors without a baseboard (blue).

The result, portrayed in Picture 11, shows the very interesting view you can create with this technique. This is perfect to showcase an interior or product design project. It also makes for a very interesting angle for any art piece and it is all achieved just by playing around with the position of the vanishing points. Play around a bit with the vanishing points' position to figure out how that changes the perspective and the angles.

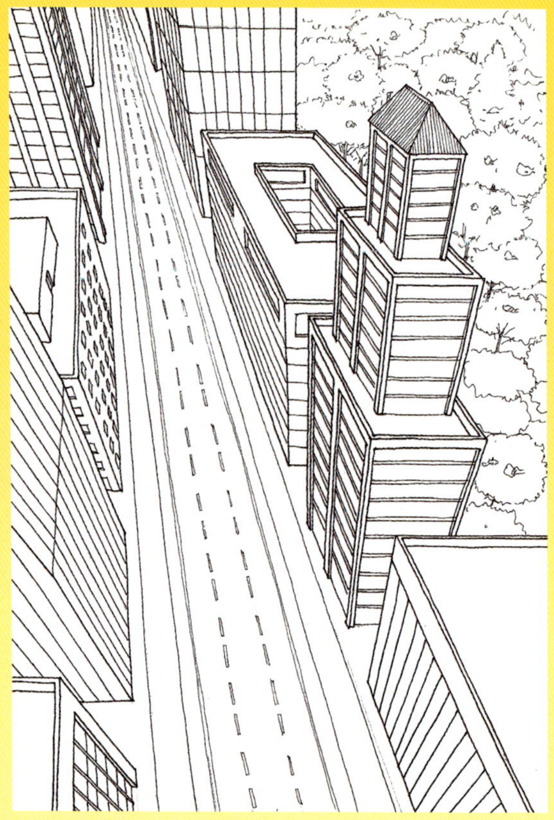

PROJECT: CITY LANDSCAPE WITH VERTICAL VANISHING POINTS

There are never too many different types of views from which to draw urban landscapes. The more options you have in your arsenal of techniques, the better prepared you will be to imagine and create interesting new perspectives that can take your work to a whole new level. Having many options can also help you develop your own unique style, which in the art world is priceless. Using vertical vanishing points in this drawing will produce a view of the cityscape unlike anything you have done so far. And, you will do it with an elastic!

Additional Materials

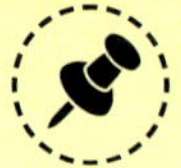
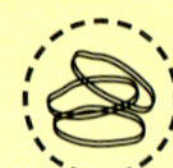
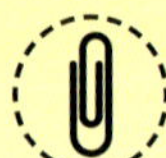

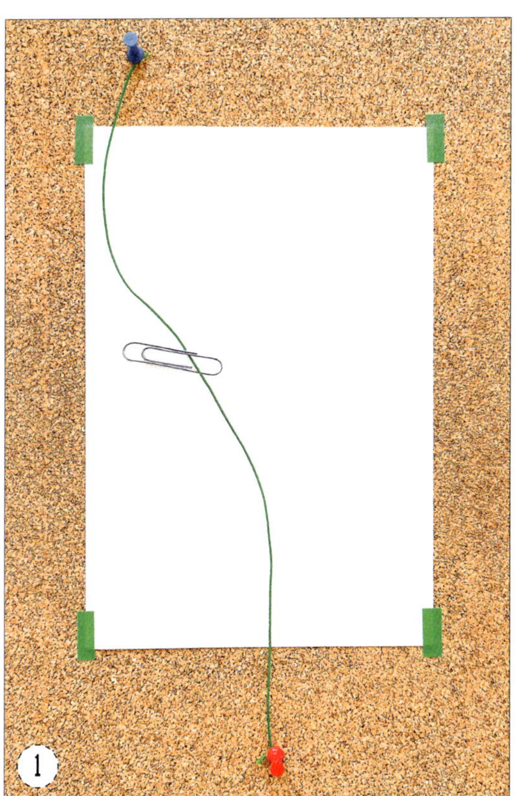

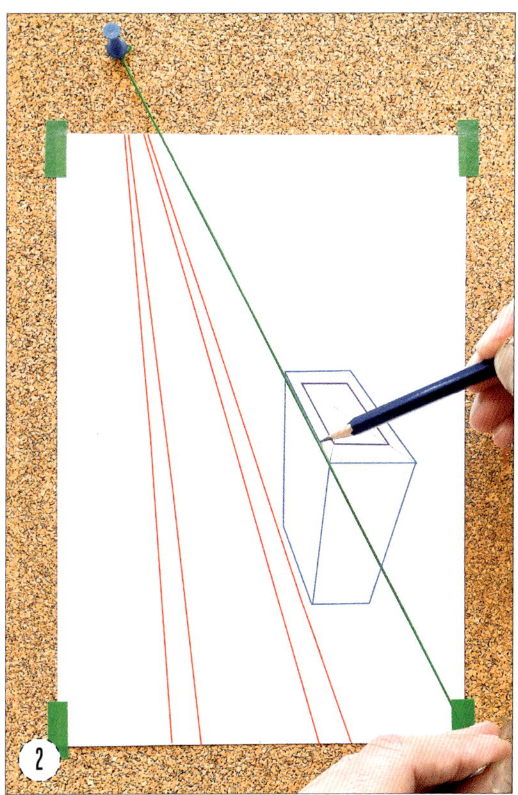

STEP 1: Use a vertical format/paper orientation. Place the first vanishing point close to the top left corner of the paper (blue thumbtack) and the second one (red thumbtack) very close to the center horizontally but a bit farther away from the paper than the first one. Attach the elastic string to each by tying a loop on either end. The distance to the paper is relative to the size of the paper so I will not give you measurements but try to use a similar proportional disposition.

STEP 2: Draw two pairs of lines (red) from the top vanishing point. They represent the street and the sidewalks on either side. Align the middle of the street with the middle point of the bottom edge of the paper. I like to start my urban landscapes with the focal point or main building. In this case, it will be located near the bottom right corner.

Draw a box (blue) with its bottom left edge aligned with the street. Remember that all verticals go to the lower vanishing point, the horizontals parallel to the street go to the upper vanishing point and the horizontals running across the street are drawn straight horizontally. Sketch an X on its top and use it as reference to draw a smaller proportional plane (purple). Do that by drawing lines that meet at the diagonals.

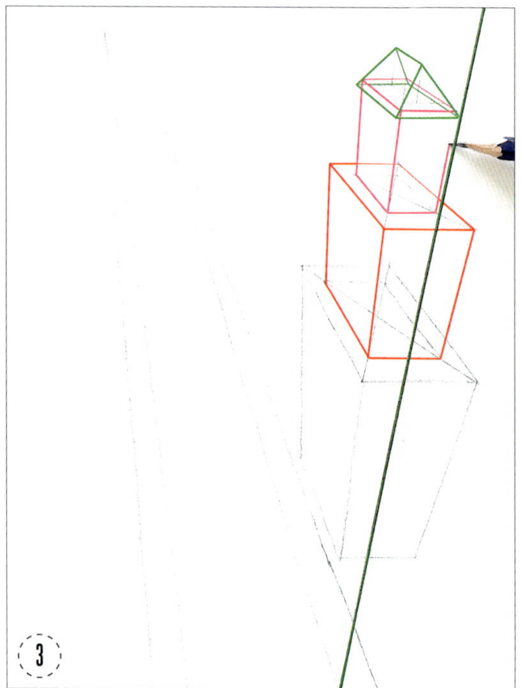

STEP 3: Using the smaller plane as a starting point, draw a box (red). Repeat the same process again for a third box (pink). Finally, draw a hip roof (green) on its top just as you learned in the Diagonals in Two-Point Perspective lesson (page 91).

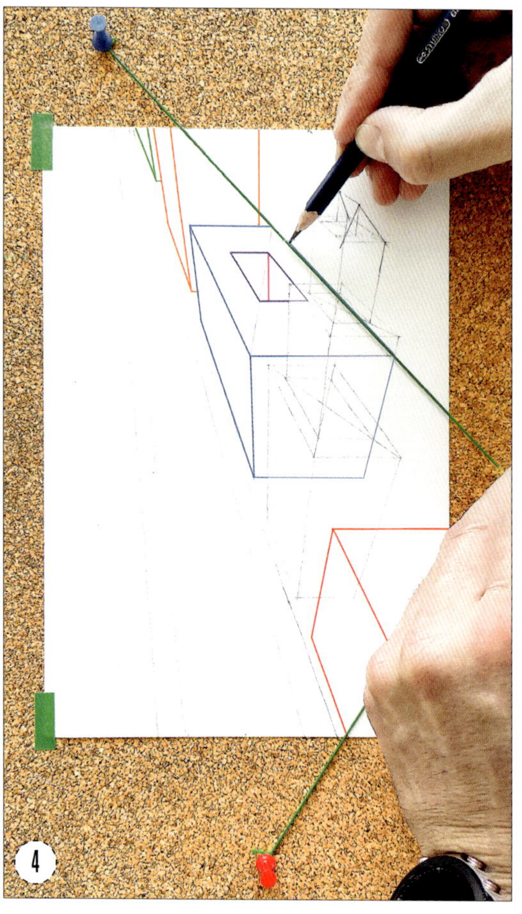

STEP 4: You will now fill the rest of the right side of the street with more buildings. Draw a box (red) to the right of the main building. This one is going to go off the paper, so only certain lines will be visible. At the left of the main building, draw another box (blue) that is a little bit shorter than the main building's first section, but longer and wider. This one is going to be a courtyard building, so sketch an X on its top and draw a plane (purple) on its top using the diagonals as reference. Then, draw a vertical (pink) from its upper right corner going down until it disappears behind the edge of the plane. Then, add two more boxes (orange and green) along the street and let their tops go off the paper.

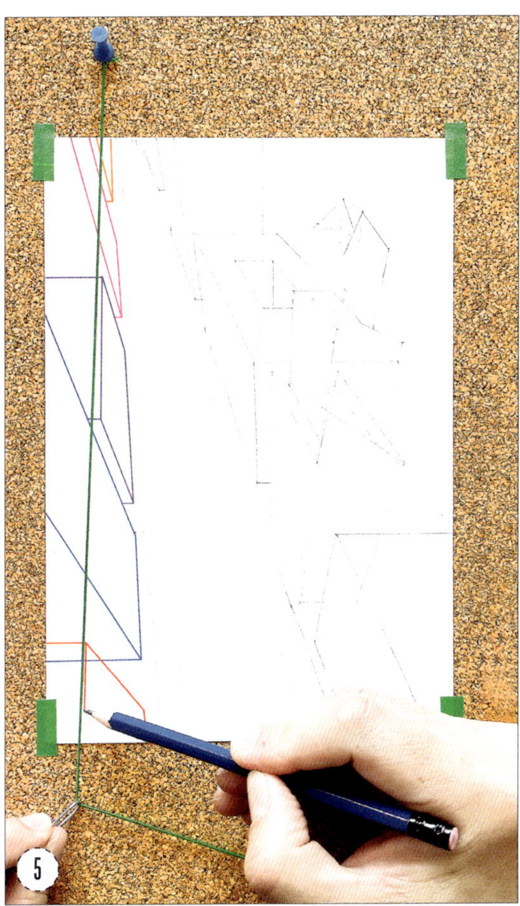

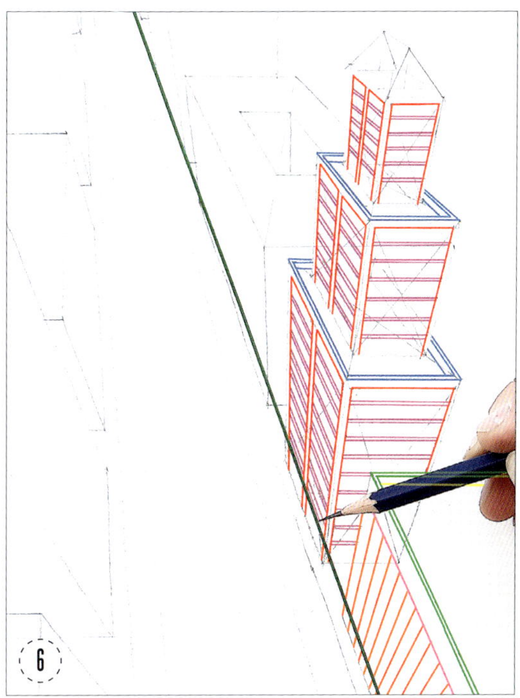

STEP 5: Now do the same thing on the left side of the street. Draw boxes of varying sizes (red, blue, purple, pink, orange) for the buildings on the other side of the street.

STEP 6: Next is the fun part: choosing the design of the buildings and drawing all the details. This is best to do in order, from the front to the back. Start from the first building on the right side going backward. On the roofs, I always add double lines all around (green) that represent the surrounding wall, and then another (yellow) below that would be its height whenever it is visible. The front of the building will have a horizontal near the top (pink) and then verticals from that line all the way to the ground (orange).

Do the same thing you did for the roof of the first building on the top of every section of the next one (blue lines). Its design is going to be simple as well. Using the diagonals and middle point of an X sketched on its front side, draw a frame all around and a division in the middle (red). Do something similar on the other side, but without the middle division (also red).

Now repeat the same process on the two upper sections (all lines in red). To wrap up this building, add double horizontal lines (purple) in both directions, inside those frames at equal distances so they look like window floor divisions.

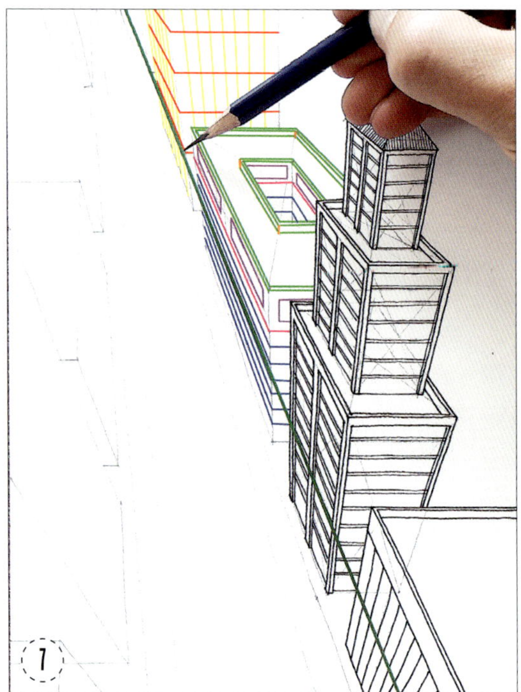

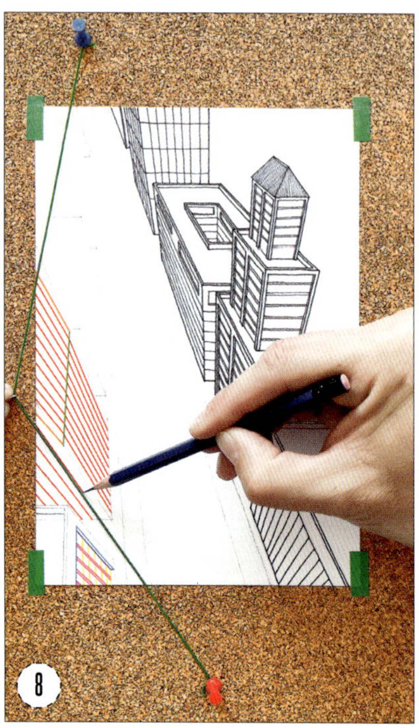

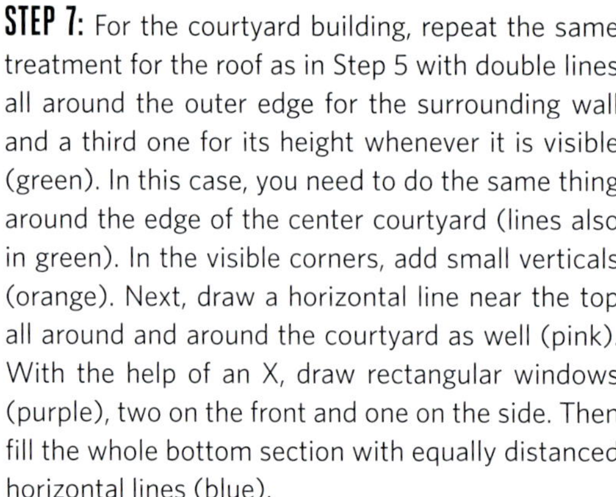

STEP 7: For the courtyard building, repeat the same treatment for the roof as in Step 5 with double lines all around the outer edge for the surrounding wall and a third one for its height whenever it is visible (green). In this case, you need to do the same thing around the edge of the center courtyard (lines also in green). In the visible corners, add small verticals (orange). Next, draw a horizontal line near the top all around and around the courtyard as well (pink). With the help of an X, draw rectangular windows (purple), two on the front and one on the side. Then fill the whole bottom section with equally distanced horizontal lines (blue).

The next building has a grid of horizontals and verticals forming vertical rectangles. Draw horizontals (red) and verticals (yellow) but leave more distance between the verticals than the horizontals. The verticals will look much closer together in the front of the building because of the observer's viewing angle.

STEP 8: You can see a little corner of the first building on the left, so start with the roof lines. Then draw a horizontal and a vertical (both in blue) around the edge of the front plane and give it a little bit of depth with a small horizontal and a parallel to that vertical (purple lines). Next, draw equally distanced pairs of verticals (pink) and horizontals (yellow) between them.

For the second building, I want to do something different and that is to create a slope on its front face after a certain height. Draw a horizontal (green) on the front, and from both front corners, draw two parallel lines (orange) with a soft slope. Then add verticals (red) all around, and when they get to the top section, make them parallel to the sloped corner lines (orange).

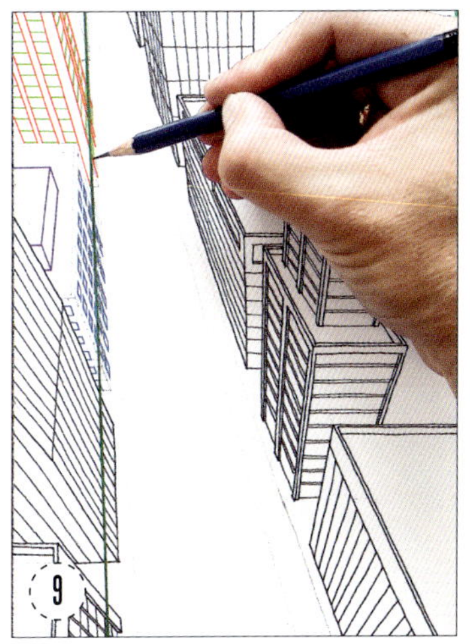

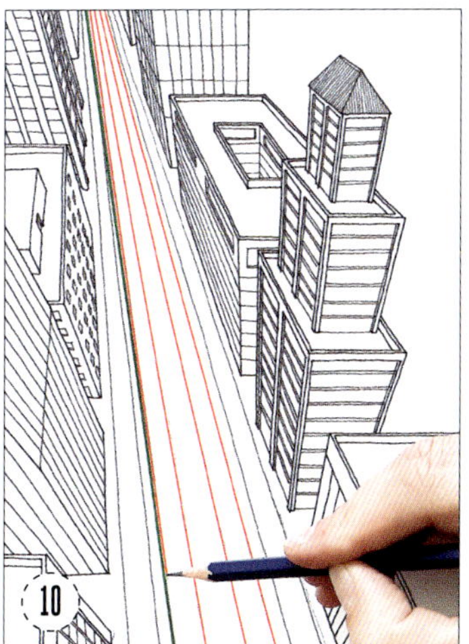

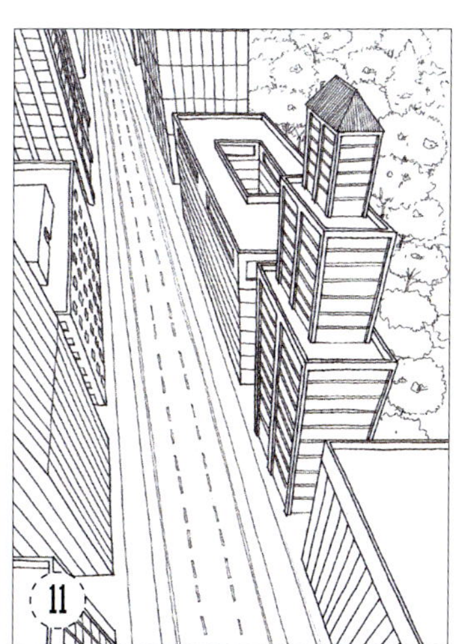

STEP 9: For the next small building, draw a box (purple) on the roof set in from the front lines to represent mechanical equipment, such as elevator shafts, air-conditioning units, ventilation systems, and so on. Next, draw a grid of verticals and horizontals and use it to draw doors (blue) on the first floor and squared windows (also blue) on the rest. For the last building on the left side, draw pairs of vertical lines (red), and then horizontals (green) between them.

STEP 10: Street lines are a must in an urban sketch where the street plays such an important role. Divide the street in equal parts using horizontals (red) going to the top vanishing point. Later when you ink it, you can divide them with small horizontals in the other direction, so they look like the usual broken street lines.

STEP 11: Check out how cool this street looks, and you did it using only two vanishing points. I decided to fill the top right corner of my example with trees to soften it up a little. So, I drew oval and random shapes with super squiggly lines and drew some trunks here and there.

I find the angles achieved with vertical two-point perspective very appealing to the eye and a cool alternative particularly for drawings where you want to place the observer in an elevated position to create this sort of semi-bird's-eye view.

3

MASTERING THREE-POINT PERSPECTIVE

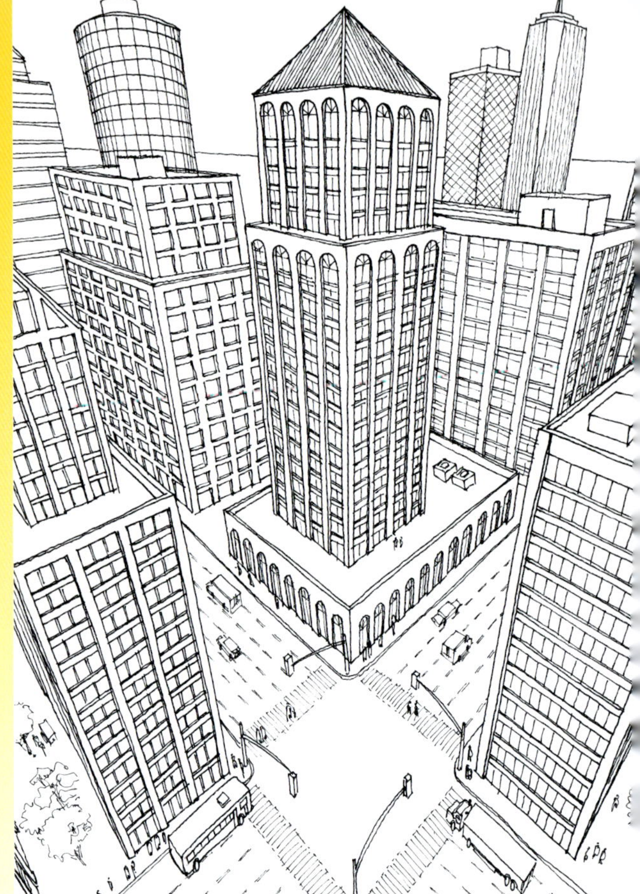

Three-point perspective completes the basic cycle of perspective learning. If you master one-, two- and three-point perspective, you will be able to draw anything you want, exactly the way you want it. In this chapter, I will show you its fundamentals and teach you the way it works.

The reason I like three-point perspective so much is that it portrays the world in the way most similar to human experience. It allows you to create depth not only from the front to the back of the drawing, but also from top to bottom (or bottom to top) making the third dimension more tangible than with either of the other two techniques. Although this description makes it sound like it is very complicated, it is not. It just adds another layer of depth that you will be able to easily understand using what you have learned so far.

First, I will teach you the basic concepts and how to draw the simplest figures and shapes in the Kitchen Corner project (page 118). Then, I will show you how to create different views by changing the position of the third vanishing point and you'll practice with the One Building, Two Ways project (page 128). Of course, I will let you know how to use elastics to sketch three-point perspective and use them to build an L-shaped staircase (page 140).

Finally, you are going to draw a bird's-eye view of a city (page 150), which is in my opinion the quintessence of architectural perspective drawing. This will be the summary of everything you learned in this book and a perfect opportunity to make sure you have all your concepts clear.

LESSON: THREE-POINT PERSPECTIVE FOR BEGINNERS

Once you have studied and understood two-point perspective, jumping to three points is fairly easy. The horizon line continues to represent the height of the observer's eyes. Two of the three vanishing points, which I will call the horizontal vanishing points, are placed on the horizon line and work the same as in two-point perspective. The third vanishing point will be located either at the top or the bottom of the setup depending on the kind of view you want to create. You will see that in more detail later.

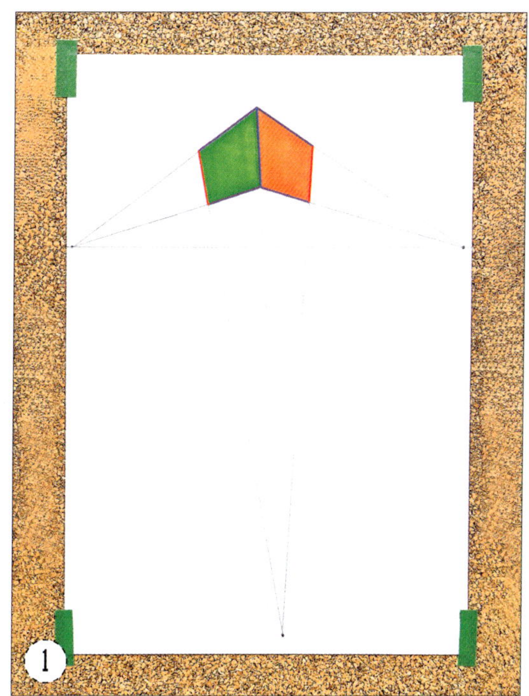

So, what does this third point do? It is responsible for every vertical line in the drawing but it means there are no straight vertical lines. In three-point perspective, every line goes to one of the vanishing points. The same rule is true though: Every time lines from different vanishing points cross each other or meet, they form a 90-degree angle.

To show you how this works, I will draw some basic shapes that will allow you to understand the concept easily. The cube is always my favorite to start with, because it is the easiest and the shape you will use the most.

First, I set up my paper in a vertical position. The horizon line is placed roughly one third of the way down, and the vanishing points are as close to the paper's edges as possible (Picture 1). I will put the third vanishing point at the bottom of the paper and a bit to the right of center. Now, I use the bottom vanishing point to draw a vertical line (blue) above the horizon. From its ends, I draw lines (purple) to both horizontal vanishing points. Now I add two more verticals (red) on either side to create two squared planes (shaded in green and orange).

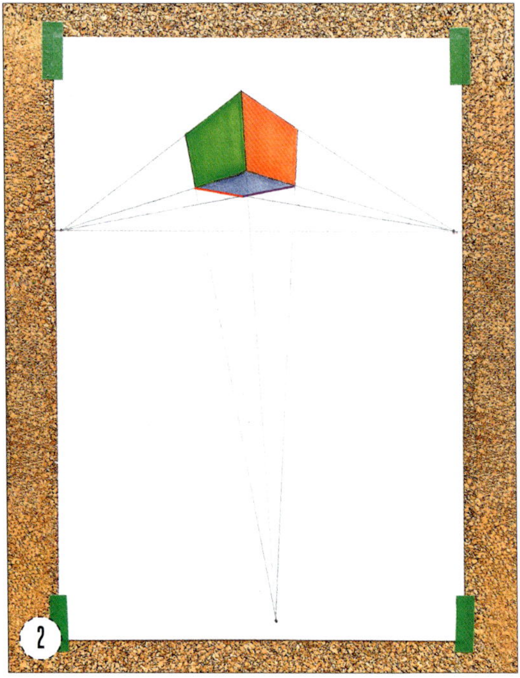

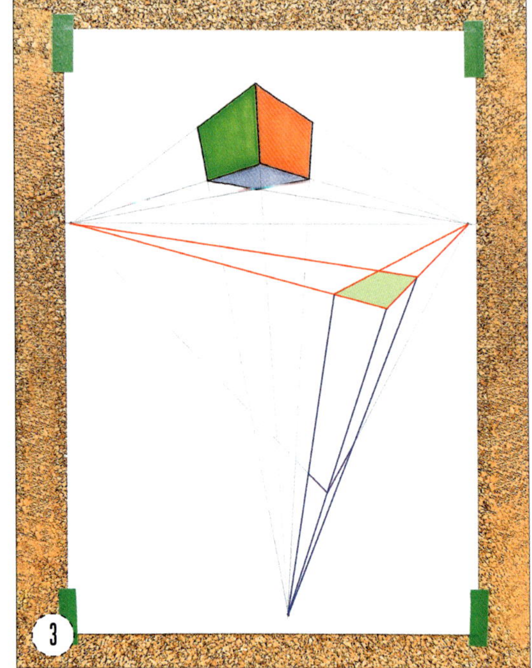

Because this shape is above the horizon line, you should be able to see its bottom plane. I find it by drawing a line (red in Picture 2) from the bottom left corner of the left side plane going to the right vanishing point. Another one (purple) does exactly the opposite on the other side. Those two lines cross each other creating a third visible squared plane (shaded in blue) that makes up the bottom of the box.

As you can see this works exactly like two-point perspective with the exception that now the verticals are not drawn straight, but go to the third vanishing point.

Now I will draw a slim rectangular shape that looks like a tall building. This one will go below the horizon line. I will start with the top plane by drawing a couples of lines (red in Picture 3) from either vanishing point and making them meet near the right edge of the paper. I am drawing them rather close together because I want it to be a very slender shape.

Next, I will draw three vertical lines (blue) going from the visible vertices of that plane (shaded in green) toward the bottom vanishing point. You can already see how it looks like a building as if you were looking at it from a high point like a helicopter or a higher building. I love how it looks smaller as it approaches the ground. That is achieved using the third vanishing point.

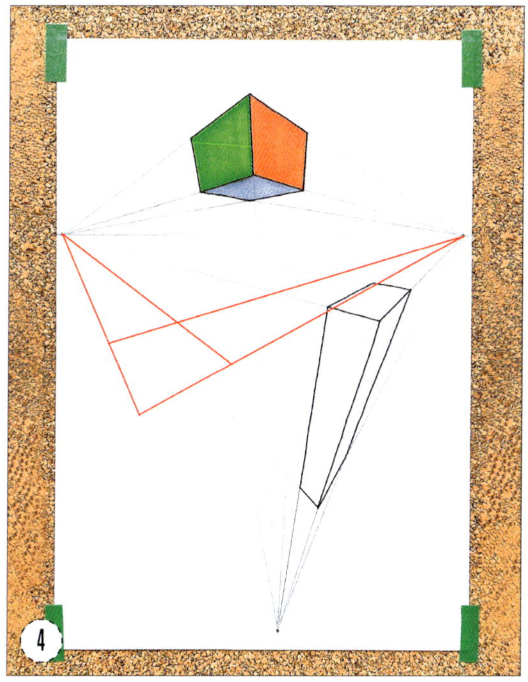

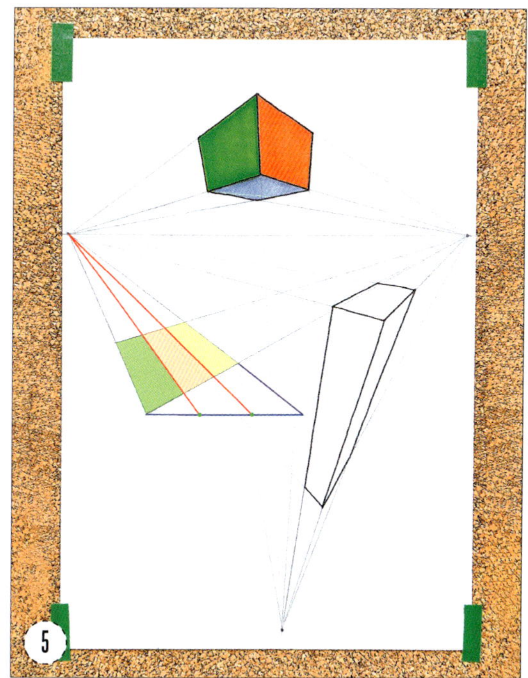

To finish it up, draw two lines (purple) starting at the same point on the front edge of the shape going to each vanishing point. Those two lines would be the place where the building meets the sidewalk.

Now I will show you how to draw a building with a more complex shape. This one will be shorter than the first one and will have an H-shaped floor plan. I start by drawing the roof with a couples of lines (red in Picture 4) from either vanishing point and have them cross and meet to the left of the first building. The roof plane should have a squared shape to start; later I will divide it into nine equal parts.

I drew a straight horizontal line (blue in Picture 5) that starts at the closest corner of that plane and extends to meet the line (purple) that is a projection of the top right edge of the plane. I divided that blue line into three equal parts using two dots (green). From those dots I can draw lines (red) to the left horizontal vanishing point. This process guarantees that the three stripes (green, orange and yellow) in the plane have exactly the same size. This works the same in two-point perspective.

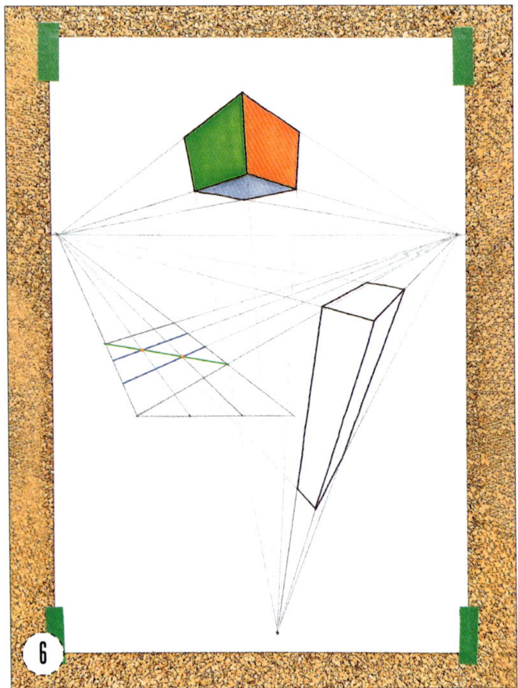

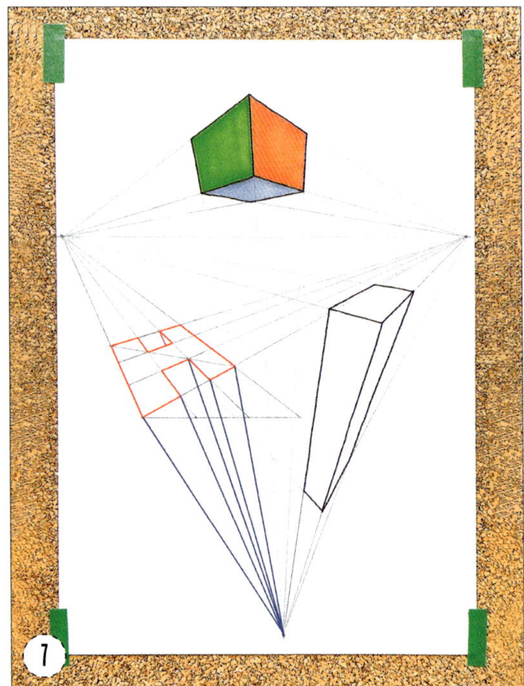

Now that I have those stripes defined, I can use the diagonal trick (see the Pro Tip on page 88) to determine the divisions that go in the other direction. To do so, I must draw one of the two diagonals of the plane. I will draw the one marked in green in Picture 6. The points (orange) where that green line meets the stripe divisions mark the correct distance of the stripes in the other direction. So, I can safely add a couple of lines (blue) to the right horizontal vanishing point passing through those points. This perfect grid will be used to draw the H shape.

As you can see in Picture 7, I drew the H with lines (red) that use the grid as reference. Now you have a beautiful H letter in perspective. Until now, I have not drawn a single vertical line in this building. But now I can start adding height so that it does not look flat but has volume. To do that, I draw lines (blue) from the bottom vanishing point to all visible corners of the H plane. I just love the way volume is magically created with those vertical lines! When doing this, make sure to look at every single corner of the top plane until you are certain that you created the visible bits of vertical lines. For example, in this case, there is a tiny vertical in the back that I marked pink so you could see it clearly.

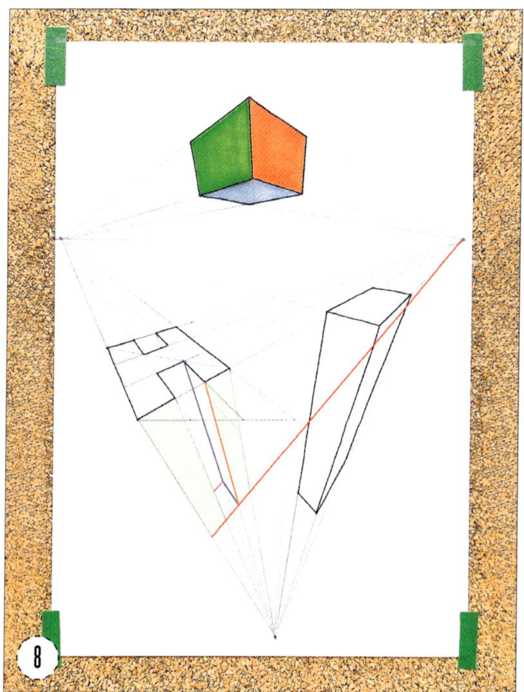

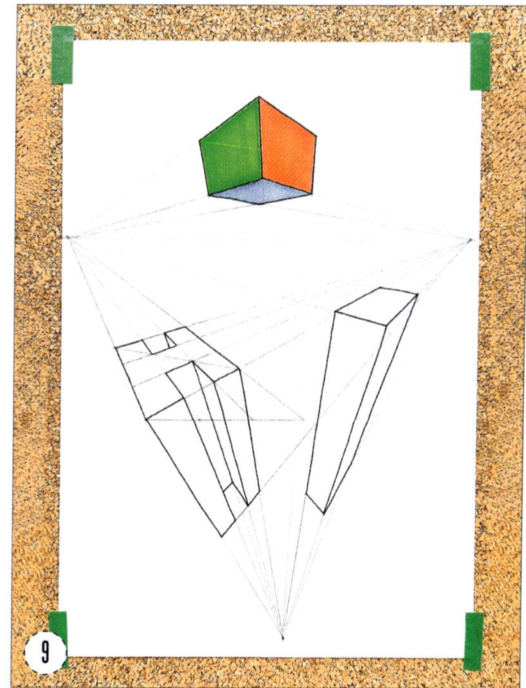

The final step is to decide how tall the building should be. Earlier I said I wanted it to be shorter than the first one so I added a line (red in Picture 8) to define its height. This line serves the purpose for the two parts of the H that stick out (shaded in green). But, what about the center part that is set back? For that I need to add a couple of lines that follow the same shape of the roof on the ground. I will start with a line (blue) going to the left horizontal vanishing point from the point where the red meets the edge (orange) that changes direction. When it changes direction again (in the edge marked purple) I draw a line (pink) going to the right vanishing point.

Picture 9 shows the result of this sketch. Three-point perspective has a beautiful appeal to it that enhances the realism of the drawing and makes it perfect for a lot of practical uses in architecture and design. For example, this is a great way of showing a client your first ideas for an architectural project or a new product or design. It allows someone that has a hard time imagining objects in three dimensions to see a first approach of how something might look. But, as cool as this looks, right now these buildings are only flying objects floating around in space. In the next project, you will learn how to ground them and position them exactly so they make more sense.

PRO TIP: You can use thumbtacks to draw with rulers also. The next Kitchen Corner project (page 118) was drawn like that. I place the edge of the ruler against the tip of the thumbtacks and use it as an axle to spin the ruler around. That way, I can keep it aligned with the vanishing point without effort and create perfectly straight lines.

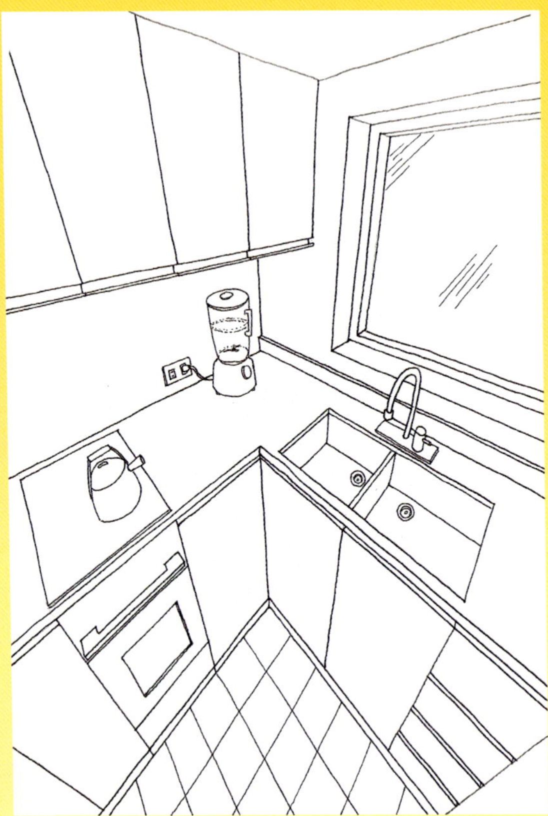

PROJECT: KITCHEN CORNER

You have heard about my corner fascination before. You practiced drawing a kitchen in a corner in the Placing Objects in Space project (page 76), but now you will be placing the observer closer to the scene, creating a more immersive experience. You will also be able to see how the third point adds a new dimension that enhances the feel of being part of the drawing. Always try to find ways to connect with your audience as intimately as possible, because in the end, in my humble opinion, that is the ultimate purpose of art. This will be your first real approach to three-point perspective applied to a tangible space with elements coming together in a cohesive drawing.

Additional Materials

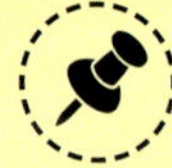

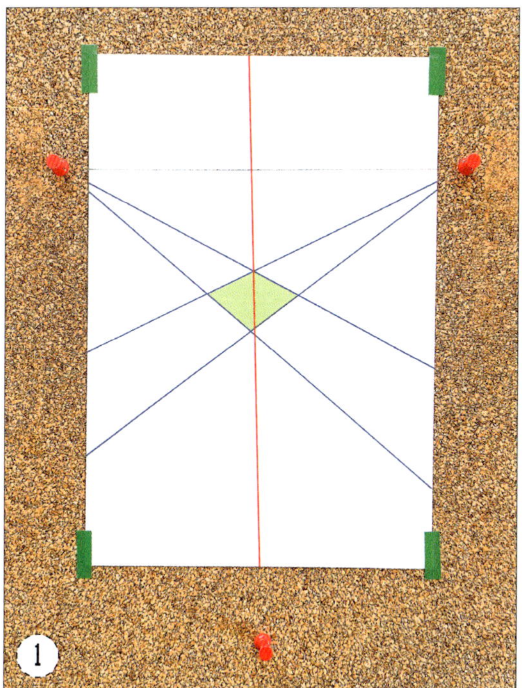

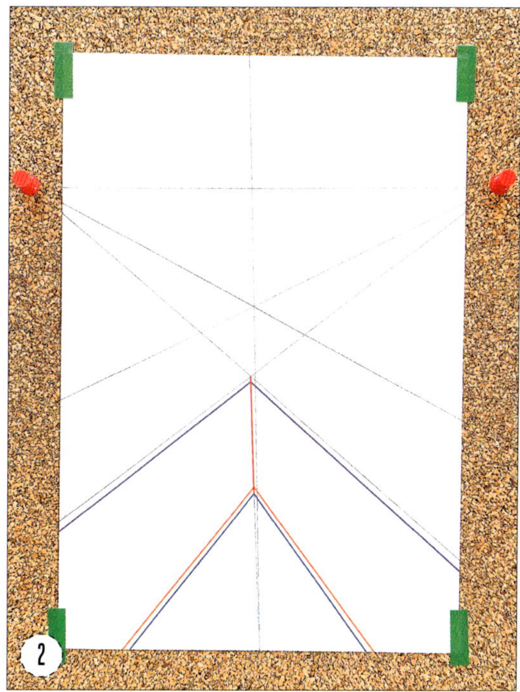

STEP 1: Set up your paper in a vertical format with the horizon line high on the paper. Place the horizontal vanishing points off the paper on either side and the third vanishing point centered horizontally. You will be placing the vanishing point at the bottom of the paper until you learn how to move it around and I recommend placing it as far off the paper as you can. The farther away you place it, the more relaxed the angles are going to look.

Start by drawing a line (red) from the bottom vanishing point all the way to the top of the paper. Note that it is not perfectly vertical, but slightly slanted toward the left. Now, draw a couple of lines (blue) from either horizontal vanishing point. The upper two should cross each other exactly over the red one. Try to make a squared plane (shaded in green) where they meet, and do not worry if the other corner does not match with the red line as well. This plane will be the countertop of the kitchen.

STEP 2: Next, add volume to the bottom cabinet. Draw a line (red) from the front vertex of the countertop to the bottom vanishing point, and from its end, lines (both in blue) going to either horizontal vanishing point until they go off the paper. Those two blue lines are the place where the cabinet meets the floor. When drawing these lines, keep in mind that the proportion between the depth of the countertop and the height of the cabinet is two thirds, which means that if the depth is 2 feet (61 cm), the height should be approximately 3 feet (91 cm). Create the countertop width with a line (purple) parallel to the front edge, and a receded base to the cabinet with a line (orange) parallel to its lower edge.

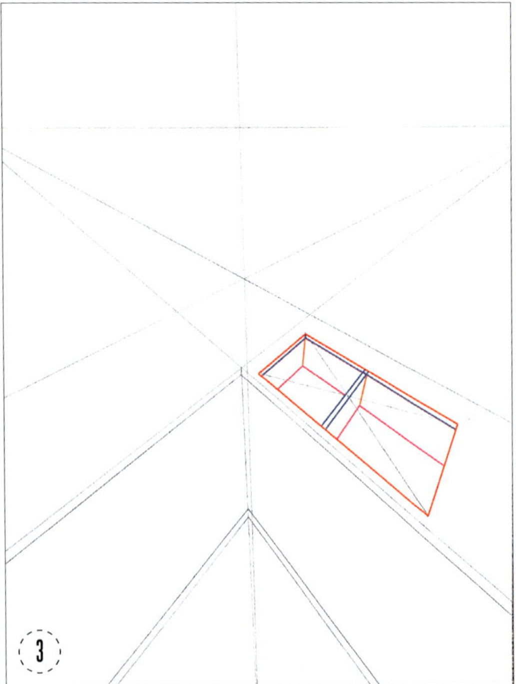

STEP 3: Time to give this kitchen a sink and faucet. Draw a rectangular plane (red) on the right side near the corner. This will be an undermount double basin sink. To create it, draw an X to find the center and draw the division lines (blue) to either side of the middle point going to the right horizontal vanishing point.

Next, trace the width of the countertop (purple lines) below and around the top edge of the sink wherever it is visible. It is made up of a small vertical from the top left corner and vanishing lines to both vanishing points from its end. The depth of the basins is created in a very similar way: verticals (orange) from both top left edges and from their ends, vanishing lines (pink) to either vanishing point.

STEP 4: Drawing the faucet starts with a horizontal rectangular plane (blue) just behind the center division of the sink. Then, draw a very thin vertical rectangular box (yellow) centered on that plane and a circle (green, which will look like an ellipse) at its top. Use them as reference to draw a curved cylinder (red). Finally, draw a small cylinder (purple) at its right side to be the control and another small cylinder (pink) attached to it with the direction of the left vanishing point.

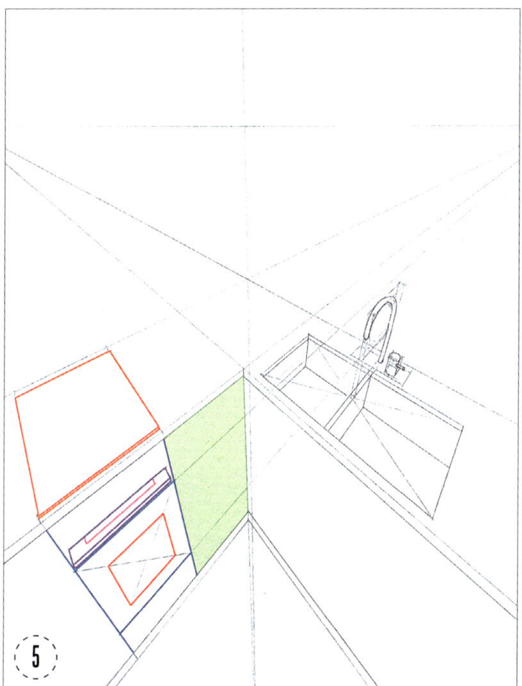

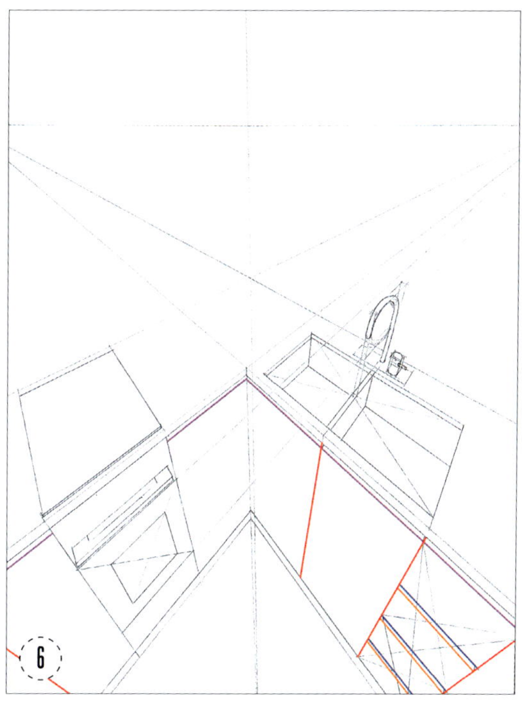

STEP 5: To add an oven and a stove, draw two verticals and two horizontals going to the right vanishing point (all blue) on the front face of the left side of the cabinet. Leave a space (shaded in green) against the corner for one cabinet door. Now, draw a horizontal rectangular box (purple) attached to the front face of the oven on its top section and a smaller horizontal plane (pink) on its top to be the oven handle. Next, draw a rectangular plane (red) on the section below the handle to mimic the see-through window. Note that I have used an X to center it on the other plane. Draw an ultra-thin rectangular box (orange) above the oven on the countertop to represent the convection burner stove.

STEP 6: To design the cabinets, draw vertical lines (red) to create the main divisions. Note that the division between the first two cabinets on the right side is aligned with the center division of the sink and the next one with its end. I want this to be a very clean design, so I am not going to put handles on the doors, just a small separation (purple) on the top against the countertop to open them. The third section will be for drawers. Divide the height into four equal parts using Xs (blue lines) and draw the double line (orange) at the top of each drawer.

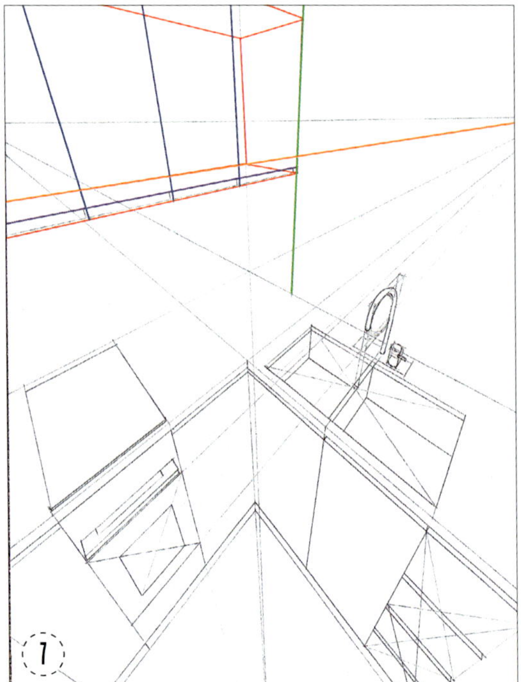

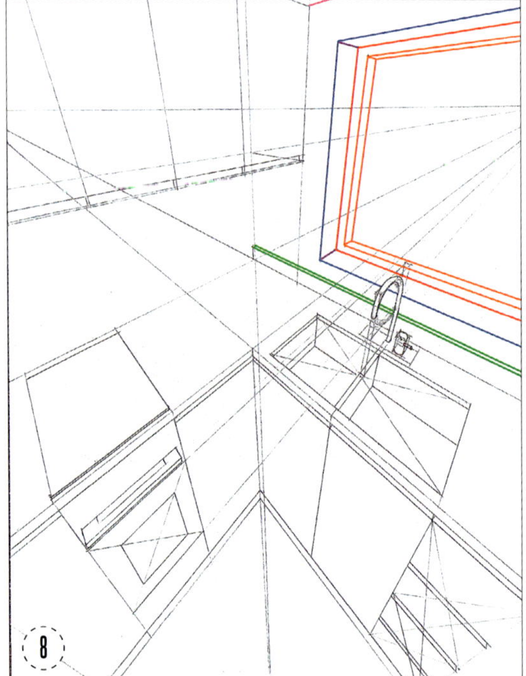

STEP 7: As I usually do, I am drawing from the front to the back so now it is time to work on the back wall. On the left side I will have a high cabinet and a window on the right.

The normal height between a countertop and the bottom of the high cabinet is $2\frac{1}{3}$ feet (70 cm) and its depth approximately $1\frac{1}{3}$ feet (40 cm), so draw a couple of lines (green and orange) to determine those measurements in proportion to the things you have already drawn. For example, the green is two thirds of the depth of the bottom countertop and the orange is a bit more than the depth of the countertop, but vertically. Using those two lines as reference draw a box (red) that is 27 to 31 inches (69 to 79 cm) tall. Then, draw verticals (blue) at equal distances to mimic door divisions. As openers for those doors, draw the same double lines you used for the drawers in Step 6 on the lower part of the cabinet.

STEP 8: Imagine that the high cabinet goes all the way to the ceiling and draw a line (pink) that starts at its top right corner and goes in the direction of the left horizontal vanishing point. That will be the edge between the right wall and the ceiling. Also draw a low backsplash on that right wall just behind the sink. This is done with a couple of very close lines (green) going to the left vanishing point at the height you choose.

The window will go in the space between the backsplash and the top edge of the wall. Draw a vertical plane (blue), and let it run off the paper on the right side. That is the window opening. To add depth, draw short lines (purple) going to the right vanishing point and then join their ends with a vertical and horizontals going to the left vanishing point (all in red). Next, draw the frame with another plane (orange), and the depth of the frame (also in orange) in the same way.

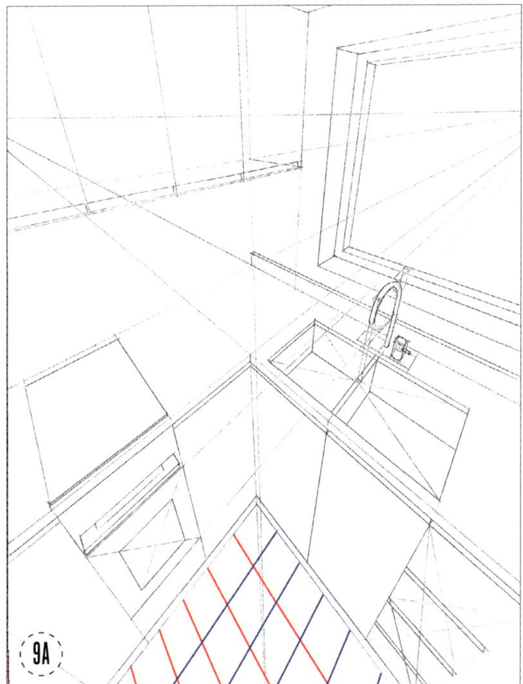

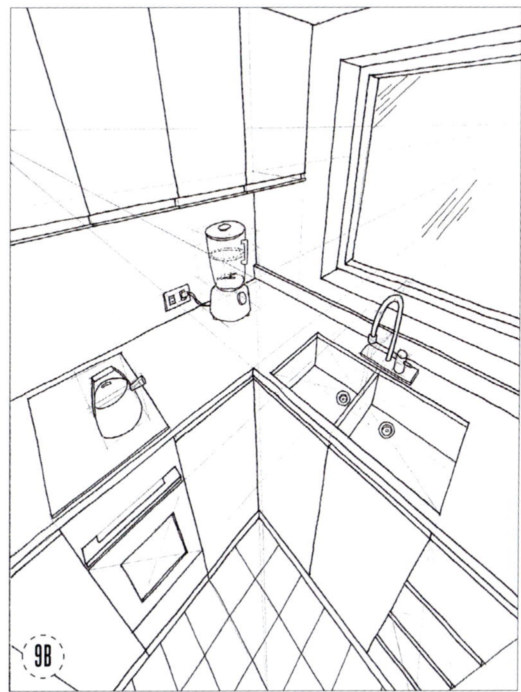

STEP 9: Draw tiles on the floor with a grid (blue and red) of equally distanced lines going to both vanishing points. Here I want you to notice that the tiles look like rhombuses more than squares and that is due to the closeness of the horizontal vanishing points. You need to place them this close so you can clearly see how the technique works, but feel free to make them farther apart to achieve a more relaxed look and avoid perspective distortion.

The inked version shows the final result. I added some details to give it more interest, such as objects on the countertop, outlets and circles for the sink drains. Never skimp on details for your drawings! One thing that amazes me as a creator is the amount of attention that people pay to the small objects and surprises that I put in mine.

I hope you enjoyed this project. Next, you will learn how to play with the third vanishing point.

LESSON: PLACING THE THIRD VANISHING POINT

When you were studying one- and two-point perspective, you saw that the placement of the horizon line and the vanishing points determines the kind of view you create. In three-point perspective, you have an additional variable to play with and I would define the purpose of the third point as the one that determines the angles for all vertical lines. The closer you place the point, the steeper vertical angles are going to look, and they will seem more relaxed the farther away you place that point.

So, generally speaking, I recommend trying to place the point far from the horizon line so you get more natural-looking perspectives. But you can also move it horizontally, and that also changes the angles of the lines. In this lesson, I want to demonstrate how different positions affect the outcome and how to choose the best one for the look that you want to achieve.

I will start with the most typical setup, which is a centered horizon line and a third point centered at the bottom. I will be drawing a container box and inserting a person in it, so you can see how that looks. Picture 1 shows the box (red) and you can see clearly how the third point makes it seem bigger at the top than at its bottom. If I had set it closer, the size difference would have been even larger and the perspective would look more forced.

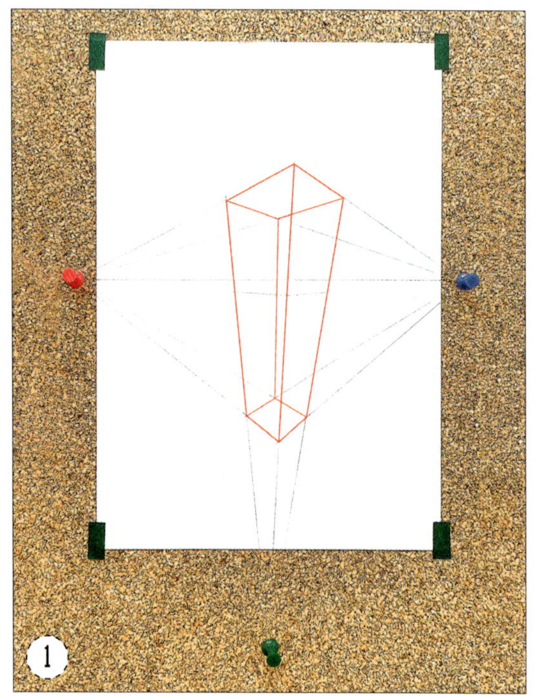

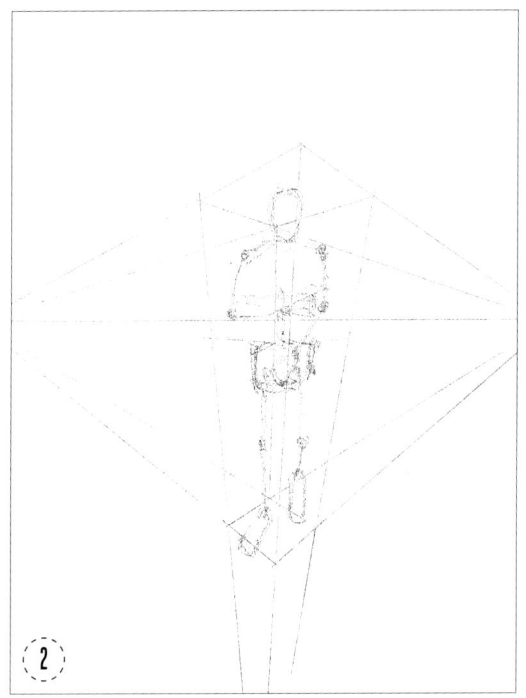

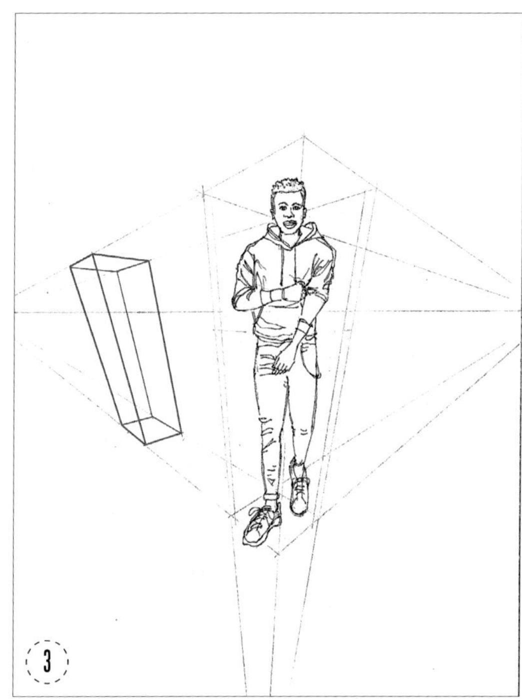

To begin, I usually draw the basic outline of the person's body shape (Picture 2) before adding any details. The head is approximately one eighth of the total height and the waist is normally near the middle of the body. Be careful to follow the shape of the box when drawing the outline.

With the outline ready, depicting the correct proportions of the body, draw all the details (Picture 3). I drew another box (blue) to the left of the first one so you can see what happens when the vanishing point is too close. If you draw something just above it, you will not have any trouble and it will look just fine, but when you start going to the sides, you will begin having problems with something called "perspective distortion." If I were to draw a person inside that box, they would look as if they were falling. The farther away you place the third vanishing point, the less problems with perspective distortion you will have.

Now I will move the horizon line to the top of the paper. By now you know that moving the horizon line higher means moving the observer to a high position and making them look down on the subject. This is when three-point perspective becomes really interesting, because it allows you to create very cool top-to-bottom and bottom-to-top views. To see how that looks, Picture 4 shows a container box (red) built with this new setup. Now you can see the top of the box, which means that you are seeing it from above. I also want you to notice that the third point is very close to the paper, because I want to exaggerate the angles and create a strong up-to-down look.

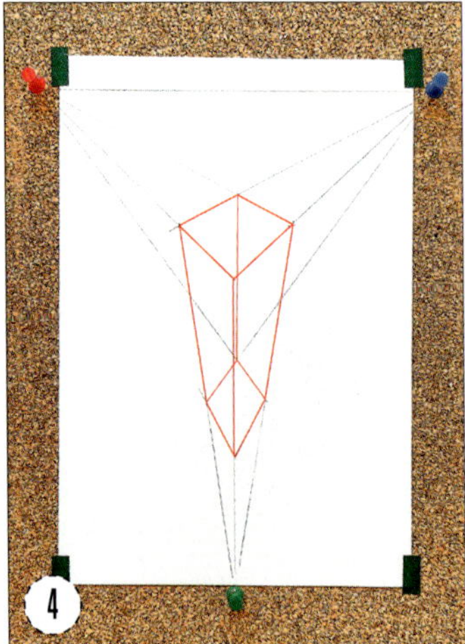

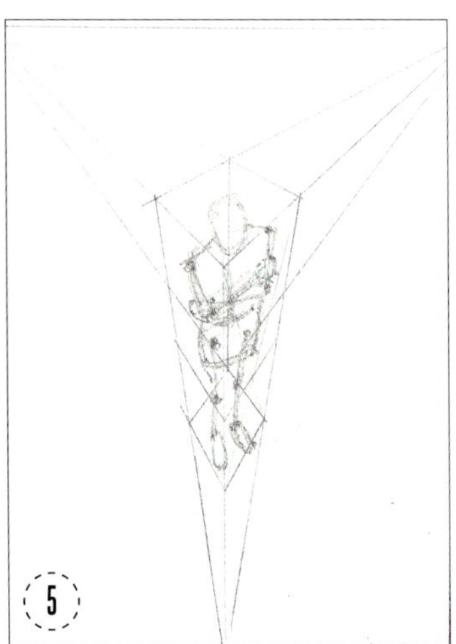

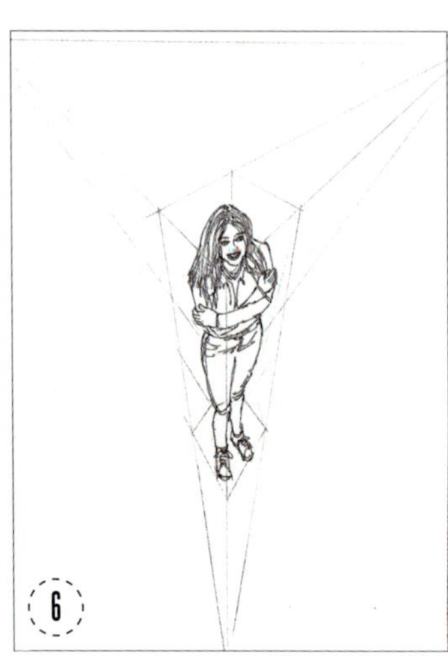

Next, I will draw the body outline again (Picture 5) fitting it well inside the boundaries of the box. This type of view is used extensively in cartoons, story-boards and manga, as well as in commercials.

With all the details added (Picture 6), the drawing acquires a new sense of depth and authenticity that is extremely appealing and that, as I mentioned in the introduction of this chapter, is very close to the kind of view that you would experience on a day-to-day basis. This looks just like footage from a CCTV camera. But there is also an ant's-eye view that you can achieve by inverting all the parameters of this sketch. That means a low horizon line and a high third vanishing point.

In the example I am about to show you (Picture 7), I will place the bottom of the box (red) aligned with the horizon line. That is because I do not want to see the soles of the shoes, but instead I would prefer to see them straight on. I also want a third point that is not too far or too close because I want it to look edgy, but not too forced. These are the kinds of considerations you need to think about before deciding on the position of the vanishing points and horizon line. If all these things are clear in your mind, the outcome will look exactly as you pictured it.

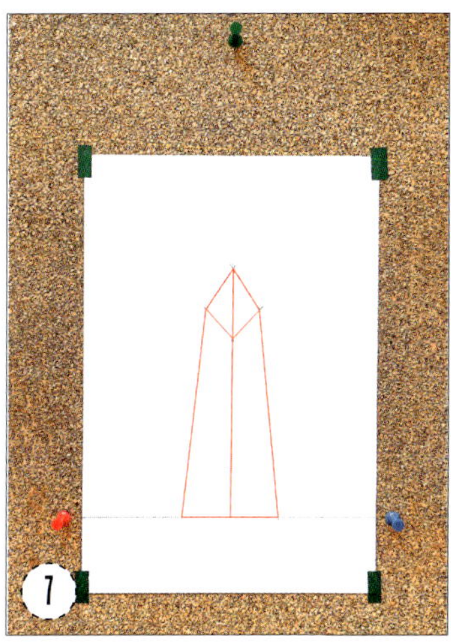
7

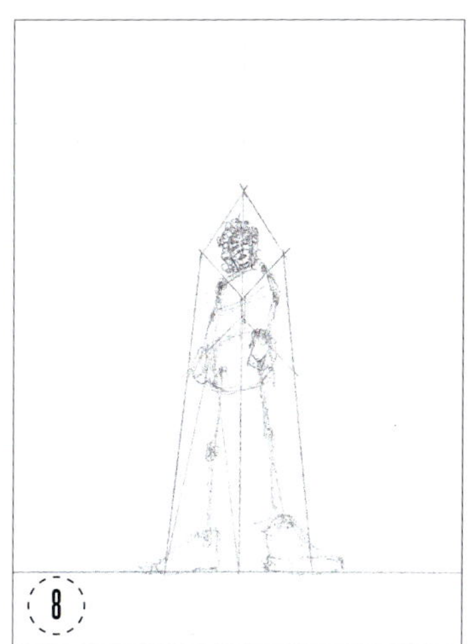
8

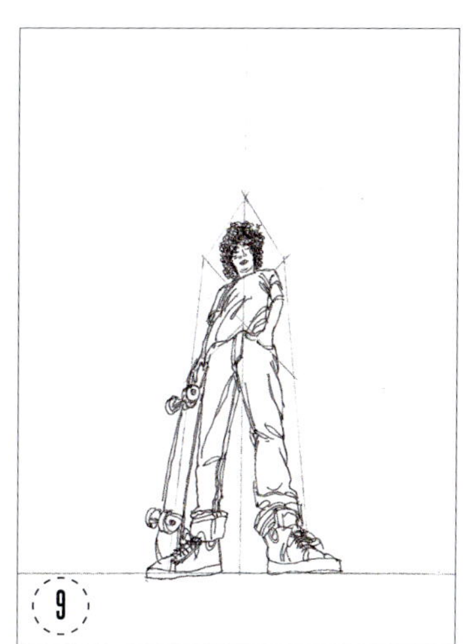
9

Picture 8 has the outline already in it. The basic shapes like the chest and hip plates should be drawn using the third vanishing point as reference so they get proportionately bigger or smaller with the box itself. Sometimes these proportions may seem a little bit off when you are first sketching them, but do not worry, just trust the process and keep going. Everything will fall in place when the drawing is done.

I would always recommend keeping your focal point very close to the horizontal position of the third vanishing point. It does not matter if the background has some skewed angles as long as the main character looks perfect. As a matter of fact, those skewed angles will help you create an even more intense focus.

This drawing (Picture 9) has the kind of view you would find in any Batman or Dragon Ball Z comic and it looks just amazing. This perspective creates a deep connection between the viewer and the character and makes you feel almost as if you were a part of the story. The same happens if you sketch architecture using this technique. It draws you inside the landscape.

In the next project, you will see how to draw the same building from a bird's- and ant's-eye view and you will be able to experiment firsthand the different feelings that each generates and how you can use them to pursue a particular reaction from your viewers.

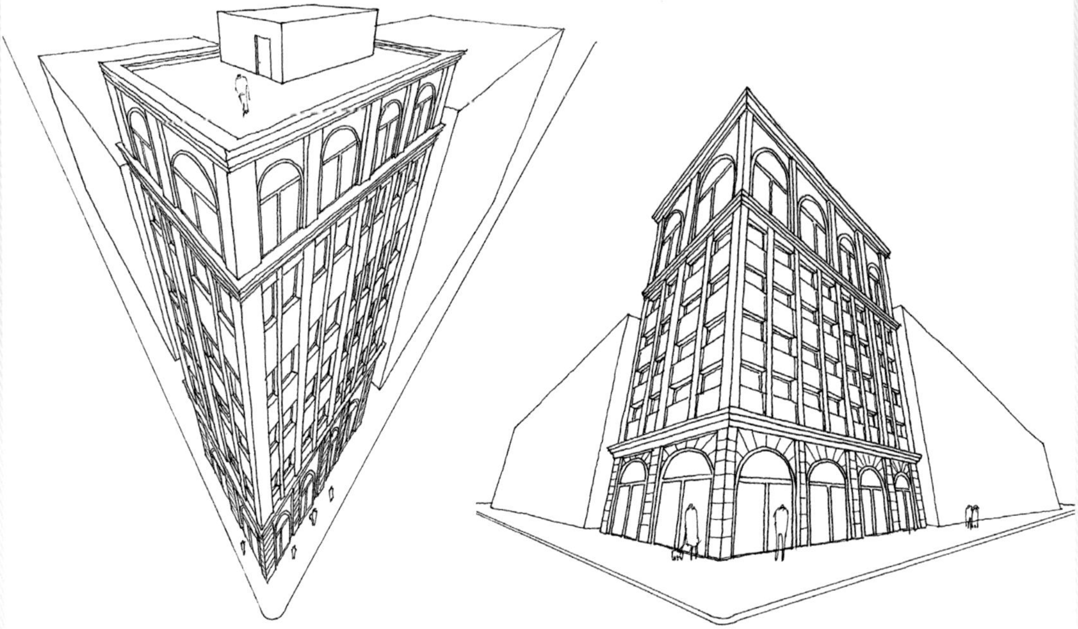

PROJECT: ONE BUILDING, TWO WAYS

This project is all about perception. How can you achieve a whole different feel and vibe when sketching the same or similar objects? Perspective! It is time to put its laws at our service and make the most of them. Building on what you have learned about three-point perspective, you will design a building and draw it from totally opposite points of view. This will also allow me to show you how certain architectural details like windows, doors, cornices and roofs need to be drawn slightly differently from different angles, which is a skill you will be using constantly.

Additional Materials

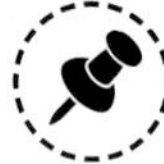

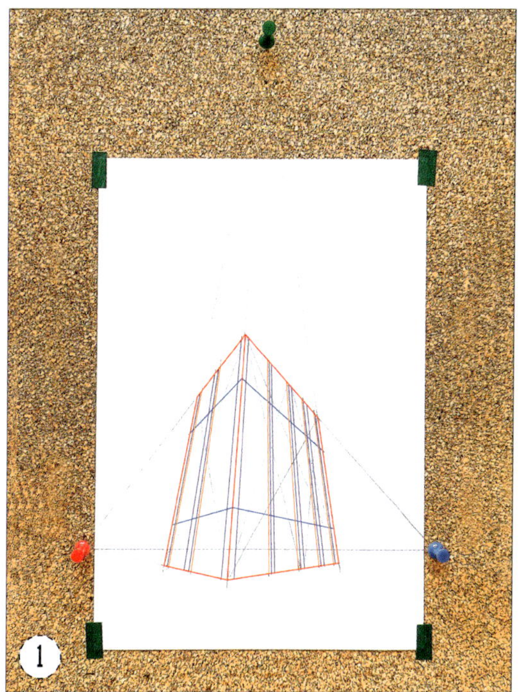

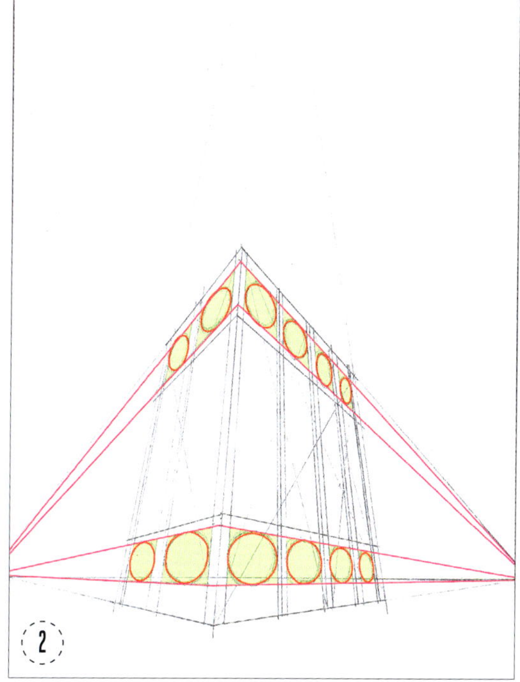

STEP 1: Place your horizon line super low on the paper, and the third vanishing point centered at the top. Draw a rectangular box (red). Try to proportion it so that the right side is double the left side. It does not have to be perfect, just eyeball it as close as you can. Then divide it into three sections with horizontal lines (blue). Now, using Xs, divide the right side into four equal vertical parts and the left one in two. Add double lines (purple) on either side of the divisions and at the edges. Add depth to those columns with an additional line (orange) wherever it is visible.

STEP 2: Next, draw two pair of lines (pink) near the top of the bottom and top sections of the building from both horizontal vanishing points, creating squared planes (marked in green) between the vertical divisions. Draw an ellipse (red) inside each one of them.

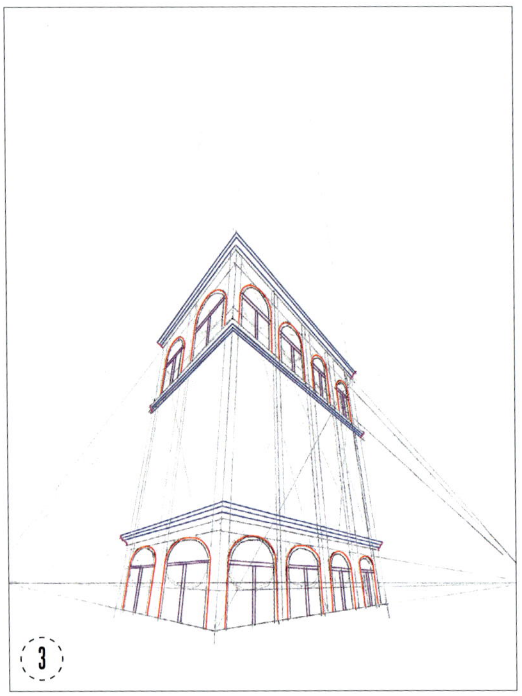

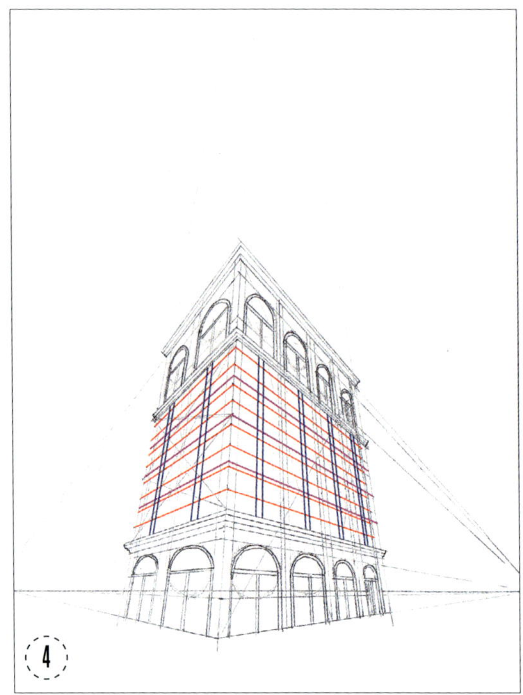

STEP 3: Use those ellipses and the reference lines that you have made so far to draw arched doors (red) on the first floor and matching arched windows (also in red) on the top floor. These doors and windows have vertical divisions in the middle and a horizontal division at the base of the arcs (all marked with purple double lines). Next, draw three additional horizontal lines (blue) at each one of the main divisions and at the top, extending their ends outside the edge of the building a bit and joining them with a bracket-like shape (pink) to create architectural details.

STEP 4: Use Xs and horizontal lines (pink) to divide the middle section in equal parts to use as floor divisions. Do as many as you need according to its height. Scale the height of each floor according to the doors you already drew. Now, divide each one of the vertical sections in two with double lines (blue). Then, add two horizontal lines (red) per floor: one passing through the middle and the other just below the ceiling line.

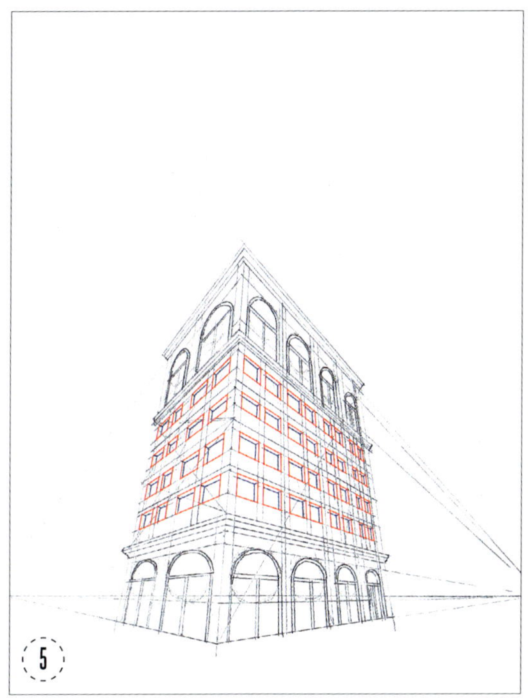

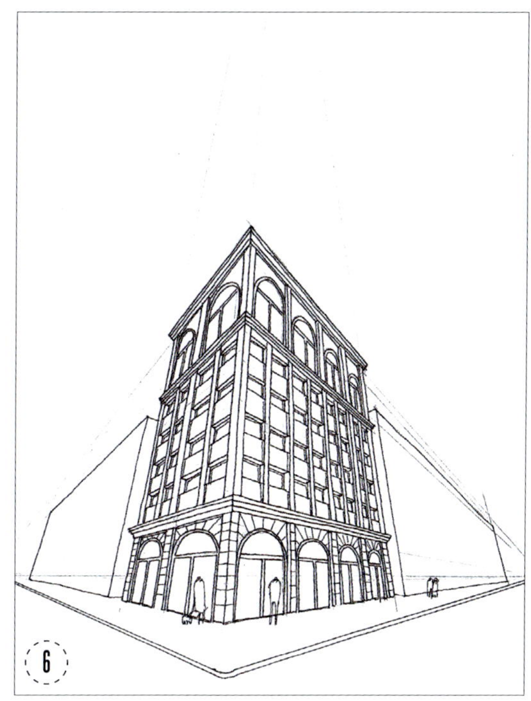

STEP 5: With the help of all those reference lines, draw pairs of rectangular/squared windows—depending on the proportions—(red) covering the middle section. Add depth to those window openings (blue) to give the building more texture and volume and double lines for the frames where they are visible. Note that from this position as the observer is lower than all the window openings, you would be able to see their depth in both the upper and farthest edges.

STEP 6: Final details for this drawing include neighboring buildings for context, some people for scale and architectural details on the first floor. These types of decoration on the front of a building vary considerably according to the style and era of the construction, so find some reference pictures according to the vibe you want to give.

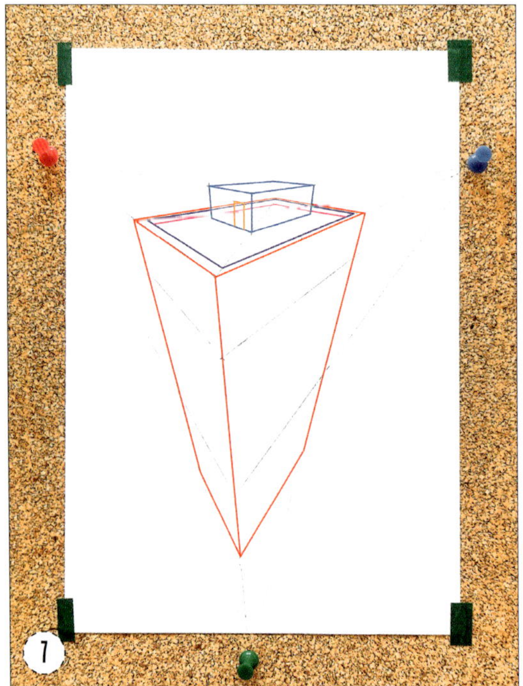

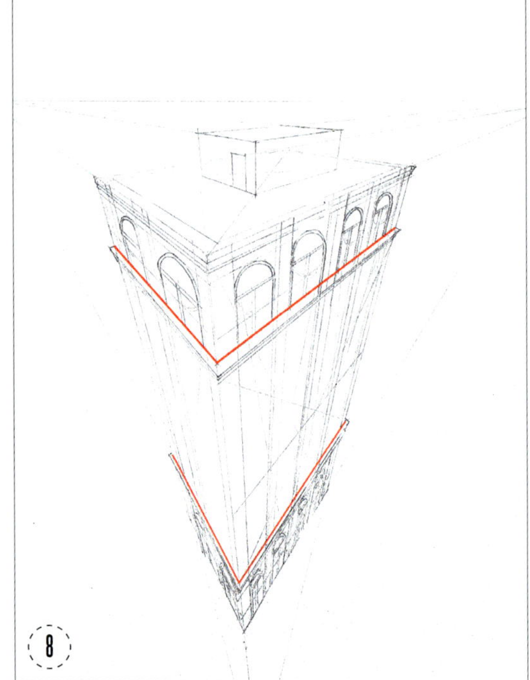

STEP 7: Now it is time to change the perspective parameters and see how this building looks from above. Move the horizon line to the top of the page and the third vanishing point to the bottom. Notice that for this drawing it is much closer to the paper than for the first one. This is my personal preference for top-down views, but I strongly recommend you play with these parameters until you find your own sweet spot.

Draw a box (red) using similar proportions to the ones you used for the first drawing. You will notice I chose a slightly taller proportion because I want to emphasize that feeling of vertigo you get when looking down.

This time you can see the roof, so you need to add some details. Draw the surrounding wall (purple) as you learned in the City Landscape with Vertical Vanishing Points project, Step 6 (page 109). Use an X so you have a well-proportioned wall thickness all around. Don't forget to add the interior height of that wall (pink) from the roof wherever it is visible. Draw a box (blue) to represent the machine room of the elevator or simply the staircase access to the roof. Of course, it will need a door and you can create it with a rectangular plane (orange).

Sometimes when you are sketching from street level but want to imagine how the building would look from a different angle, you will have to make up parts that you cannot see, and that is perfectly ok.

STEP 8: For the façade of the building, you need to follow the exact same steps you did for the first view. In Picture 8, you can see Steps 1 through 3. The only small difference here is that from this perspective, you can see the top of the architectural details you drew as horizontal divisions, so you need to add their depth (red lines) relative to the front walls.

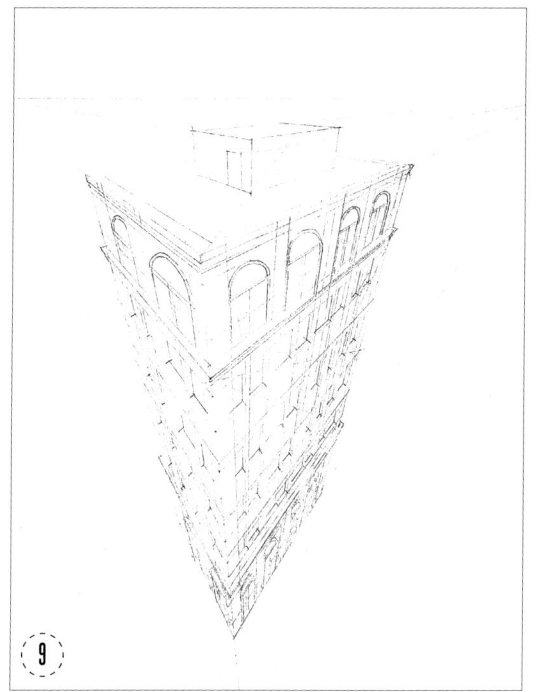

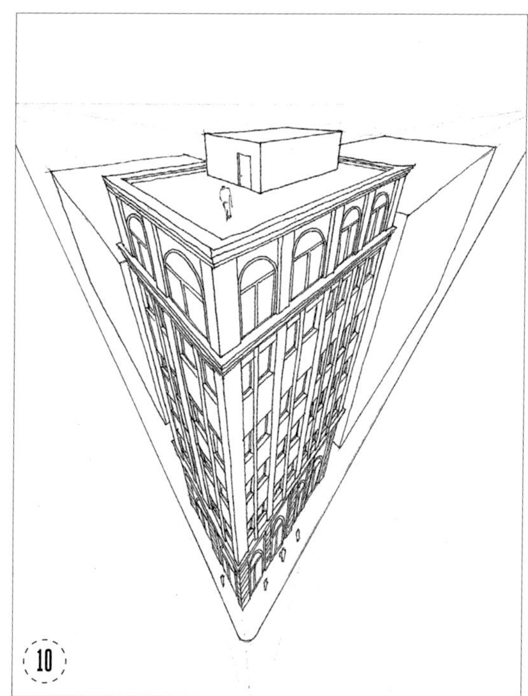

STEP 9: Picture 9 shows how Steps 4 through 5 look from this perspective. Be careful when adding depth to the windows in the middle section. From this point of view, you will be able to see it on all lower edges of every opening plus left-side edges on the left side and right-side edges on the right one.

You can see the dramatic difference between the final version in Picture 9 and the one from Step 6 (Picture 6).

STEP 10: Just like in the first view, final details include adding some neighboring buildings for context and some people for scale.

Make sure to keep the same proportion of the buildings on the sides and scale people according to the size of the doors on the first floor. Note how in this view, I didn't need to add architectural details to the first floor because it is not the focal point of the drawing.

You followed pretty much the same steps for both drawings, but they look absolutely different. They convey totally different sensations, but you did not have to rent a chopper or go to the top of a skyscraper to feel them. And that my friends, is the power of perspective. You can create a thousand more different views just by tweaking the parameters.

LESSON: USING ELASTICS TO REFINE THREE-POINT PERSPECTIVE

One of the reasons I like elastics so much is that they allow you to understand in a direct and visual way what is happening in a perspective drawing. One of the most common struggles with three-point perspective is trying to figure out which lines go where, but having a clear, tactile reference of the vanishing points and the direction of the lines going to each one of them is a game changer. It connects very closely with another big question: How do you decide the position of the vanishing points?

The possibilities are literally infinite. Having three points that you can place anywhere can be daunting and make you want to quit before even starting. But do not worry! If you learn how to work with a few basic dispositions, you will be more than ready to go. Being able to change the position of the vanishing points just by moving the pins around makes it so much easier. Do not be scared about filling your paper with holes or getting some weird-looking perspectives while you figure it out.

In this lesson, I will do an exercise that I love and that you have done many times in this book: Draw the same thing from different angles. This is the best way of understanding how a view changes when you see the differences side by side. I have chosen a chest of drawers with an open shelf for books placed near the corner of a small room. I also want to slightly change the drawing style that I have been using so far and shift toward a sketchier and looser one. This may help you realize that you do not have to change your own drawing style to apply the rules of perspective effectively.

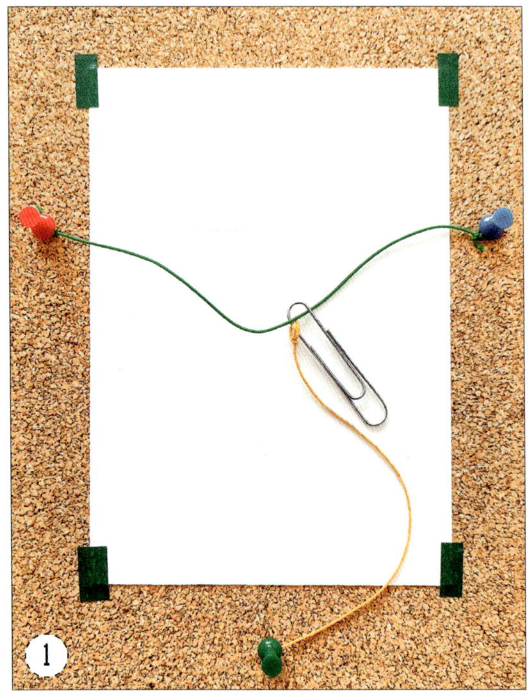
1

Set up the elastics as follows: First, join the horizontal vanishing points using one elastic (green in Picture 1). Cut it long enough so that when you are not pulling it, it is very loose. It must be able to reach all the corners of the paper. Tie a loop on either end so you can insert the tips of the thumbtacks, then pass the paper clip through it before pinning it to the board. The other elastic (yellow) also needs a loop on both ends: one for the thumbtack to hold it in place and the other end through the paper clip.

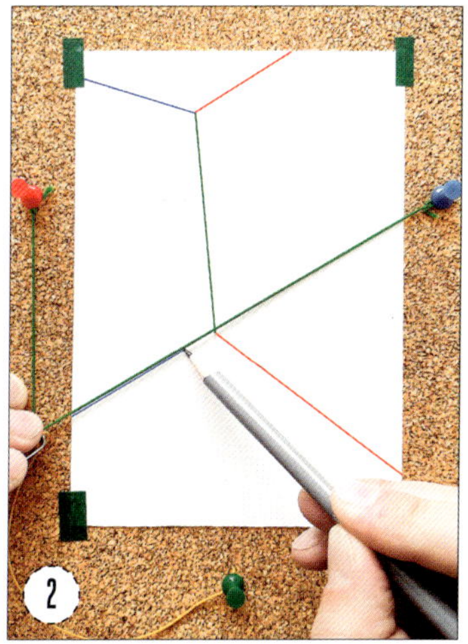

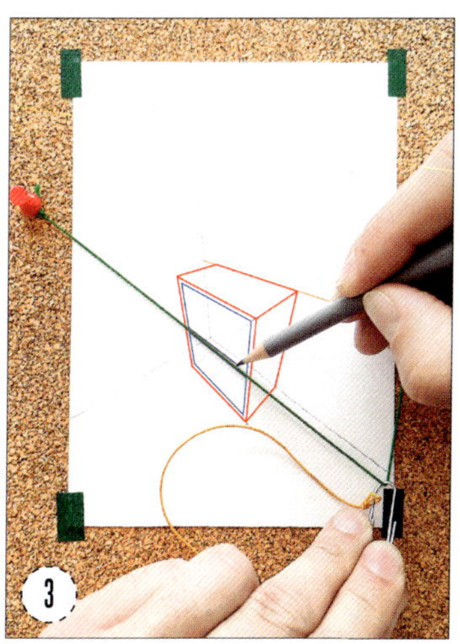

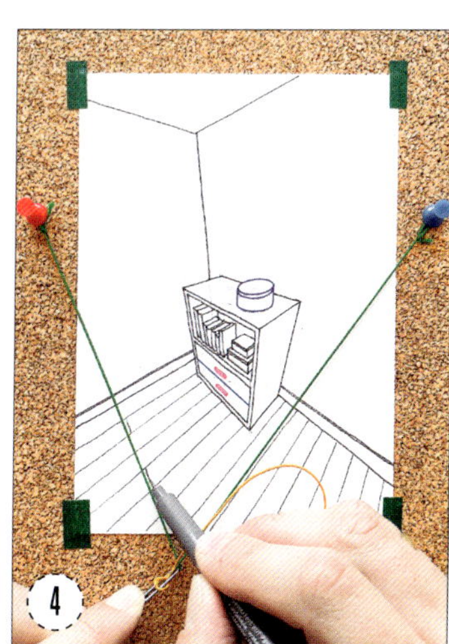

The first kind of view I will show you is similar to the ones you have done so far and it will be the base reference. I will place the horizon line about one third of the distance from the top of the paper with vanishing points on either side (red and blue thumbtacks in Picture 1), and the third one (green thumbtack) centered at the bottom. I will start by defining the corner of the room with a vertical (green in Picture 2) and then lines going to either vanishing point from its ends (red and blue lines).

Next, I will draw a box (red in Picture 3) that is one third of the total height of the room. It should have a square front plane and its depth should be approximately half its height. Notice that I placed it a bit separate from the corner but still drew a reference line from it (orange) to determine its height. Now, I will draw the thickness of the frame all around the front plane with parallels (blue) near the edges and divide it horizontally in the middle with two lines (purple). The top part will be the bookshelf and the bottom part will be divided into two equal-sized drawers.

Picture 4 shows how I created drawers with a horizontal line (blue). I also drew a couple of super small and long boxes (pink) centered in the drawers to mimic handles. Next, I filled the shelf with some books and boxes (see The Elastic String Technique lesson on page 81), and added a cylindrical cookie box (purple) on top. To finish this version, I drew hardwood floors going to the right vanishing point and added the baseboard.

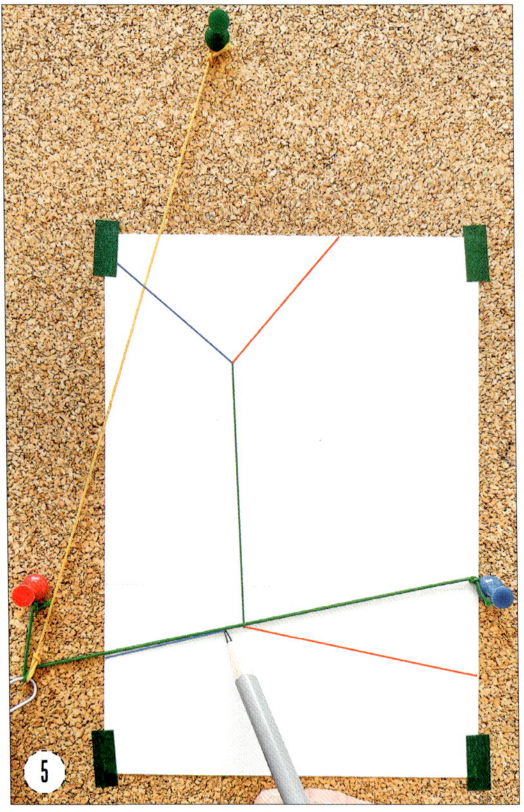

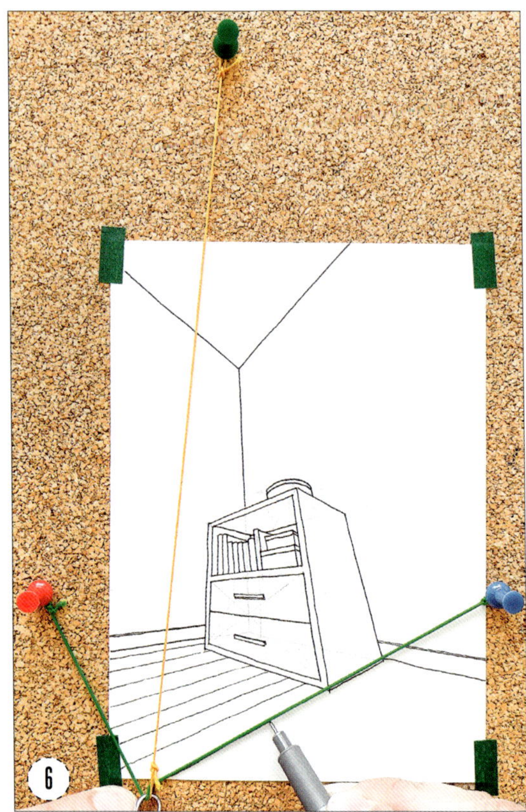

To invert the setup, I moved the horizon line to one third of the distance from the bottom and moved the third vanishing point to the top and a bit to the left (Picture 5). Note that the right vanishing point is closer to the paper than the left one. I repeated the same process to define the corner with a green vertical line and lines from both horizontal vanishing points (red and blue).

The rest of the steps are the same to build the chest drawer and all the objects in and on top of the chest (Picture 6). So far, this is very similar to what you did in the One Building, Two Ways project (page 128). These two drawings still work very much like a two-point perspective, but with verticals going to the third vanishing point. However, there is a way of making three-point perspective look more like one-point perspective and thereby create a whole different kind of view.

In the setup for this third example, one of the vanishing points (red thumbtack in Picture 7) is going to be placed inside the paper and there will be an inclined horizon line (Picture 7). The second vanishing point (blue thumbtack) is outside the paper and aligned with the horizon line. I placed it far from the paper to keep the distance between the horizontal vanishing points similar to the one on the first two examples. The third vanishing point (green) is on the bottom of the page and I want it very far away to avoid perspective distortion.

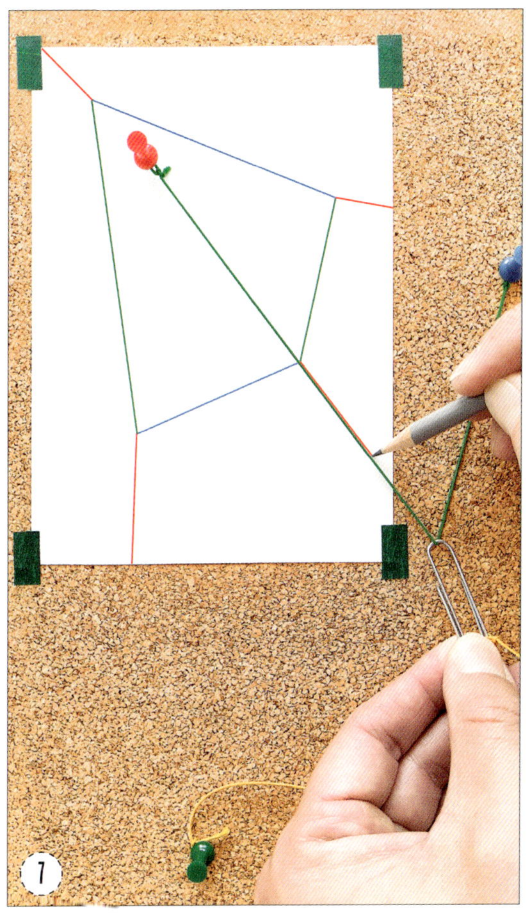

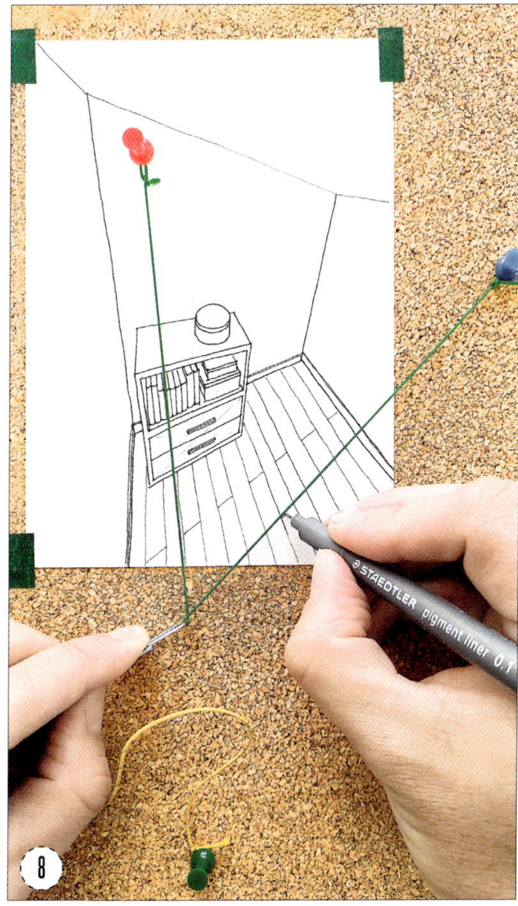

So, here is the main difference: In the first two examples, the horizontal vanishing points were used to draw horizontal lines going to the right or the left side of the observer's eyesight, but now that one of them is inside the paper, it is handling all horizontal lines going straight from the observer's eyes to it. The one on the right side is used for all horizontals running across the observer's visual line. In that sense, now it looks like a modified one-point perspective. In both cases the third vanishing point is responsible for all verticals.

Now you are not just seeing the corner but the whole back wall and here is how I drew it: I joined two verticals (green) and two horizontals (blue) going to the right vanishing point from their ends. From all four corners I drew lines going to the red vanishing point (red thumbtack) until they went off the paper. Notice that the scale of this drawing is a bit smaller because now you can see the whole wall, so the chest will look smaller too.

Picture 8 shows the chest completed. As you may see, this option is better if you need to show a little bit more of the room and not just the corner. I could have drawn the back wall even farther away and shown much more of it. In this case, the hardwood floor lines all go to the red vanishing point to keep them consistent with the first two drawings.

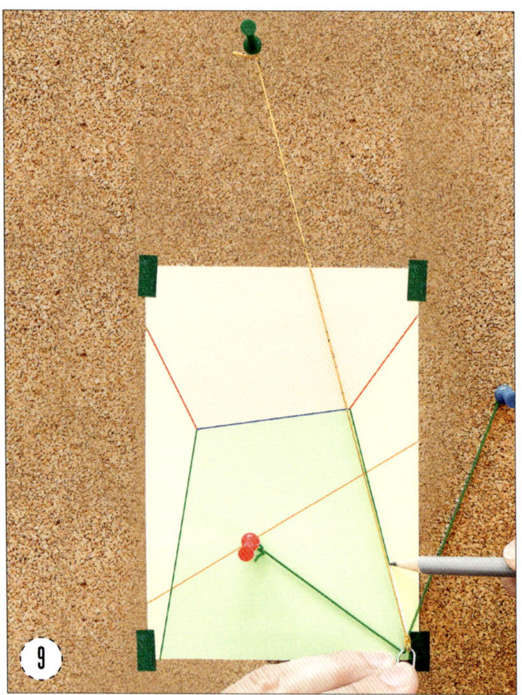

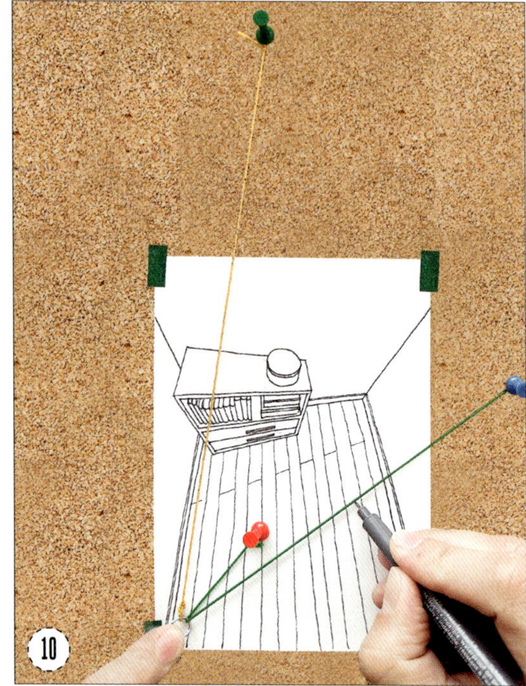

Finally, I want to shift the observer's position from looking straight ahead to looking from above to show how you can also use three-point perspective to create a bird's-eye view. This is similar to what you did in the Upping Your Floor Plans lesson (page 61). I moved the left horizontal vanishing point (red thumbtack in Picture 9) to the lower part of the paper and positioned it left of center. The horizon line (orange) will have a steeper inclination, leaving the right vanishing point (blue thumbtack) higher. The third vanishing point (green thumbtack) is on the upper part of the setup and a bit toward the left of the center.

Now the verticals are all going to the left horizontal vanishing point because of the observer's change of position. I drew the floor with a line in the direction of the right vanishing point (blue) and a couple of lines (green) from its ends going away from the top vanishing point. From the corners, I added two verticals (red). Now there is a top view of the floor (shaded in green), the back wall (shaded in orange) and the two side walls (shaded in yellow).

Check out the finished drawing (Picture 10). Using this technique is a perfect way to create immersive floor plans or designs. The true challenge here is to have the direction of the lines clear. Whenever one of the three vanishing points is inside the paper, just remember that all lines going in the same direction as the observer's eyesight will go there.

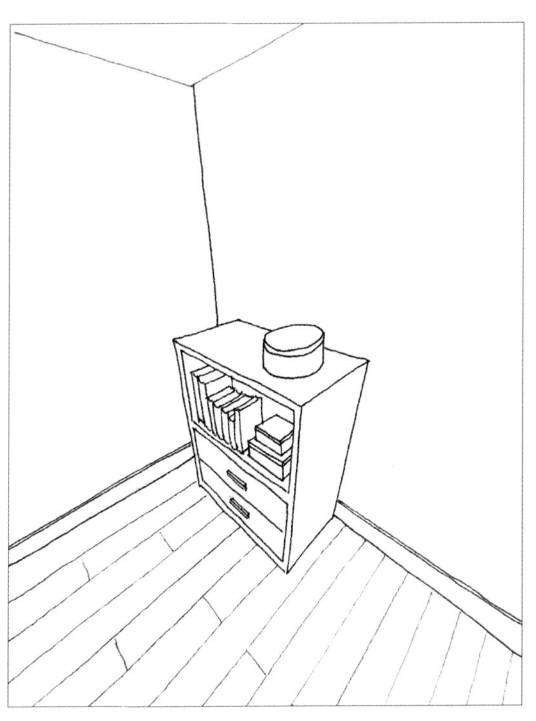

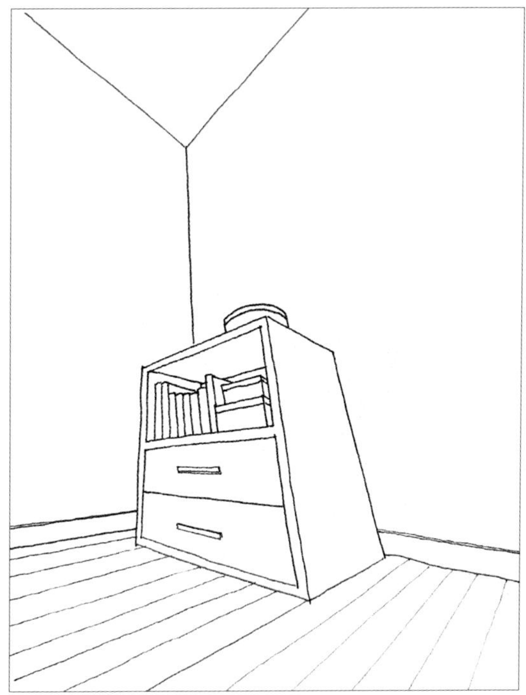

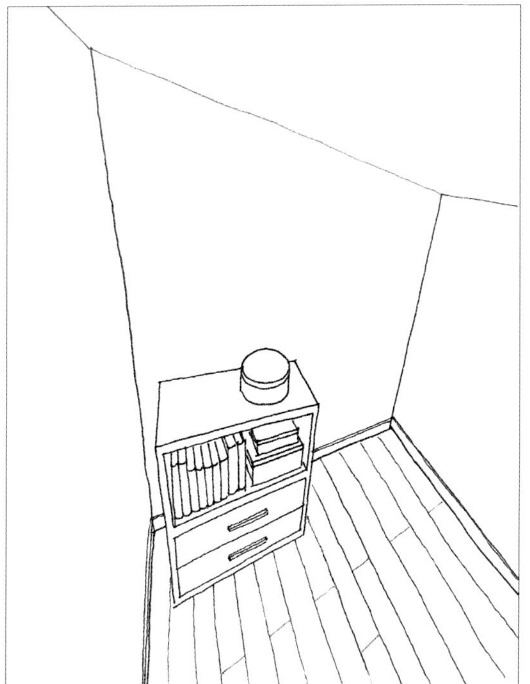

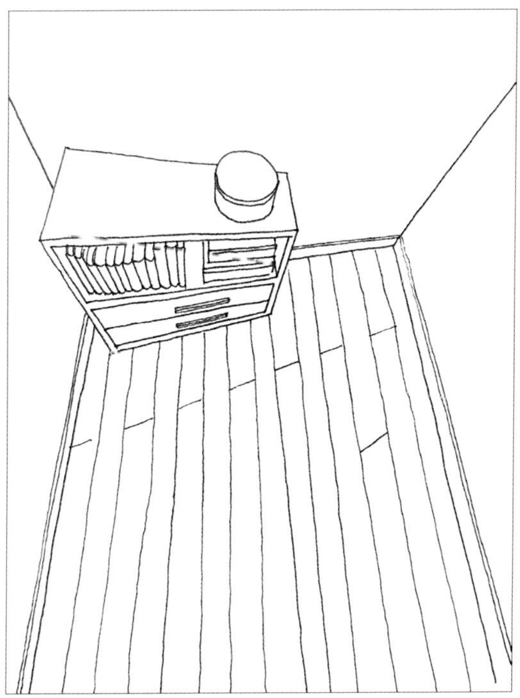

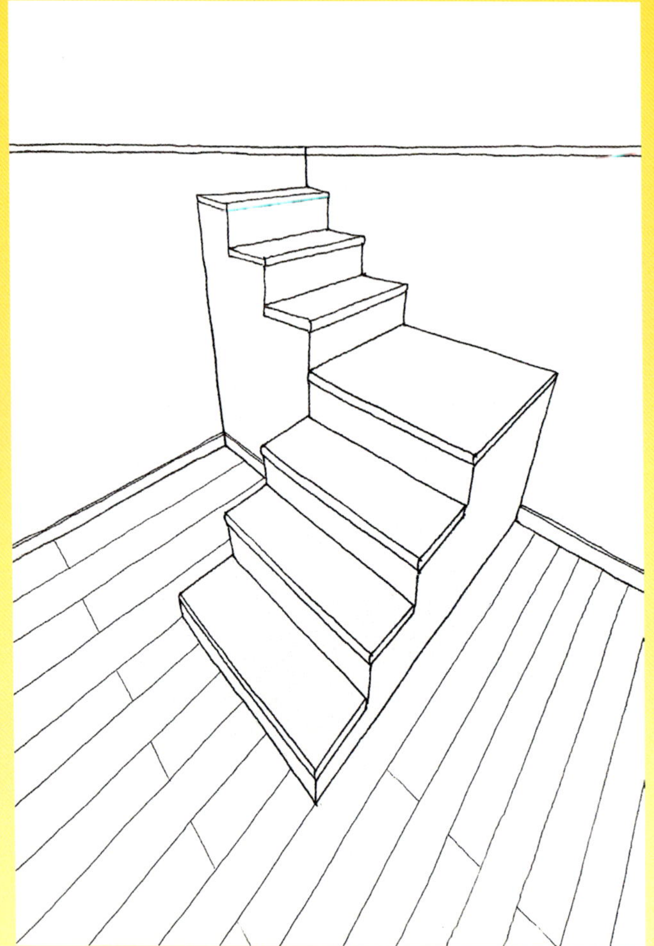

PROJECT: L-SHAPED STAIRCASE

Time for another exciting staircase project: the return of the super useful L-shaped staircase. In this project, I not only want to teach you how to draw it, but how to use it to join two levels. This is something that you will need to do over and over in architectural design and the technique I will show you can be used with almost every staircase design.

Additional Materials

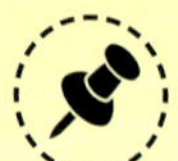
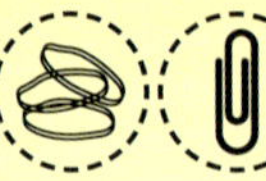

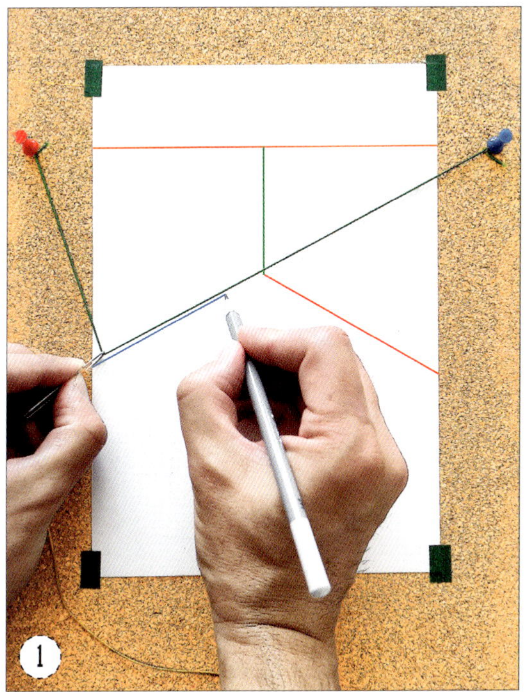

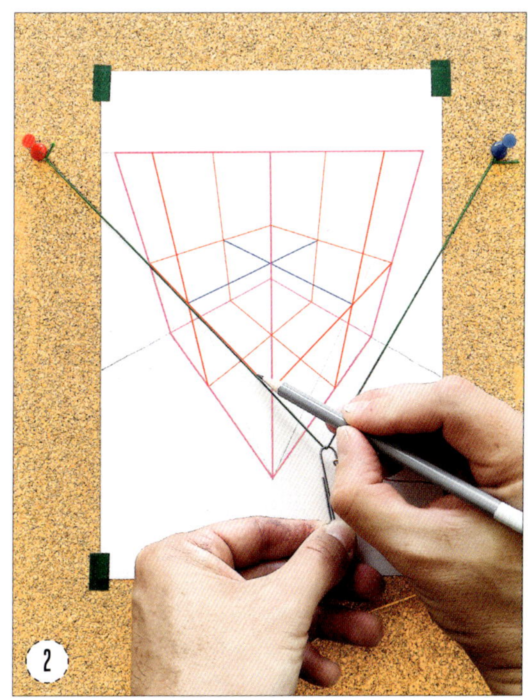

STEP 1: Place the horizon line high on the paper with the two horizontal vanishing points at equal distances from it. Center the third vanishing point at the bottom. Start by drawing the two levels you want to join. The height of the upper floor should align with the horizon line (orange). Then, build a corner into the lower floor for the staircase. Draw a vertical line (green) and lines (red and blue) in the direction of each horizontal vanishing point from the green line's lower end.

PRO TIP: L-shaped staircases can usually be inserted in cube-shaped boxes, because they normally have the same number of steps in both directions.

STEP 2: Draw a cube (pink) that has the same height as the distance between the two levels. Divide all the faces of the box down the middle vertically and horizontally (red lines). Transfer those divisions also to the interior of the box (blue lines).

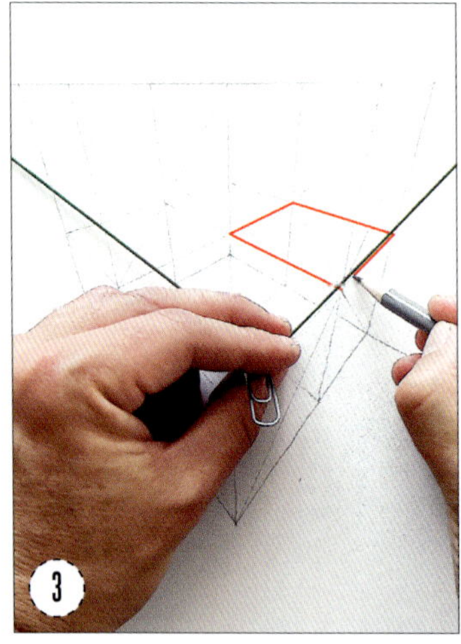

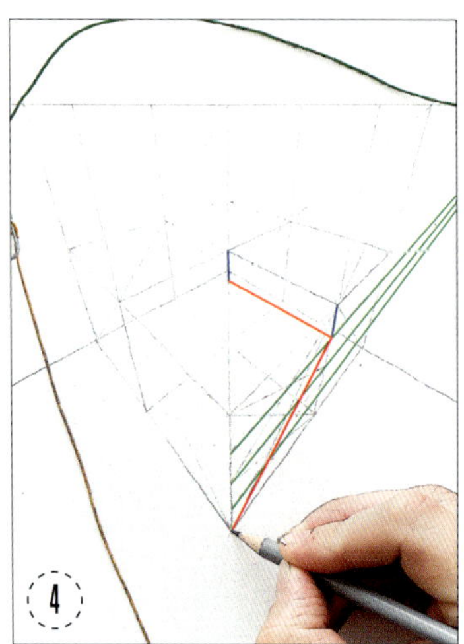

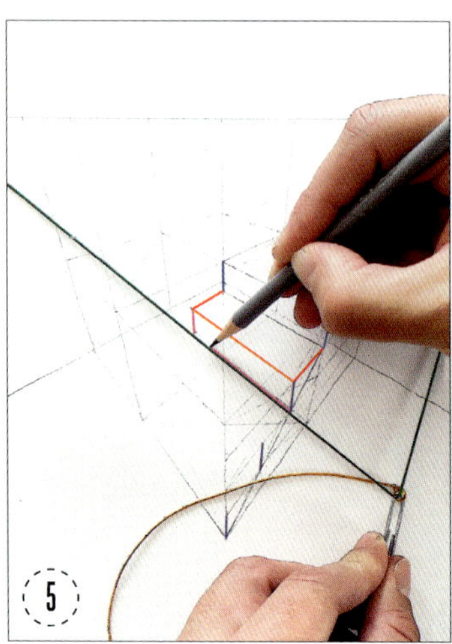

STEP 3: To establish the position of the landing tread (which is going to be squared), draw a horizontal plane (red) located on the back right quarter of the second tier. Then, start working on the steps from the floor leading to that landing.

STEP 4: There will be three steps from the floor to the landing and three more from the landing to the second level. Divide the distance between the floor and the landing in four equal parts with three lines (green) going to the right vanishing point. Draw a couple of verticals (blue) starting at the front left corners of the landing until the right one meets the height of the first step going down. Next, join their lower ends with a line (orange) going to the left vanishing point. From the bottom end of the right blue line, add a diagonal (red) all the way to the front corner of the box. That diagonal is the inclination of the staircase.

STEP 5: Draw verticals (purple) between the step height divisions every time the diagonal crosses them. Now, draw two lines (red) that start at the bottom of the blue lines, until the right one touches the top of the first purple. Join their ends with a line (orange) going to the left vanishing point. Close the front of the step with a vertical and a horizontal (pink) coming from both corners until they meet.

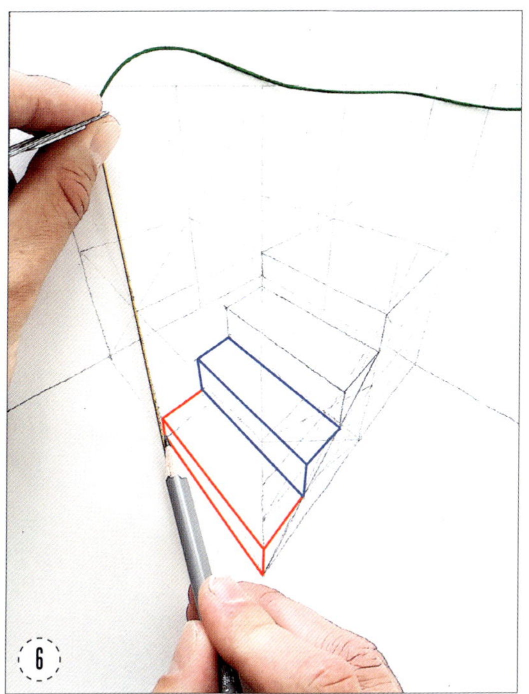

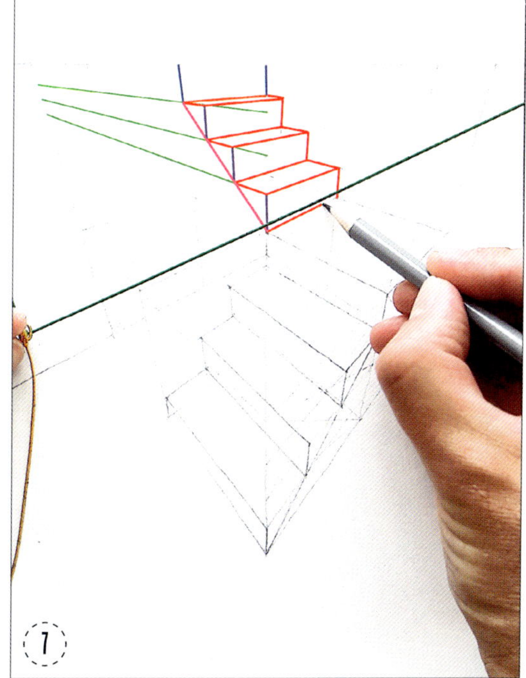

STEP 6: Repeat the same process for the next two steps (blue lines for the second and red for the first).

STEP 7: The other flight of stairs turns to the left after the landing. Follow the same process as before to draw those steps. Add height division lines (green) going to the left vanishing point in the middle wall of the box. Then draw two verticals (blue) that start at the front right corners of the second level landing and join their bottom ends with a horizontal (orange) going to the right vanishing point. Add the diagonal (pink) from the bottom end of the left blue line until it reaches the corner of the middle landing. Next, draw verticals (purple) between the step height lines wherever the diagonal crosses them. With all those reference lines build the steps (all in red).

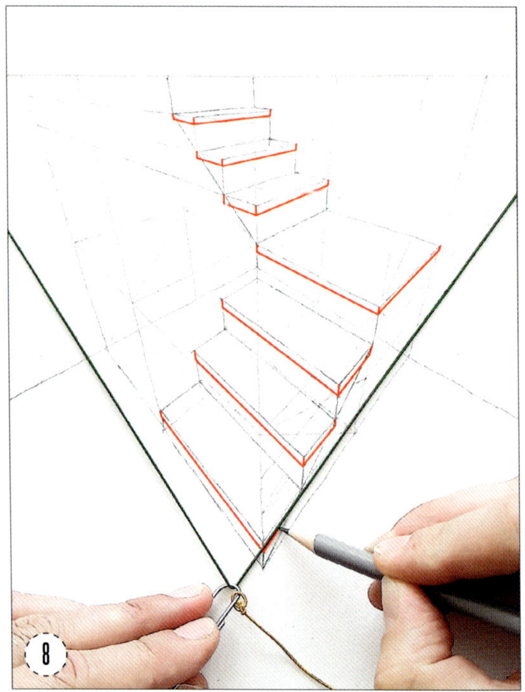

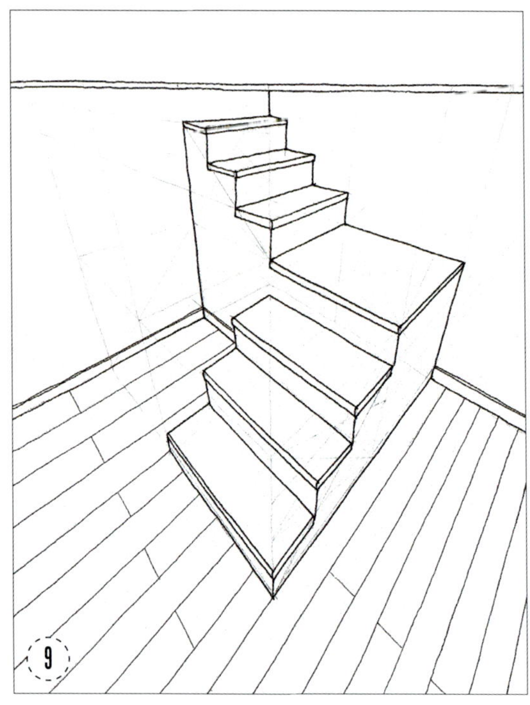

STEP 8: The top of the steps is hardwood, so draw a thin horizontal box (red) in each one of them to mimic the wood slab.

STEP 9: Time to ink the drawing. I will leave all the construction lines so you can see how everything was built and how light these lines are supposed to be. Notice how I drew a box under the whole staircase to make it look solid. I also drew hardwood floors on the lower level and added a baseboard.

LESSON: TYING IT ALL TOGETHER

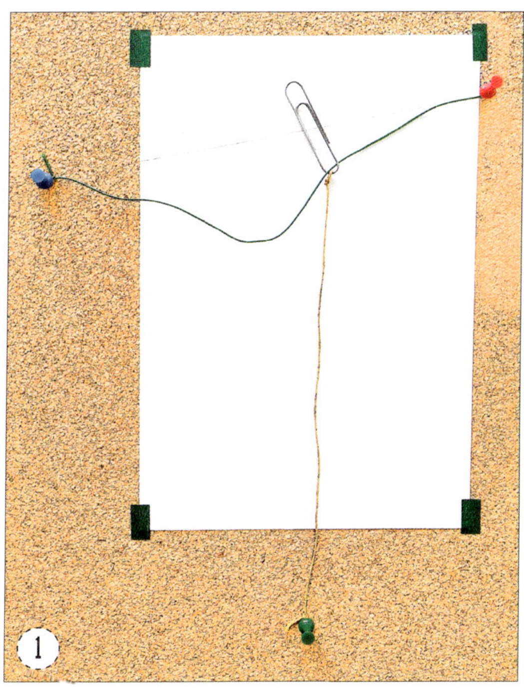

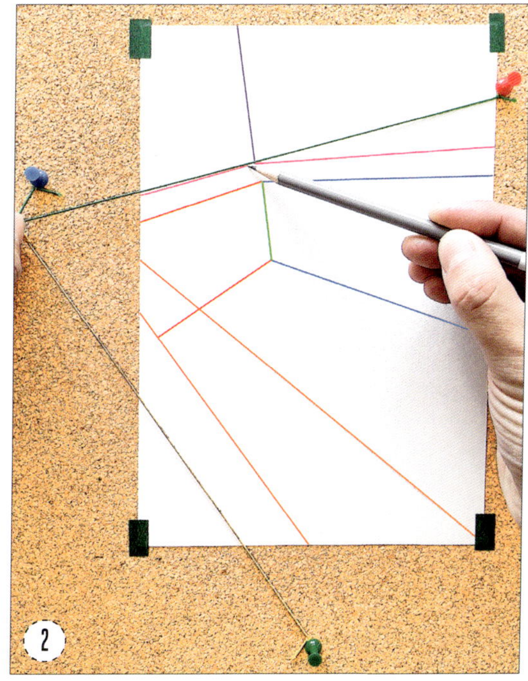

This final lesson summarizes the most important techniques you have learned so far and shows how harmoniously they interact in a single drawing. The horizon line will be inclined at the top of the page (Picture 1). The right vanishing point (red thumbtack) will be very close to the paper, while the left (blue thumbtack) will be further away. The third vanishing point (green thumbtack) will be centered at the bottom.

PRO TIP: When thinking about the layout you want for your drawing, play around with a couple of fast sketches first, so you are sure that the horizon line, vanishing points and main lines are exactly where you want them. As an example, I drew four versions prior to the one I will be describing ahead. If you are working with a bigger format, make thumbnail-size sketches but make sure they have the same proportions.

I will start by defining the main lines of the drawing. First, two lines (orange in Picture 2) come from the left vanishing point. One of them starts at the bottom right corner of the paper and the other at the middle point of the bottom edge. Next, draw a vertical line (green) that starts around the center and a bit to the left and finishes around the same height as the left vanishing point. From both its ends, add lines going away from both vanishing points (red and blue). Finally, draw another vertical (purple), that starts a bit above where the green one ended and just a bit to the left. From its bottom end, add lines going away from both vanishing points again (pink). Do not worry, you will understand everything in a minute.

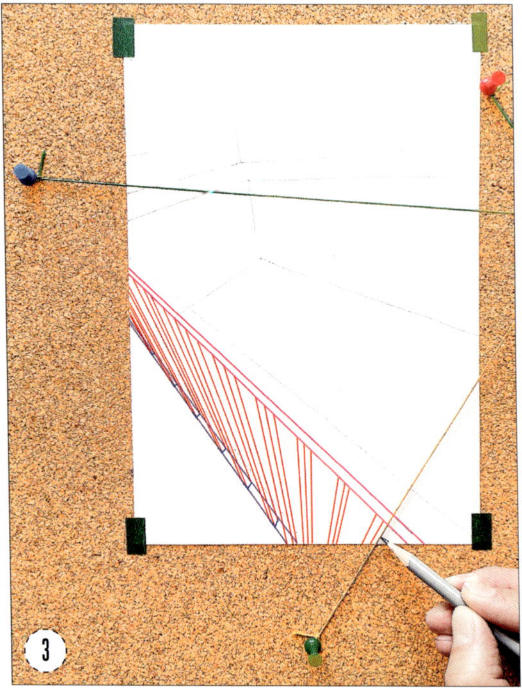

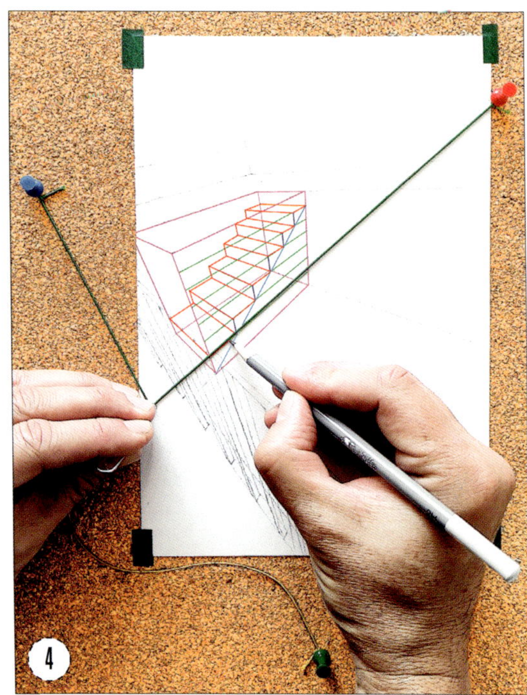

I have mentioned that I like drawing from the front to the back. The two lines at the bottom left corner are going to be a railing, so I will start there by drawing two lines going to the left vanishing point close to the top one (pink in Picture 3), and two more (purple) close to the bottom one. Now, I will draw equally distanced groups of three vertical lines (red) between the pinks and the purples. For each baluster, the red lines farthest to the right end on the top purple line and the other two end on the bottom purple line. Close the lower end of the balusters with lines (blue) going to the corresponding vanishing point depending on their direction.

Now, I will create a staircase on the corner that goes from the lower level to the mezzanine. You can review the process for staircases in the Drawing a Simple Staircase (page 44), U-Shaped Staircase (page 96) and L-Shaped Staircase (page 140) projects. First, I will do a 2:3 rectangular box (pink in Picture 4) that has the same height as the mezzanine. Its height will be approximately 4½ feet (1.4 m) so I will need seven steps. That means I need to divide the height of the box into seven equal parts with six lines (green).

I then drew a line (orange) going to the left vanishing point from the first step height going down, until it reached the other side of the box, and from its right end, a diagonal (blue) that goes all the way to the front right corner of the box. Next, I drew verticals (purple) in every cross point between the greens and the diagonal. Now I can use the purples, greens and the diagonal to build all the steps (red).

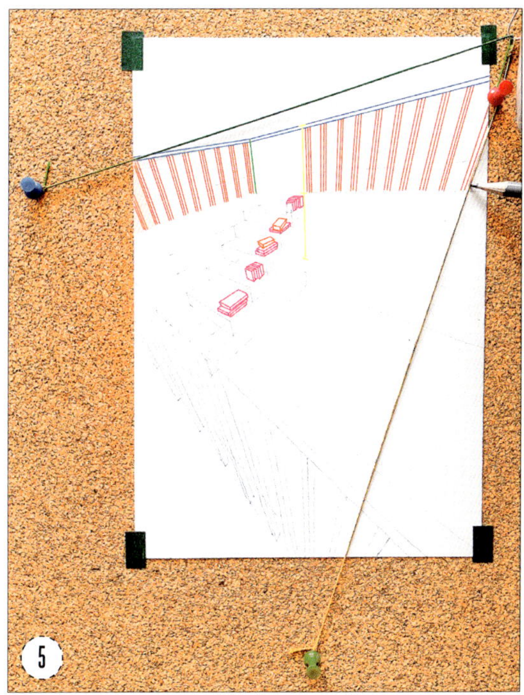

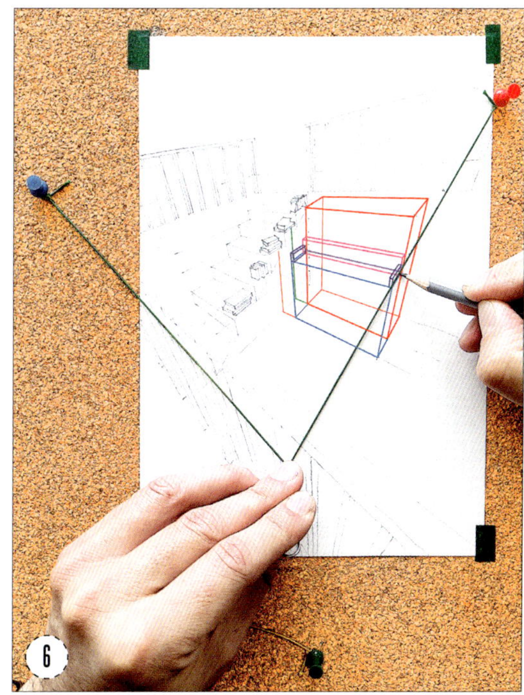

To finish the staircase, I want to put some books at the right end of each of the steps. These do not have to be all perfectly aligned with the vanishing points. Draw some using the vanishing points (pink in Picture 5) but change the angle slightly for a couple (orange), to make them look more natural.

To create the railing all along the mezzanine, I will draw a couple of very close double lines (blue) above its edge with a height of approximately 38 inches (97 cm). I used the steps as reference. They should be five steps high (yellow reference line). They need to change direction where they meet at the corner (green line).

Next, I will draw balusters between the blue lines and the edge of the mezzanine with triple lines (red) mimicking the ones I did on the front, but I must be careful because these are much farther away and I need to modify the scale accordingly. Afterward, I will erase the section of the blue lines that is in front of the stairs.

I would like a piano in the corner between the wall and the stairs, so I will build a box (red in Picture 6) for it. It should be a bit shorter than the height of the mezzanine, and longer than it is tall, approximately 4¼ feet (1.3 m) tall by 5 feet (1.5 m) long by 1½ feet (46 cm) deep. For the depth, I will be using 1½ steps as reference (green reference lines). Next, add another box (blue) joined to the first one a bit taller than its half and with the depth of one step (orange reference lines). Then, just add a couple more details: a smaller box (pink) and two small boxes (purple) on the sides, on top of the blue box.

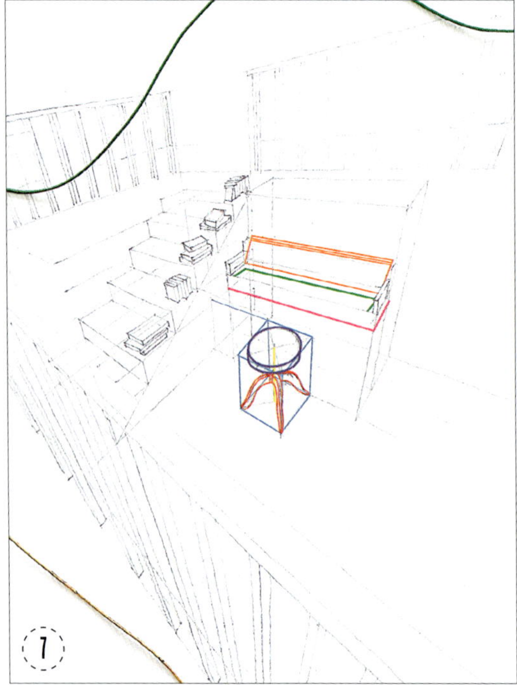

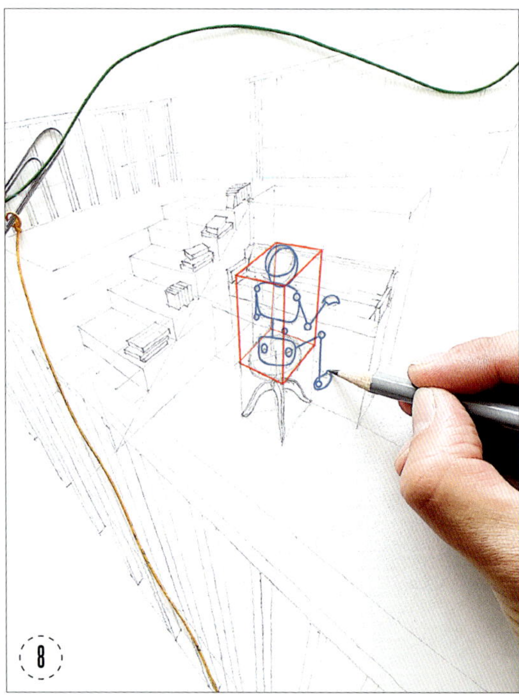

Picture 7 shows how I drew a couple more lines to define the keyboard box (pink), the plane where the actual keys (green) will go and their lid (orange). To review a little bit about inclined surfaces, check the Conquering Diagonal Lines (page 40) and Diagonals in Two-Point Perspective (page 91) lessons. All these reference lines will allow me to draw the details later.

I would like to include a round surface and human figure in this review lesson. I will start with a round piano seat, and to draw it I will create a rectangular box (blue) that is approximately 2½ steps high and with a squared top. Then, I will insert an ellipse on the top plane (purple) and give it thickness. For the legs, I will draw curved ones (red) that go to all visible corners. See that I sketched their center axle (yellow) so I know their starting point.

The human figure will be a little boy playing the piano. To find the proportions of his torso, I build another box (red in Picture 8) on top of the seat's box with its exact dimensions, but just a little bit taller (just make sure that it is not higher than the piano itself). Using the red box as a reference I can draw the basic outline of his body (blue). For more details about sketching human proportions, see the Vertical Vanishing Points lesson on page 101.

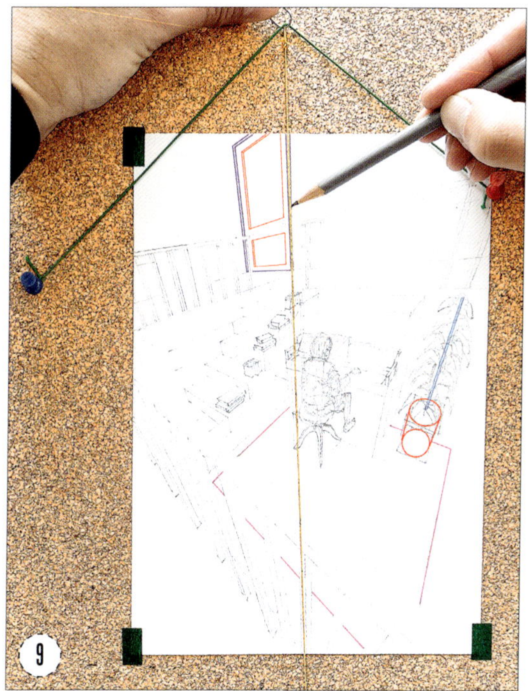

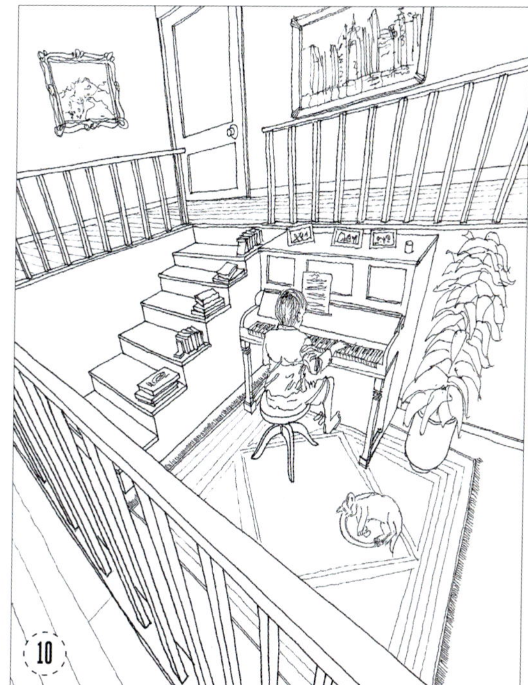

I used that basic outline to figure out the details of his body (Picture 9). Next, I want to draw a plant next to the piano. I will draw a cylinder (red) for the planter and a vertical (blue) starting at its center going up that will be the trunk. Then, I can draw leaves all around it to the top. To wrap up the lower level I will add a carpet (pink) below the seat that covers a good section of the floor. On the mezzanine I will add a door (purple) on the right side of the corner. It has a very simple two-panel design (orange).

Once I have all the details sketched in pencil, I can ink the drawing (Picture 10). Remember to wait until you have completed a drawing before you ink. Otherwise, you may ink lines that should not be seen because they are covered by an element of the drawing that is closer to the observer.

For this scene, final details I added include some pictures on top of the piano, sheet music in the keyboard lid, hardwood floors, baseboards, wooden steps in the staircase, some paintings on the mezzanine walls, an area rug and a kitten sleeping on the rug.

This is actually a very complex drawing and you should feel very proud that you were able to complete it. You should also pat yourself on the back for how far you have come. Now, you are ready for our very last project.

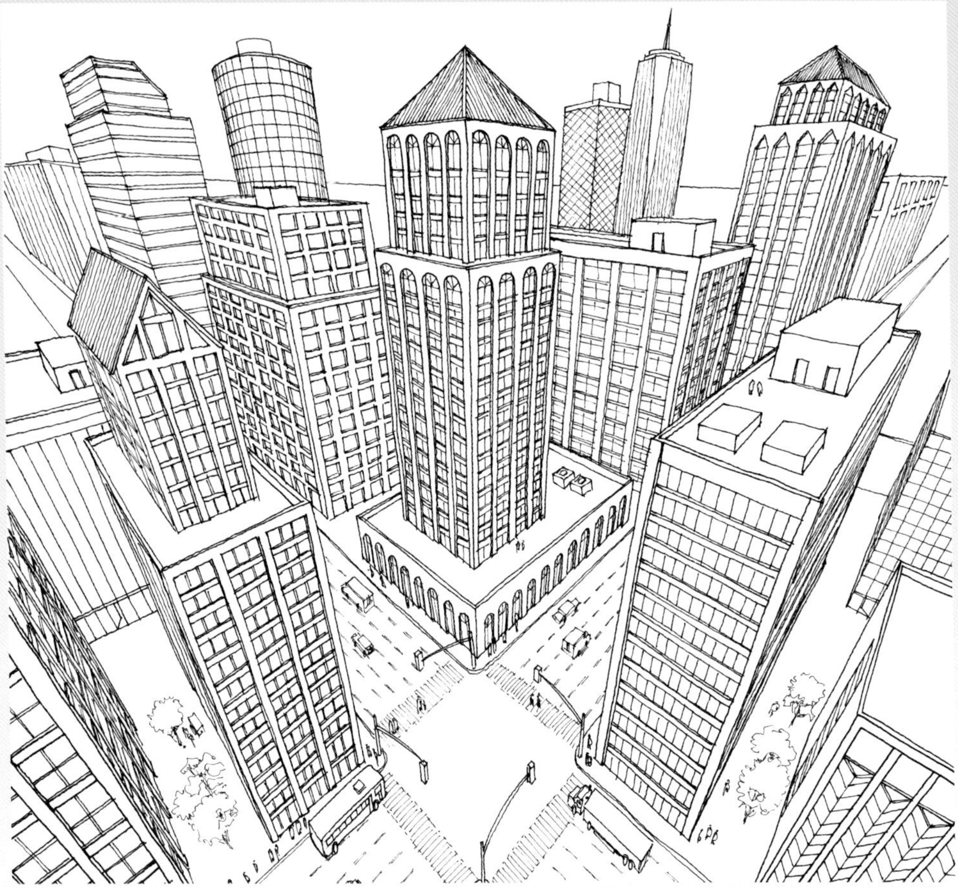

PROJECT: BIRD'S-EYE VIEW OF A CITY

For me, as an architect, this is the drawing that I wanted to do since I first started learning: a three-point perspective city landscape from above. It may seem like a super complicated drawing to do, but it is not. It is actually rather easy and fun, but when finished, it looks absolutely amazing and you will be able to brag about it to your friends. What it does require is a bit of patience, because there are a lot of lines involved in drawing a city, but this is where the elastics do their best work. Besides, the sense of fulfillment that these more intricate artworks produce once you finish them is well worth the effort.

Additional Materials

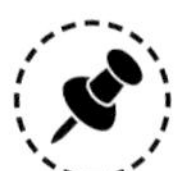
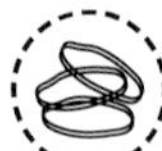
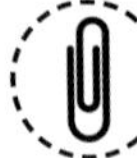

STEP 1: You will use a square format for this drawing. Place the horizon line very high on the paper with vanishing points at equal distance on either side, and the third vanishing point centered at the bottom. Start by drawing two pairs of lines (reds and blues) coming from each vanishing point. These lines will be the basic layout of the city—that is, the streets and the blocks—so the crossings of the streets should be squared planes (shaded in green), as well as the main block in the middle (shaded in orange).

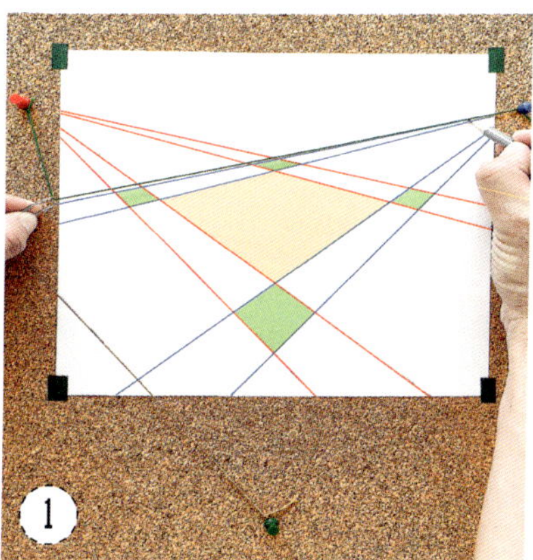

STEP 2: Each of the buildings is going to be a box or a sum of boxes. You should draw all their outlines before doing any details, starting with the main building or focal point located in the closest corner of the main block. Draw a rectangular box (blue). On top of its closest corner, draw a vertical rectangular box (red) with a squared bottom and top planes. Draw another shorter box (purple) with similar shape but smaller footprint to sit on top of the red one, and a pyramid-shaped roof (orange) to top it off.

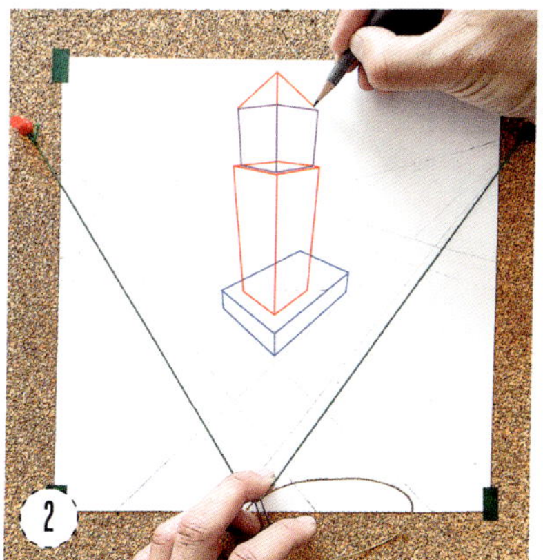

STEP 3: Draw another couple of main, yet less important, buildings on each one of the adjacent corners. Start with the one on the left. Draw a vertical rectangular box (red). On top of it place another box (blue) that is narrower and put a gable roof (orange) on top (see the Diagonals in Two-Point Perspective lesson [page 91] to review roof shapes). On the opposite corner, draw a tall and long rectangular box (purple).

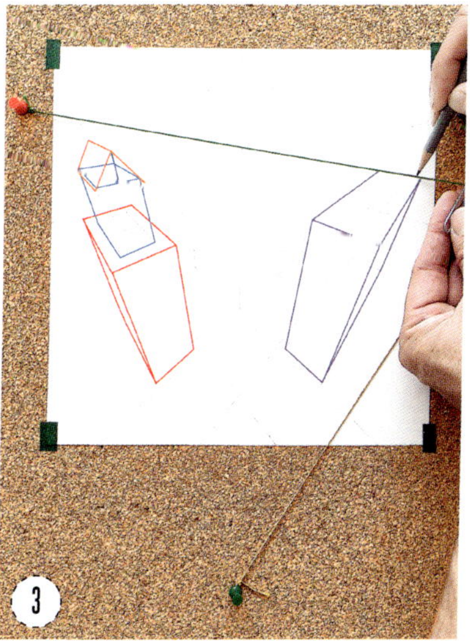

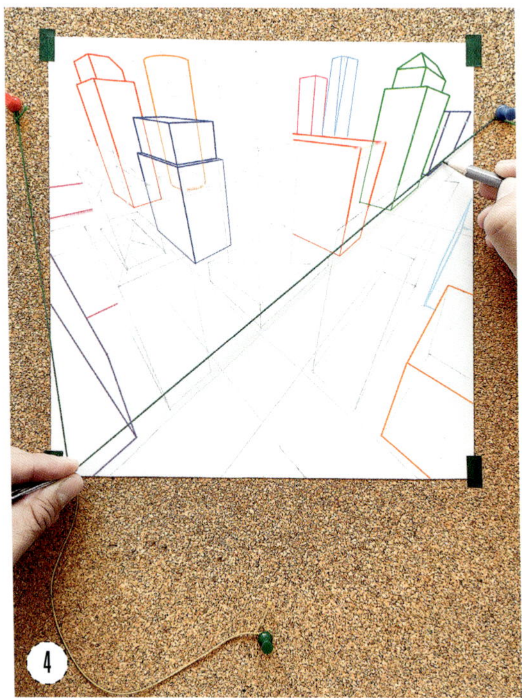

STEP 4: Now, fill the rest of the layout with more buildings (all colors) so that it looks like a city. Here, I want to encourage you to try different sizes and shapes so that you create a drawing that is a little different from mine. Use reference pictures to get ideas. Note that I am being very careful with the position of the streets so I know where to place them, and I am also making sure that none of the buildings overshadows the focal point.

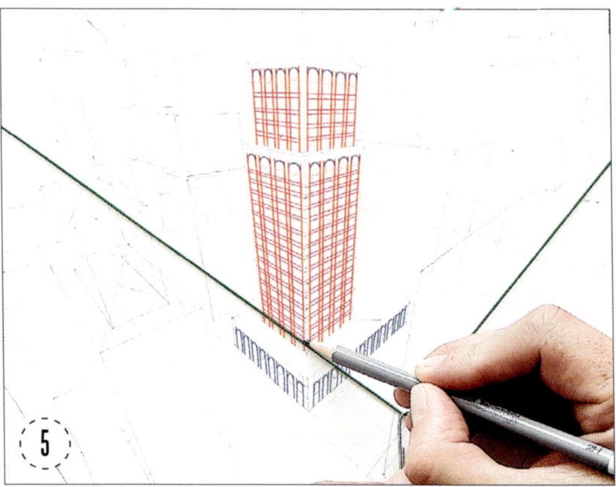

STEP 5: When you are happy with the general layout of your city, start working on the details. As I usually do, I will start with the main building. I will divide all the sections in equal parts with verticals using Xs. In the top two sections I will make four on each side (red lines) leaving a small frame against the top edge. In the bottom section, I will create divisions (blue) that have the same width as the ones above.

Next, I will draw arched windows (purple) at the top of every section (check the Corner Building Sketch project [page 86] to remember how to draw arched windows). Then, divide the rest of the height with double horizontal lines (pink) to create the windows. I will eyeball the distance between them according to the overall height of the building.

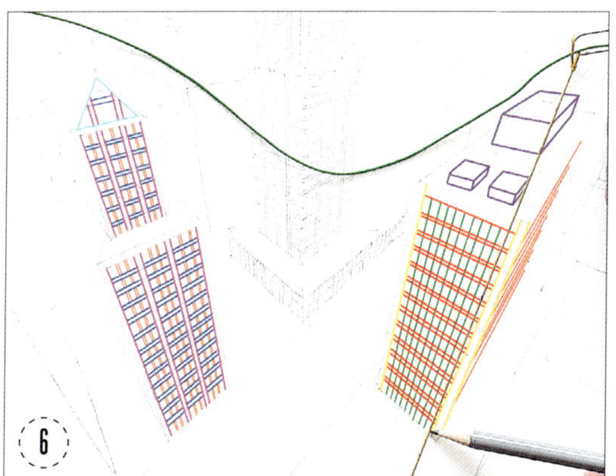

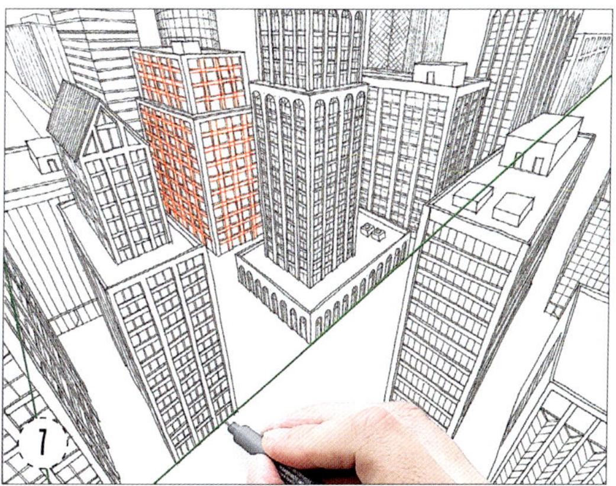

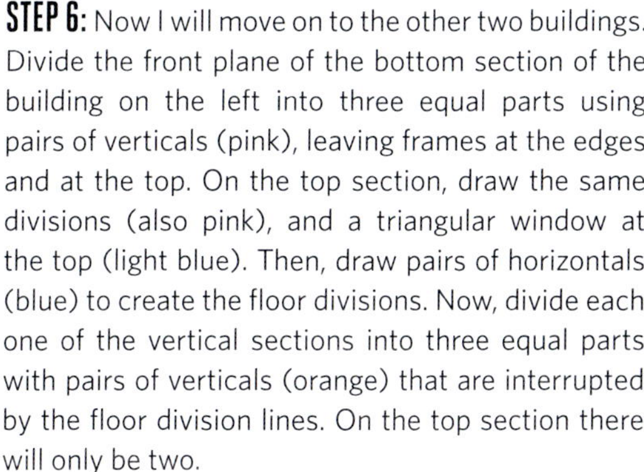

STEP 6: Now I will move on to the other two buildings. Divide the front plane of the bottom section of the building on the left into three equal parts using pairs of verticals (pink), leaving frames at the edges and at the top. On the top section, draw the same divisions (also pink), and a triangular window at the top (light blue). Then, draw pairs of horizontals (blue) to create the floor divisions. Now, divide each one of the vertical sections into three equal parts with pairs of verticals (orange) that are interrupted by the floor division lines. On the top section there will only be two.

The building on the right will have some structures on the roof that you can draw with simple boxes (purple). For a refresher on how to approach roofs, review the City Landscape with Vertical Vanishing Points (page 106) and One Building, Two Ways (page 128) projects. The front planes will have columns on the corners drawn with vertical lines (yellow), pairs of horizontals (red) for floor divisions and verticals (green) to mimic the window panels. The horizontals will look very close together on the right side because of the viewing angle.

STEP 7: Continue drawing the details on all the buildings (Picture 7). You can see that I inked the rest of them directly. I did a lot of different versions that you can copy, but again it would be great if you tried creating your own designs. Also, note that the farther away the buildings are, the finer point I use, and the simpler I make them so they do not look too heavy.

When I want to do squared windows—for example, the one to the left of the focal point—I draw a pencil grid (red) first so I make sure that they are equally distanced both horizontally and vertically.

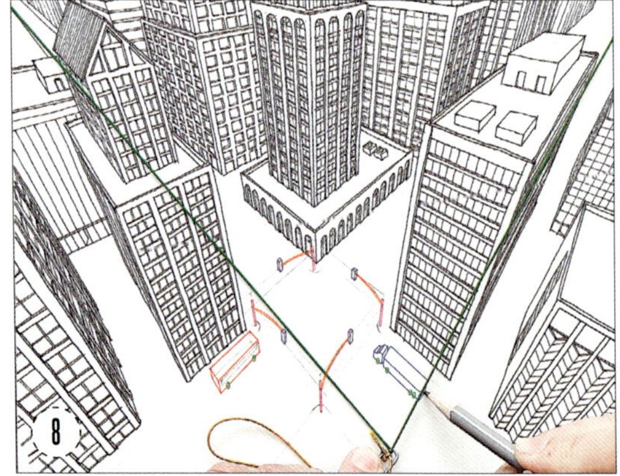

STEP 8: Round the corners on the street intersection. Then draw traffic lights in the corners using a vertical (pink) and an arched inclined line (orange) attached to it. At the end of the arched line, draw a rectangular box (purple).

Some buses or trucks on the streets would look great and help with scale. Draw a rectangular box (red) that has approximately the same height and width as one building floor. Then draw two ovals (green) on the lower edge that will serve as tires. Also, draw a rectangular plane on the side as a window. Next, on the street on the right side, draw another box of similar dimensions (blue), and very close to it, another one with two different heights and a diagonal joining them (also blue). Add ovals as tires (green).

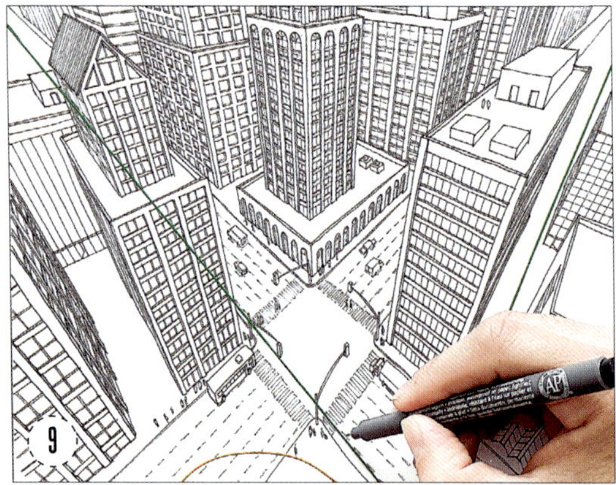

STEP 9: Add some people on the sidewalks and more vehicles on other streets. Draw the people according to the size of the bus, the truck and the height of the floors. Finally, add street lines, such as lane separations and zebra crossings.

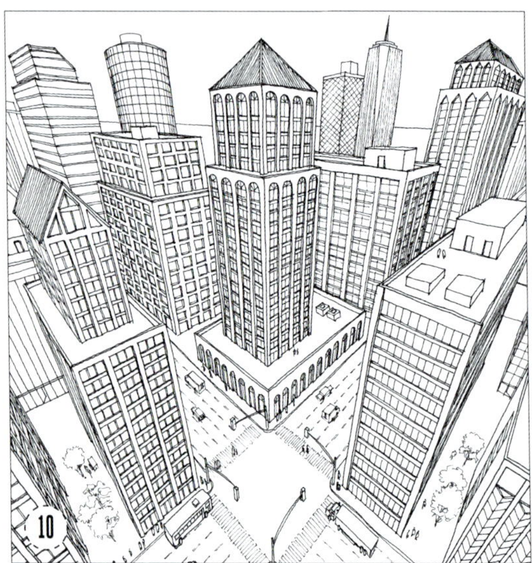

STEP 10: Take a look at the final version. Remember to add depth to windows and architectural details wherever they are needed to create volume and realism. I also added some trees in the alleys between the buildings. Go crazy with the details.

You did great! I hope you enjoyed this quick look at perspective. I am sure that by now you feel much more confident when you pick up your pencil, and if that is the case, my purpose has been fulfilled. Drawing requires practice and discipline to get really good, but with the foundations that you learned in this book, you have all you need to continue your journey. It has been an absolute pleasure teaching you and please let me give you one last bit of advice: Your art is yours always. As long as you are happy with it, no other opinion should matter.

ACKNOWLEDGMENTS

I thank God for His guidance throughout my life and for the gifts and talents He has given me. My wife and daughter are the motor that moves my life and my team accompanying me in every new adventure. I love you guys. My father inspired me to become an architect and has supported me through every crazy twist and turn of life. My mother was always there for my siblings and me growing up and taught us important values like excellence, hard work, honesty and responsibility. My brother and sister always bet on me and backed me up. My parents-in-law love me as if I were their own son. Thank you all.

ABOUT THE AUTHOR

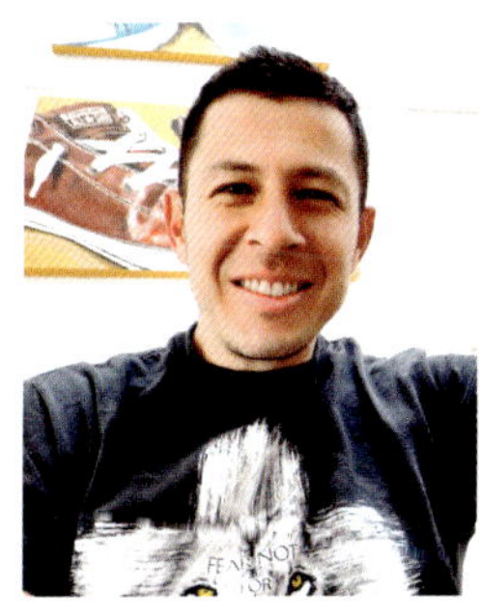

ROBERTO BERNAL is an architect, artist and content producer from Colombia. His career as an architect led to his career as an artist, which then led to his career as a content producer. The common denominator of this path has been his love for architectural art, sketching and perspective drawing. Over the years he has developed techniques that mix his architecture school teachings with his own particular experimentation and practice journey. This has led to a new approach to perspective and a fresh and innovative way of teaching it that has been widely embraced.

INDEX

E

F

G

H

I

K

L

M

N

O

P